Please remember that this is a library book,
and that it belongs only temporarily to each
person who uses it. Be considerate. Do
not write in this, or any, library book.

The Crumbling Walls

The Crumbling Walls

TREATMENT AND COUNSELING OF PRISONERS

EDITED BY

Ray E. Hosford and C. Scott Moss

University of Illinois Press
Urbana Chicago London

Library of Congress Cataloging in Publication Data

Hosford, Ray E   1933–
    The crumbling walls: treatment and counseling of
prisoners.

    Includes bibliographies and index.
    1.   Rehabilitation of criminals—California—
Addresses, essays, lectures.   2.   Correctional psy-
chology—Addresses, essays, lectures.   3.   Corrections—
California—Addresses, essays, lectures.   I.   Moss,
Claude Scott, 1924–   joint author.   II.   Title.
[DNLM: 1.   Counseling.   2.   Criminal psychology.
3.   Prisoners—Case studies.   4.   Prisons—United States.
5.   Psychotherapy.   HV6089 H825c]
HV9305.C2H68   1975   364.6   75–23266

ISBN 0–252–00424–8

*To our wives, Phyllis and Bette,
who are not only our girls Friday,
but Saturday, Sunday, and always.*

If you treat an individual as he
is he will stay as he is, but if
you treat him as if he were what
he ought to be and could be, he will
become as he ought to be and could be.

GOETHE

Contents

Foreword

Norman A. Carlson
Director, Federal Bureau of Prisons

Because of what is seen in movies on television's late, late shows and read in books which frequently tend to sensationalize the subject, most people have a distorted perspective as to what goes on in prisons. The Atticas and the Cumminses highlight prison problems, but the day-to-day efforts to help correct society's rejects often go unnoticed. The walls which have served to keep prisoners in have also served to keep the public out, thereby encouraging rumor, malevolent fantasy, and (most unfortunately) occasional unacceptable practices. As the title of this book suggests, these walls are crumbling.

The chapters in this book are a remarkable compendium representing the diverse kinds of people we now find working in our institutions. Prison administrators and inmates have frequently written about their experiences; but it is quite unusual to read chapters written by line officers and staff professionals. Dr. Bliss's article, which depicts a male prison as seen through the eyes of a woman psychiatrist, gives a refreshingly different view even to professionals who have been in corrections for many years.

The diversity of personality types dealt with in the case study section as well as the variety of treatment approaches touched upon throughout the book lend further support to my firm conviction that there are no panaceas in the treatment of offenders. There is no single modality, whether it be reality therapy, transactional analysis, behavior modification, group counseling, or whatever, which is appropriate for all inmates, under all conditions. Rather, the thrust which is evident in these chapters, is the direction in which I see the programs of the Bureau of Prisons moving. We've called it differential treatment—finding which treatment approach is appropriate for which kind of offender under which circumstances as implemented by what type of treater.

The commitment we have made is that federal prisons exist to correct offenders. The need is to develop new kinds of correctional environments in which this objective can be achieved more effectively. The search is for new kinds of programs which can "reach" those offenders we have been less successful with in the past. It is hoped that in time, through intensive in-service training such as described in the chapter by Hosford and Moss, more and more staff members, e.g., case managers, correctional counselors, and line staff, will take active roles in the resocialization process. This will allow the few highly trained psychologists and psychiatrists to step back, at least in the less acute cases, and act largely as consultants, trainers, and program evaluators.

A prisoner in a federal penitentiary sent the following comment in a letter recently: "My primary training (Ph.D. Psychology) and experience were in other forms of social dysfunction—mental health and mental retardation. Even now, although incarcerated, some might judge that no valid claim could be made by me as to any expertise in penological or correctional reform procedures. However, it is interesting to note the striking parallels between the problems of the three social institutions." The point being made, from this unusual perspective, is that institutions housing society's misfits (no matter how defined) are not that different from one another. Just as institutions for the mentally ill and mentally defective have finally become a matter for public concern, so have those of corrections; however, all three have a lot of catching up to do.

As the walls crumble we invite our fellow citizens to help us bridge the gap which has so long separated our correctional institutions from our communities; the cooperation between the University of California, Santa Barbara, and the Federal Correctional Institution, Lompoc, is a step in the right direction. We need to work together so that released offenders can "make it" in our world.

Introduction

The programs and courses of treatment described in this book were conceived and carried out for the most part at the Federal Correctional Institution (F.C.I.) at Lompoc, California. The institution was originally constructed as a maximum security disciplinary prison by the United States Army in 1947, on part of Camp Cooke (now known as Vandenberg Air Force Base). The United States Department of Justice negotiated a lease on the property in 1959, and it was transformed into a correctional facility for adult civilian male offenders, largely those serving their first felony convictions. The main institution complex is a series of stark concrete buildings, resting on twenty acres and surrounded by two double-link chain fences, with six guard towers. It is located 60 miles northwest of Santa Barbara in what the natives like to call the "Valley of the Flowers," which is not an exaggeration, since the area produces about half of all commercial flower seeds in the world.

F.C.I., Lompoc, has currently about 1450 felons, the majority being between the ages of 18 and 26 (recently with the building of new institutions, the population is changing, growing older with longer sentences). The majority of residents are serving sentences for taking cars across state lines, smuggling or selling drugs, robbing banks, pirating commercial jetliners, counterfeiting, and so forth; a few are in for murder. In racial composition, about 40 percent are equally divided between Blacks and Chicanos, 55 percent are Caucasians, and 5 percent are Indians. Most of the inmates are within the prison proper, but there is an appendage in the form of a recently initiated camp with minimum security precautions. It was this camp which achieved a temporary notoriety as the "Watergate prison" when some of the offenders convicted in the Watergate affair served their time at it. Selected minimum-custody, nonviolent inmates throughout the western part of the United States are transferred here to begin their re-entry into society. The staff of F.C.I., as a whole, numbers approximately 390 persons, and by far the greatest number by discipline are the officers (170).

Recently there has developed an increased public concern about the role that prisons play in society. While many people are under the impression that correctional institutions act as rehabilitative agents of society, the facts refute this belief in the great majority of cases. Prisons, for the most part, are not rehabilitative, but custodial institutions designed primarily to separate the offender from the "outside world." Indeed, even the stereotyped prison which one usually envisions—the massive gray structure, tall guard towers, rows of barbed wire—supports the general assumption that these facilities exist primarily to punish the inmate and to isolate him from society. The inmate is regimented, institutionalized, not taught to make decisions, nor to accept responsibility. And when the institution has finally taught him to lead this abnormal life, and he has served his time, he is expected to adapt to a normal society. It is simply impossible to teach a person to be able to live successfully in society if you isolate him completely from that society; that is, if an individual is taught only abnormal behavior and is exposed only to abnormal behavior, few opportunities exist for him to learn how to behave in normal ways.

Fortunately, many people now realize that punishment per se does little to rehabilitate an individual. Support for this view is found in the high recidivism rate of prior offenders as well as in the findings of correctional and experimental psychology. Rather than punishment, the evidence overwhelmingly suggests that if we are to rehabilitate an individual effectively, we must help him acquire the kind of knowledge and skills that he will need in order to be a useful member of society. To accomplish these goals, correctional programs need to be implemented which are designed specifically to help inmates respond appropriately to the variety of program situations which they will encounter during and after incarceration. To be effective, i.e., to rehabilitate the inmate to the point that he will not engage in subsequent antisocial behavior, such programs must set as their objectives not punishment (because it doesn't work) but results that are related specifically to the kinds of personal, social, and vocational skills these individuals need to learn in order to function successfully and appropriately in society. Individuals who have learned to communicate effectively with others and to do the types of behaviors society as a whole reinforces so that they feel positive about themselves as persons, and who have learned those vocational and academic skills which pay off in life, have little need to use inappropriate (criminal) behaviors in order to receive the type of reinforcements they seek.

The first section of the book deals with correctional programs and issues and presents a general outline of some key programs which we hope will begin to reduce some of those inmate behaviors which are counterproductive to functioning successfully in society, e.g., hostility, bitterness, depression, and social withdrawal. Inability to make effective personal, educational, and vocational decisions; being unable to satisfy the expectations of families, peers, and society; withdrawal from social situations; or just being unable to relax are but a few of the examples of the kinds of behaviors which are often related directly or indirectly to the individual's continuing criminal involvement. On the other hand, when individuals learn more appropriate positive social skills, then the utilitarian value itself of this new behavior serves to enhance and maintain the new socially acceptable ways of behaving.

In the second half of the book, which deals with illustrative counseling cases, there is a heavy emphasis on short-term, time-limited, crisis-oriented counseling in contrast to more traditional psychoanalytic psychotherapy. While the latter utilizes a historical approach to understanding the individual, the former is essentially nonhistorical. The emphasis in counseling is on the person's current problems and ways of behaving rather than "insight" as to how they developed, i.e., new behavior rather than insight per se is considered curative. The interaction between the therapist's personality and that of the client is also deemphasized with the result that little stress is placed on transference and the danger of countertransference. Finally, this approach attempts to work within the individual's present frame of reference or life style rather than attempting to bring about basic changes within the client's personality. The limited professional mental health staffs of correctional institutions alone would necessitate short-term therapy, but it goes much deeper than that, signifying subscription to a markedly different treatment philosophy. This is the type of treatment now conducted in most comprehensive community mental health settings—it is also taught by many graduate schools of clinical or counseling psychology under the guise of behavior modification. For correctional institutions, it encompasses training other staff as the change agents—including the line officers—to become skillful in the performance of psychological functions; at the Federal Correctional Institution at Lompoc we are even exploring ways to place certain selected inmates in a counseling role.

We are under no delusion that we have taken a traditional prison and magically transformed it into an open system, but we do think that we have taken several giant strides in that direction. However, we are pragmatic in the recognition that, whether we like it or not, society will demand prisons for a long time to come. But we do believe it is possible to change these prisons from the traditional cages to something more rehabilitative than what has been imagined to date.

We think that what is happening here is exciting and provocative. To grossly simplify, our program is the amalgamation of Warden Kenton's progressive thinking based on thirty years within the correctional setting; Dr. Moss's orientation taken from community mental health, combined with the promising developments of behavioral counseling; and an endeavor of cooperation between two institutions serving the public—the correctional facility and the university.

As this book neared publication, we noted the appearance of a second book about the Federal Correctional Institution at Lompoc, written by Lewis Merklin, a psychiatrist assigned to the prison to fulfill his alternative Selective Service requirement. The book, *They Chose Honor* (Harper and Row, 1974), depicts Merklin's experiences during the period 1967 to 1969. It focuses on a small number of draft resisters organized within the institutional group-psychotherapy program, and their tribulations within the context of being treated as criminals. Not surprisingly, Merklin identifies with their plight; he equates incarceration with dehumanization, which leads inevitably to "petrification" of all inmates. However, we take exception to Merklin's total pessimism about the rehabilitation process within the prison walls, although we realize that it is shared by many authorities, including other psychologists and psychiatrists. While we agree that rehabilitation following the conventional model is not sufficient, what we advocate is a new treatment approach in which both inmates and staff are totally involved. Taken together, these two books should, however, give the broadest representation of two different varieties of mental health programming within the single prison.

Lompoc, California, 1974   RAY E. HOSFORD
                                              C. SCOTT MOSS

I

Issues and Programs

1

Prisons: Rehabilitative or Custodial Institutions?

Frank F. Kenton

To understand the problems involved in the rehabilitation of inmates, it is necessary first to have some understanding of the concept
of the correctional institution in the United States. Traditionally, the
correctional institution has been viewed as being outside the perim-
eters of society as a whole, as existing to serve society's needs while
being at the same time unworthy of reciprocal assistance. There has
been a reluctance to recognize that the correctional facility exists as
one of society's legitimate institutions with the same needs for support, cooperation, interchange, and interaction as exist among other
institutions. The pervasive feeling has been that we function as a convenient garbage can. Society sweeps in its misfits with cries of "rehabilitate! reform! restructure!" and closes the lid and forgets them.
In effect, society has said to us, "Here is an individual whom we have
been unable to help, even with all the resources and all the institutions
which we have available to us. Because we have failed, we are banish-
ing him from our midst. It is your job to succeed where we have not,
but don't expect any help from us."

Recently, however, lay and professional people have begun to
realize that prisons do not exist in isolation, that they are indeed a
part of the total society. With this realization has come a recognition
that we cannot succeed alone. We need a lot of help if we are to do
our job effectively. Most of all we need to be brought back into society and to be allowed to work side by side with other institutions if
we are to solve society's problems together. Only when the correctional institution is allowed to move back into society can it possibly
prepare its inmates to do the same.

The individuals society places in prisons cannot be forgotten. They are real people with real problems who are struggling in the most unreal of all worlds—the prison—to learn how to make it in the real world outside. It is completely unrealistic to isolate these individuals from the real world and then to expect them upon release to become useful citizens. By restricting the individual exclusively to the prison setting, we are helping him learn how to live within the prison setting, not how to live in the real world outside.

Fortunately, society is beginning to pay more than just lip service to the rehabilitation role of the prisons by increasing cooperation between various institutions and resources of society and the correctional institution. A good indication of this can be seen in the rationale behind the location of many of the new correctional facilities. The aim is no longer isolation from the community. Instead, we try to locate in proximity to population centers, for it is there that we find these resources—religious, social, educational, and vocational—which are so necessary to the rehabilitative effort. At the same time, the community recognizes that it too is an instrument of society and that as such it has certain obligations to cooperate with society's other institutions.

A good example of community involvement is an educational program undertaken in an institution in Connecticut, where the instructor of a community adult education course in industrial psychology agreed to accept some local prison inmates as students in his class. The same course was later held inside the prison for those inmates who, for security reasons, could not attend downtown with a class made up of people from the outside community and of inmates. After the first week the instructor and outside students requested that the prisoners be allowed to wear civilian clothes to avoid making an artificial distinction between the inmates and themselves. These men weren't "prisoners" or "bad guys" but were rather students like themselves. Also, the inmates began to realize that the "good people" on the outside whom they hated or envied or resented were really just ordinary people, that they were in fact just students like themselves. As these people responded to the inmates as fellow students the inmates' own self-perception began to change, and the real world began to be seen as a place less hostile toward them than they had thought. This experiment accomplished more than increasing the interaction between inmates and persons on the outside. It also changed attitudes of persons in the community toward men in prisons. Many of those participating began seeing the inmates not as criminals, but as individuals like themselves—as real men with real problems who, never-theless, had something positive to offer society. Even more important was the effect this acceptance had on the inmates themselves. To find that they were not hated or feared by individuals from the outside went a long way toward promoting changes in their attitudes and subsequent behavior.

It is time that we recognize that society is made up of several different parts, none of which can afford to be exclusive if each part is to do its job effectively; their separation serves more to fragment society than to solve problems. We must promote continual intercourse between each institution and instrument of society. Otherwise, when we are forced to come together—as upon the release of an inmate into the community—we may find that we have defeated ourselves through isolationist policies.

This same principle of avoiding fragmentation within society is also applicable to the process of rehabilitation within the correctional institution. Just as we need to avoid the isolation of the prison from society as a whole, so must we avoid establishing autonomous mini-institutions within the correctional facility which cut the individual into little pieces, allotting so much to education, so much to religion, so much to vocations, and so much to therapy. When each of these rehabilitative programs has completed work on its respective piece, we then try to glue the individual back together again, only we frequently find that the pieces do not fit together the way they should.

If we are serious about trying to rehabilitate the inmate, we must equip him with the skills and knowledge he needs for life on the outside. We cannot accomplish this by running him through a series of semi-related programs. Educational programs can give the individual knowledge; vocational programs can give him skills; religious programs may strengthen his faith and his moral fiber; but what he needs is a way to bring these together and make them work for him so that he can learn to live again in society, in the family, and on the job. Psychological counseling is very important here, but the psychologist cannot do it alone. Instead, counselors, officers, teachers, case workers, ministers, other staff members, and the inmates themselves must work together with the whole individual in the whole situation. Ideally, of course, all those who come into contact with the inmate should cooperate in giving him the kinds of help and support he needs in order to learn how to function successfully as a member of society. Just as cooperation and interaction are vital to the relationship between society and the correctional facility, so are they vital to the relationship and to the effectiveness of programs which exist within the institution itself, for it is only through a real sense of mutuality that we can begin to help the inmates.

At F.C.I., Lompoc, we have recently begun involving our line people more and more in the rehabilitation process. Our correctional officers represent one of our richest sources in the institution for therapy and rehabilitation. These men are an integral part of each inmate's environment. Because they are with the inmates twenty-four hours a day, they are in the prime spot to counsel individuals who are trying to establish goals for themselves and to work out programs within the institution to achieve these goals. We have discovered what others may have known for a long time: for therapy or rehabilitative programs to be effective, they must take place in and utilize all aspects of the individual's environment. Now we are trying to provide opportunities for training which will elicit, extract, and exploit this kind of potential. Not only is the individual inmate benefited, but the rehabilitation program has become much more satisfying, rewarding, and fruitful to the professional practitioner. I no longer say that I have one psychiatrist, two psychologists, and eight social workers, but that I have educators and consultants who assist in the training of others. We are just beginning to discover how much capability we have for true rehabilitation within the institution.

That such changes have had a positive effect on the inmates can be seen in the fact that more inmates than ever before have voluntarily sought personal counseling. As the editors describe in Chapter 9, we have taken psychological services out of the hospital and have put them into contact with the general prison population. Separating adjustment problems from the concept of hospital sickness provided us with some valuable insights within a very short time. For example, we have noticed that the inmate no longer considers himself sick when he says "I am going to a headshrinker" as he did when he saw the same person in the hospital setting where he was expected to behave accordingly—sick. There are now no white coats, no thermometers, no stethoscopes, but instead a variety of humanizing services available.

The program has had an equally positive effect on our various staff members. For example, when everyone is a participant and each is as important as the other in the rehabilitation or counseling process, morale improves. We have developed the unit type of case management whereby case workers, correctional counselors, and psychologists work as partners in the particular unit in which a group of inmates live. We are now working the unit officer—once called the disciplinarian or correctional mechanic—formally into the counseling process and have found many of his insights valuable to the total rehabilitative process of the inmate. We hope that as the unit officer finds himself more involved with others in the rehabilitative process, he will think of himself more as counselor than as custodian.

It is imperative that we implement training programs designed to promote interpersonal communication and other counseling skills, not only for the unit officers, but for every staff member who is willing and able to become involved. When we do that, we will have taken a long step toward the ideal of the professional correctional officer, and toward the unification of the facility into an integral whole. When we can bring together all the elements of the smaller society which constitutes the prison and all of the institutions which constitute the larger society of the world outside, then, and only then, will the correctional facility become more than a custodial servant, more than society's garbage can.

A good instance of cooperation between the total correctional facility and society's other institutions can be seen in that between the Federal Correctional Institution at Lompoc and the University of California, a reciprocal involvement which led to the publication of these essays. While this book offers many important techniques for helping the inmate psychologically, perhaps its most significant contribution lies in its example of the establishment of a cooperative bond between institutions and thus between the individual members of those institutions and between the various mini-institutions which exist within the facility itself. If we are to deal successfully with correctional problems, there is going to have to be more of this kind of breaking down of walls, of reunification, of coming together. If we are successful, perhaps one day even the physical walls may come down.

2

The Development of a Correctional Human Resources Program

C. Scott Moss

Until recently the mental health division has played a relatively restricted and conventional role in the Federal Correctional System. Now, however, the system is expanding along many dimensions and the Federal Correctional Institution at Lompoc aspires to take the leadership role in a number of areas, including an "experimental" effort to extend what ordinarily might be called Mental Health Services, but which we prefer to call Human Services or Human Resources. The following discussion of the highlights of relatively recent developments in Human Services within the Lompoc facility is intended to provide part of the context for training not only of psychology graduate students but for all of those staff members who come into contact with the inmates and who are thus in positions to influence inmate behavior.

The inception of the Human Resources Center at F.C.I., Lompoc, can be traced to early 1970. Indeed, when I came to the facility for a job interview in the spring of that year, one thing which impressed me was an escorted tour of the prison hospital by the chief medical officer, who indicated that serious consideration was being given to converting the then-vacant third floor into some type of mental health center. When I returned as the chief psychologist in the fall, I was given a copy of a proposal for establishing a counseling center which had been drawn up in the interim, the product of an ad hoc committee under the direction of the chief medical officer, but also bearing the unmistakable imprint of another psychologist in the institution, Burton Kerish. The document provided the beginning of a rationale for the center which to some extent still holds. The stated objectives were

(1) to unify the then badly fragmented services—education, social service, the chaplains, mental health, etc.—into a centrally located place; (2) to maintain a higher standard of guidance through much needed coordination; and (3) to provide a training institute for graduate students in counseling psychology who were beginning to come here from the University of California, Santa Barbara.

It was also evident that the warden had decided against establishing the counseling center on the third floor of the hospital, ostensibly because he was thinking of a more accessible place. The proposal had generated quite a bit of interest, but when I did not hear any more about it for two months, I decided that the notion had probably died on the proverbial vine. Unbeknownst to me, however, the warden was simply waiting for a strategic moment to present the idea to the director of the Federal Bureau of Prisons, which he did the following October.

At the very first meeting after my arrival, the warden asked if I had any objections to being allied with case management rather than with the prison hospital. It was his feeling that those working in Human Services should not in any way be connected with the old medical model approach to mental health. I replied that I not only had no objections, I was really most enthusiastic. Over ten years ago I had begun making the transition from clinical psychology to community mental health and was thus pleased to learn that I was being placed in close proximity to the eight adjustment or treatment teams, at the heart of decision-making about the inmates. In retrospect, it is clear that this was one of the most crucial decisions made in respect to setting up the center.

The psychiatrist, Barbara Bliss, who was hired next, similarly was placed out of the hospital, although being an M.D., she was given special liaison with the physicians. Shortly thereafter, Burt Kerish was also brought out of the hospital, thus ending the formal alignment of mental health (Human Services) to physical medicine. And on the arrival of the second Ph.D. psychologist, Kenneth Lebow, who was placed in charge of the drug abuse program (part of Human Resources), there was no hesitation in placing him away from the hospital setting as well.

Let me, without going into extensive detail, point out a few basic differences between community psychology and psychiatry or clinical psychology. Community psychology is simply a discipline which addresses itself to pressing social problems for which at this time adequate solutions do not exist. Clinicians, on the other hand, deal with mental abnormalities of individuals. The objective of community psychology is *prevention;* the focus is on the mentally healthy and on trying to structure the environment in such a way as to prevent people from developing mental problems. The primary difference between the two lies in the separation of community psychology from any adherence to the medical model and in its close alliance to education and learning theory.

To my mind, the introduction of a community psychology program at F.C.I. meant doing away with the prison environment as far as and as rapidly as possible, and bringing in the more positive aspects of society at large. The development of modern, productive prison industry and the increase of work and study furlough programs are steps in this direction (Nietzel and Moss, 1972). Family-oriented or conjoint group therapy is another. Homosexuality could be largely controlled through the granting of conjugal visits, although home furloughs would be even better. But of all the current innovations in corrections, none perhaps offers as much promise in terms of rehabilitation as that of handling of individual offenders within the local community, e.g., in halfway homes and similar facilities, rather than in county or city jails. In terms of expense, recidivism, employment, and reintegration into society, community-administered programs have the advantage over institutional handling. In my opinion, insofar as possible prisons should be used only for the chronic and/or violent offender. Open institutions can and should become commonplace for juvenile and even adult offenders without histories of violent acting out (Warren, 1967, 1968, 1969). In this way the disabling effects of institutionalization can be largely avoided, while rehabilitation is promoted. And only in this manner will the high rate of recidivism be markedly reduced.

After a decade of promoting a national community mental health program, first as a consultant for the National Institute of Mental Health and later as a professor of psychology at the University of Illinois, I found a fascinating and happy coincidence between these objectives of community psychology and their application to the Human Resources Center we were developing at F.C.I., Lompoc. Every prison is, in effect, a self-contained community like that of the state hospital system; this containment is at the same time its greatest detriment. Like the old state mental hospitals, the prison must be opened up to the greater outside community and the latter must bear a much greater responsibility for the prevention and rehabilitation of its own social deviants. Such reforms will minimize the unhealthy aspects of incarceration. To my way of thinking, there is no scientific proof that placing human beings in cages for any period of time has the slightest beneficial effect on the imprisoned individual. Prisons, in and of themselves, are a detriment to the rehabilitation of the individual. It was because I held this point of view that the warden invited me to join the staff at F.C.I. and eventually placed me in charge of developing a Human Resources Center employing the principles of community psychology.

The warden's first memo in respect to the center, issued in January 1971, designated a Human Resources Advisory Committee to plan and develop the center, and stipulated that the committee would be made up of the two associate wardens for programs and operations, the captain, the chief of case management, the hospital administrator and the four key mental health professional people, with me as chairman. The composition of this committee gave evidence of the warden's plan to thoroughly integrate the center with the total correctional program. Consistent with the principle with which we were developing the center, at each meeting all other programs represented by the participating members of the committee receive equal consideration. The theme that is being fostered is coordination and integration, which in my opinion is essential for any community mental health program to be truly effective.

The implementation of a Human Resources Center concept serves as an important step toward achieving a more humanitarian program for the inmate to compensate partly for the fundamental factor of prison life—keeping the individual locked up for the protection of society. Another result of the implementation of this concept is that it should change the viewpoint of inmates, staff, and students toward psychological services per se. What we state about the new center is somewhat factual, somewhat speculative, since it involves a radical change in the thinking that remains to be translated into the actions of all staff members. In a sense the presentation at this time may be premature. However, it is important to point out that the concept of such a center is essentially new to the Federal Prison System.

In May, 1971, the concept of the center was given official recognition by the United States Public Health Service through a new reorganization plan which placed the position of the mental health coordinator on par with that of the chief of the health services within the institution and that of the hospital administrator officer. Now all three are responsible directly to the warden.

About this same time (May, 1971) the mental health service at

F.C.I. became the recipient of an innovative treatment program called transactional analysis (TA). An associate warden who had been transferred from the federal penitentiary at Marion, Illinois, which had a therapeutic community utilizing TA, arranged for the transfer to Lompoc of two prisoners to begin teaching fundamentals of transactional analysis to volunteer inmates through the education department. However, shortly after initiating the program, the associate warden left the correctional system and the mental health section was given administrative responsibility for the program. Quite deliberately we began introducing other schools of psychotherapeutic thought into the curriculum, and in time, under the direction of Burt Kerish, TA was expanded into the peer counseling program (see Chapter 5). The single, most important element in the program is that it is inmate-conducted and inmate-directed, under the nominal supervision of mental health personnel, and thereby escapes the usual resistance on the part of inmates to staff-led counseling groups. Another form of lay therapy, reevaluation counseling, was also started by Dr. Bliss, our psychiatrist, with the help of a reevaluation group from Santa Barbara. This program too, was eventually incorporated into the peer counseling program. Reevaluation differs markedly from TA in that it is very positive and supportive throughout rather than focusing on confrontation as does TA.

In September of the same year, we opened up the brand new Human Resources Center—which lasted exactly six weeks. It was a combination of mental health and drug abuse counseling, but a short time after the opening, an edict from the central office in Washington arrived requiring the separation of drug abuse programs from mental health, thus ending the "marriage." In addition to the desires of the central office, there was a concern on the part of the warden with the isolation of the mental health staff from the rest of the prison programs. His concern fitted our own private trepidations. Thus we moved out of the center, dispersed along the main corridor of the institution, and again became closely allied with the case manager. At my request, my office remained in the retitled Drug Abuse Treatment Center because of the added space needed for consultants and graduate students in training, and because I felt that my presence would also serve to maintain some articulation between the drug abuse and human resources programs.

During the last quarter of 1971, we added a pilot program of nine UCSB graduate students in counselor training at the institution. Six of them were taking two courses, a practicum and a seminar on behavioral counseling, taught by Ray Hosford. In addition to setting up a specific training program in which students were assigned inmates to see individually, we attempted to provide them with some feeling for the correctional facility as a whole and at the same time to give the staff some information on the students and what they were doing. The students were a small but important part of a comprehensive inservice training program that was gradually evolving.

Before coming to the institution, the students were given an initial indoctrination at the university by Dr. Hosford. As a matter of policy, each year F.C.I. schedules a refresher course of several days duration to bring the staff up-to-date on the latest correctional techniques, and the students were also included in this instruction. During the practicum training period, the students ate lunch at the institution and as typical of visitors to the prison setting, isolated themselves at a table in the officer's dining room. This situation was changed when they were asked by us to disperse themselves throughout the dining area in order to converse with staff members, thus enhancing both their learning and that of staff members as well.

Originally the practicum and seminar were both set up to take place on the third floor of the hospital, but the warden again perceived that this was a mistake since it simply perpetuated the conceptualization of counseling or therapy as a medical regimen, and the training was transferred to the education department, where even the individual sessions took place behind large transparent windows. This did much to dispel for the students, staff, and inmates alike the mystique of the counseling sessions. Hosford invited the case management staff members to enroll in the course, and two of them did. In addition, I went out of my way to announce weekly to the staff that they were all invited to attend the afternoon seminars. Although only a few of the staff came, they did know that the seminars were open to them.

During the course the students were given the opportunity to take a tour of the F.C.I. Because their guide was the chief of case management, this also gave them the opportunity to acquaint themselves with some part of the case management function of the institution. In the final session of the course, the warden provided the students with a summary session of his view of the role of correctional institutions in the rehabilitation of inmates. He took the opportunity to show them a film on the work release program which he had instigated previously at another institution. As a final formal consequence of the course, each participant worked up a case summary of his particular inmate and the results of the counseling, which collectively were presented to the warden and the remainder of the staff. Two of these reports—those by Boulette and George—constitute chapters in the second section.

Since the inauguration of this pilot seminar, F.C.I., Lompoc, has continued to serve as an expanding training center for counseling psychologists. Since the initial experience of UCSB graduate students, we have striven to provide the students with a more realistic and comprehensive practicum experience. We have wondered, for instance, how we might simulate a part of their experiences so that they have an idea what it is like to be incarcerated. We are, of course, aware that on a few occasions it has been possible to pass students off as patients in mental hospitals. And we are cognizant of Zimbardo's work at Stanford in which he exposed volunteers to simulated prison conditions (1971). But we thought having students admitted as inmates in a real prison setting was far too great a risk to take. The inmates are too sharp and too suspicious—they are always looking for "FBI plants." The result could be catastrophic and even if perpetuated would be almost impossible to repeat again. To date the best we have done has been to have each of the male students join in-coming inmates and participate with them in week-long programs in the correctional setting. Interestingly enough, the students' identification with the inmates is something almost too complete and sometimes serves to the detriment of the relationships with the correctional officers. Partially to offset this tendency, we have recently added to the orientation program a three-day session for new students by the custodial staff.

In addition to providing the students with individual counseling and group experiences, we have also undertaken to provide them with some exposure in data collection, evaluation, and applied forms of research. One student, for example, is collecting pre- and post-tests from inmates who are involved in plastic facial surgery (rhinoplasty) to try to determine what immediate psychological changes are experienced; a second student attempted to determine what benefits (if any) are accrued by the process of categorizing inmates during the initial admission interview into different categories of predicted adjustment within the institution; a third counselor is attempting to monitor the changes within an experimental unit that has been set up within F.C.I. and to compare these observations with those made on another unit that was selected to serve as a "control"; and a fourth student is evaluating the effect of formal drug abuse information given by Operation Breakthrough (see Chapter 7). None of these has the rigorous control that we would like, but each serves as an introduction to program evaluation and as a possible pilot study to future research. With the support of the central office in Washington, in 1972–73 we received our first full-time, year-long counseling psychology intern, who is completing, as the first doctoral dissertation at this facility, a study comparing and contrasting two modes of teaching behavioral counseling procedures to personnel.

Relative to this study, in recent weeks arrangements were made for personnel in case management to receive an intensive (forty hours) in-service training package in the fundamentals of behavior counseling. We were fortunate to be able to set it up in a paradigm we could study. Half of the case managers and counselors were exposed to the training by the actual instructors (composed of Ray Hosford, Jules Zimmer, and Don Atkinson, all from UCSB, plus the warden and me); the other half were exposed to the same training "symbolically" by videotape. It is hoped that the two versions will prove to be more or less comparable because then we will be in a position to share the training with other departments and/or across institutions, without elaborate consultation being needed. As an additional part of the training, case management staff members, having gone through the course, meet on regular weekly sessions with three advanced graduate counseling psychology students in discussion of particular problems in the application of behavioral techniques to their caseloads. At this writing we are six months away from any definite results; however, regardless of the outcome of this experiment, we are again sharing our expertise with the other change agents within the prison, and they with us. Further, there is discussion of taking a unit and running it according to behavioral principles.

In summary, the question may well arise for some as to the relationship between community psychology and the behavioral orientation, since both are integral parts of our program. Community psychology to my way of thinking is little more than an attitude or a philosophy rather than a particular body of knowledge. This attitude is best represented as *seeking* into social systems rather than *waiting* to treat the chronic disability or a *preventing* rather than a *repairing* attitude. The defining characteristic seems to be the effort to reach out beyond the office, clinic, or hospital directly into the community

—in the beginning, starting with a community that is defined by a state hospital or the walls of a prison.[1] On the other hand, the tremendous conceptual and practical strides which have characterized the social-learning behavioral approach to human problems in general have focused the attention of psychologists more and more sharply on the environmental determinants of human behavior. The development of requisite skills and motivations, through appropriate environment structuring and enrichment, is seen with increasing clarity as a major goal of community psychology and behavior modification. Thus we are bringing to bear the two leading innovations that have influenced applied psychology in the past decade.

The nation's penal system has been described increasingly by vociferous critics as a miserable failure as a crime deterrent, and certainly if the success is to be measured in terms of returning an offender to the community without further involvement in crime, then there is no question that the traditional penal institutions often intensify and compound the problem. But the basic question is where does the fault lie? As seen now, to a very large extent the penal system is simply an outmoded community gesture toward the misguided belief that social misfits can be punished into becoming socially acceptable persons; unfortunately, it has been proven that punishment in and of itself does not lead to rehabilitation. The solution must be found within society itself, rather than in warehousing people away. There is an expanding chorus that advocates a shift toward community-based correctional programs geared to the early release of offenders on parole or probation, with the assistance in rehabilitation

---

[1] The characteristics of a solidly trained community psychology person, as I see it, are as follows: (a) The community psychology person does not hide behind such shields of professionalism as a white coat, a mantle of diplomas, or the term "doctor." He is known by his deeds rather than by indicators of status and prestige. (b) He is trained as a generalist and has the broadest possible perspective. He is at home in all sorts of institutions and community settings and is able to establish collaborative relationships with a wide range of agencies and disciplines. (c) He thinks of the concept of "mental health" (human resources) as a striving for normality rather than as some illness or sickness or some psychiatric nosological entity in his training. (d) He largely foregoes individual and even group treatment in favor of a consultative and training relationship in which services are provided through paraprofessional, semi-professional, and allied professional people. (e) He is trained in how to provide the very best coordination of available services, since too often clients fall between the cracks left by uncoordinated/and duplicated agency programs. (f) He has sophistication in comprehensive mental health planning on a large scale. He realizes that in the past, planning grew out of crisis; he sees a future where problems can be anticipated. (g) Finally, he engages in social innovation based on applied research. He has knowledge of program evaluation and research utilization, i.e., putting research knowledge to work.

from local residents and groups (e.g., National Advisory Commission on Criminal Justice, 1973). One has only to witness the success in the transition from an antiquated, overcrowded state system to a viable comprehensive community based mental health program as testimony to the fact that active community involvement is possible; similarly the idea is to prepare the offender to carry on life in the community, not to prepare him to live in an unnatural lifestyle of an institution.

Yet, where it was generally accepted that no more than 5 percent of the mentally disturbed patients were ever a threat to society, the figure must remain open at the moment in terms of the adult male prisoner, and one suspects it would be a higher proportion. Even when the transfer of responsibility is accomplished, there will be a residual population of both chronic and hostile acting-out individuals that still requires institutional treatment. Bringing about this critical shift will require constant evaluation and continuous public education (convincing the correctional staff of such a radical alternative will not be as difficult as is often assumed, since they bear daily witness to the inefficiency and ineffectiveness of the present methods). Being a pragmatist, I believe that we are bringing about a partial solution during this time of transition—that it is possible, using social learning techniques, to rehabilitate some proportion of the residents even within the confines of this changing setting.

REFERENCES

National Advisory Commission on Criminal Justice. 1973. *Preliminary report on standards and goals.*

Nietzel, M. T., and Moss, C. S. 1972. A reformulation of the role of the psychologist in the criminal system. *Professional Psychology* 3 (3): 259–70.

Warren, M. Q. 1967. *The community treatment project after five years.* California Youth Authority, Div. Research.

———. 1968. Classification of offenders as an aid to efficient management and effective treatment. In President's Commission on Law Enforcement and Administration of Justice, *The Challenge of crime in a free society: A report.* New York: Dutton.

———. 1969. The case for differential treatment of delinquents. *Annals of the American Academy of Political and Social Science* 381: 47–59.

Zimbardo, P. G. 1971. The psychological power and pathology of imprisonment. Statement prepared for U.S. House of Representatives, Committee on the Judiciary, Oct. 25, 1971, pp. 1–11.

3

The Group Leadership Training Program at F.C.I., Lompoc

Stewart B. Shapiro

INTRODUCTION

In August of 1969 the chief psychologist and the psychiatrist at the Federal Correctional Institution at Lompoc, California, requested my services as a consultant to help organize and conduct a group counseling program there. My initial function was to train a group of leaders drawn from various parts of the staff, including correctional officers, medical personnel, case workers, and people from industry, education, and the personnel department.

The long-range objectives for the total program were to reduce alienation among inmates and to improve staff-inmate relationships at all levels. The short-range instrumental objectives were to train group leaders and develop staff-led voluntary inmate counseling groups.

As a result of the original contact, a memo was sent to the staff by the acting warden, indicating that the institution had acquired my services as a consultant from the University of California, Santa Barbara. All department heads were urged to attend an initial scheduled meeting, as were those of their respective staff who could be spared from normal line duty. Staff members who had had previous contact with group work and all others interested in an innovative program were urged to ask their supervisors for permission to attend.

ORGANIZING THE PROGRAM

Thirty-four staff members attended the first session, including Dr. Norman Barr, chief of psychiatric services of the Federal Bureau of Prisons.

After I was introduced, I opened this meeting by asking each participant to answer the following question: "How can I become more productive and what can I learn here that will enable me to perform my function within this institution?" I then asked for six volunteers to sit in a circle in the middle of the room and discuss the above question for thirty minutes, while the remainder of the group, acting as observers, was asked to comment on the issues raised by the volunteers. At the end of the thirty-minute period I summarized the discussion in terms of the four major areas of concern which I heard emerging from the participants: (1) a need for increased understanding of self; (2) improved understanding of inmates; (3) more effective staff communication; and (4) a better definition of the mission and "product" of the organization.

The entire group was then divided into four voluntary interest groups corresponding to these areas of concern with instructions to (a) go deeper into what was desired and to list the interests of the participants; (b) rank lists of interests by priority; and (c) state an ideal picture of what the institution would look like five years from now if everything was as they desired it to be. Following this exercise, which took thirty minutes, each group reported its findings to the rest and feedback was again received. My summary of the "products" of these interest groups emphasized growth rather than deficiency. In effect, I was looking for ways of improving what "is" by concentrating on positive goals and by using imagery which would promote the attainment of these goals. This method, called "path-goal" imagery, is used to help negotiate goals of groups by searching for common grounds. At this time I also introduced the method of sensitivity training as one way of developing both individual congruence and interpersonal empathy in achieving common organizational goals.

Following what appeared to be a very successful beginning—judging from the quality and amount of participation and the flow of ideas and feelings—I met briefly with the medical staff and we decided to begin the group leadership training program per se with a group of twelve staff members (including the psychologist and psychiatrist) meeting for eight two-hour sessions once a week. My rationale for this experienced-based form of training was that in my opinion the best way to become a group leader is first to have some experience as a group member.

After the eight sessions of leadership training, five staff members were to be selected to be co-leaders with the psychiatrist or the psychologist conducting inmate groups for eight additional sessions.

Depending on progress made, each staff member there would be expected to lead subsequent groups independently with only weekly supervisory sessions or "clinics."

DESCRIPTION OF TRAINING SESSIONS

The following account of the first series of eight leadership training sessions is fairly representative of all those which followed. Even though subsequent training sessions were different in at least two very important respects—inclusion of inmates as trainees and significant extension of the number of sessions—the style and pattern of techniques and theory presentations were essentially the same.

SESSION 1

The first session utilized the "fish bowl empathy exercise" in which the group members were paired off in two concentric circles: an inner circle made up of "participants" who were asked to discuss what being in such a training group meant to them, and an outer circle made up of "observers," each of whom was asked to act as an "alter-ego" feeding back the feelings, perceptions, and ideas expressed by his pair-partner in the inner circle.

After the feedback from the "alter-ego" observers, each pair of participants "de-briefed" the experience by moving to the center of the total group and talking about such questions as the accuracy of the "alter-ego's" feedback, the feelings of what it's like to be observed and the behavioral cues which made it easy or difficult for the observers to "read" the inner participants, etc.

In summing up this "fish bowl" method, I stressed the differences between interpretation, clinical observation, mere factual description, and genuine empathy; I defined empathy as the ability to put oneself accurately in the shoes of another . . . to feel, think, and see in some degree as the other. This, I felt, set a tone for one of the major themes of the Leadership Training Program: one of empathy and understanding as contrasted with mere observation, clinical analysis or judgmental criticism of one another.

Following the first group session I met with the psychologist and psychiatrist to discuss and evaluate the session and in particular the implications of the presence of the warden and the chief medical officer, who had participated in the first session with the rest of us. It was felt that the inclusion of these two officials should be discussed further at the next meeting.

SESSION 2

All members of the group were present at this session. The warden announced that he would have to miss several meetings and asked the group how they felt about his irregular attendance. He offered the alternative of leaving this group or of possibly attending a later one. Much discussion followed and the warden was asked to leave in order to allow the group to come to a decision on what appeared to me to be a very important issue. The group spent the entire session on this issue and ended with such divided opinions that a decision could not be reached. At the end of this meeting I asked the members to list: (1) their feelings (e.g., anxiety, frustration, hope, anger, indecision, etc.); (2) group issues which had emerged (e.g., the "price of admission" to this group, membership norms, authority problems, etc.); (3) other salient issues (e.g., the politics of having the warden in or out of the group, inhibitions in his presence, possible consequences for the future of the entire group program, etc.).

By way of summary, I indicated that the central issues that had emerged were (a) the development of trust and (b) the group issue of inclusion-exclusion, and I encouraged the group to continue to work with these problems in the next session.

In the clinic following this meeting, I expressed strong satisfaction with the group, for I felt there was an unusual degree of honesty, especially given the coercive nature of the institution and the high-risk value of the issues involved. I felt that this group did not back away from these very sticky, difficult issues and from its beginning showed an encouraging willingness to deal with its internal problems.

SESSION 3

The warden was not present at this meeting and left word with the group that he would have additional engagements making his attendance even less frequent than originally planned. Apparently there had been considerable discussion about his inclusion or exclusion among many of the group members during the week between meetings, for in his absence arguments continued in full force, with much ambivalence in many members. However, a gradual "hardening" of the position of some of the members against his irregular attendance influenced the group and it decided that if the warden could not attend the great majority of the meetings, he should be excluded from the group. The chief medical officer, who could attend most meetings and who was therefore included in the group, was chosen as emissary to inform the warden of the group's decision to exclude him.

Since these decisions, which gave great relief to the group, appeared to provide emotional closure, I took the opportunity to outline what I thought had happened in the three sessions up to this point. I divided my summary observations into three headings: (1) Self, (2) Group, (3) Other Learnings.

1. *Self:* (a) If I withheld personal feelings in my role as leader, they tended to come out too strongly later; (b) indecision is frustrating and disturbing to many people compared to the more desirable image of being strong, firm and decisive; (c) leadership styles differ and their effects on groups differ significantly; (d) the ability to change one's mind during a session may not be an indication of weakness, but rather an example of appropriate flexibility.

2. *Group:* (a) In the influence process, each person tries to make sense and to be persuasive, he depends on past relationships, listens to others, and is able to show respect for minority opinions and for those holding them; (b) the development of trust in a group takes "testing time," and passing through group crises; (c) the group decision on the inclusion-exclusion issue was important—nearly all groups sooner or later deal with this basic issue of group life; (d) the process of delegation of authority and its relationship to group development and trust should be noted (e.g., sending the C.M.O. to inform the warden of the group's decision to exclude him); (e) the existence and evidence of strong informal leadership in the group was demonstrated; (f) growing groups, self-conscious about process, tend to make "mountains out of molehills"—issues which may *appear* trivial to the groups become enlarged as symbols of importance for them.

3. *Other Learnings:* (a) The manner in which a group deals with crucial or difficult decisions or situations helps to shape its destiny; various decision-making alternatives could be: postponement; airing of individual feelings and opinions on the issue; respect for and listening to others' feelings; appeal to an expert or professional leader for the "right" decision; (b) double messages in which there are contradictory elements often produce such responses in the receiver as alienation, despair, hostility, or self-doubt; (c) some of the above phenomena are frequently found in the communications and images in any large organization or institution.

SESSION 4

This session was characterized by considerable carry-over of the inclusion-exclusion issue from the previous sessions. Group members appeared to be very reluctant to abandon this topic, and I pointed this out to the group. After my process intervention, the discussion gradually turned to specific "here-and-now" communications between group members. Personal feelings and problems were aired and two members in particular solicited feedback from the group on these problems. I pointed out the importance for the group of both the request for feedback (trust) and its being given (a norm for the helping process in the group).

SESSION 5

In this meeting I presented my theory of interpersonal contracts (Shapiro, 1968), and the contract exercise which is derived from this theory. My major points were that there is much unnecessary conflict in interpersonal relations due to violation of *implicit* agreements. Because these "agreements" are seldom made explicit, there is a tendency to rely on undisclosed expectations, which may result in considerable distortion.

The interpersonal contract exercise was demonstrated to the group as a possible corrective for these difficulties. Each member was then asked to interview each other member and to list: What do I want from him? What does he want from me? What do I want from myself in the context of my relationship to him?

I pointed out that there are three basic dimensions of contracts: social (interpersonal), task, and learning. Also, I instructed each pair of members to negotiate interpersonal, task, or learning contracts or a combination of all three. That is, if one member of a pair could not meet certain expectations or wishes of the other member, he was to agree to discuss the problem openly so that a viable agreement could be reached. The group members were also advised to make their contracts renegotiable so they would not become too rigid, legalistic, or binding.

There was time for approximately four series of pairings in which the participants exchanged wishes and expectations in order to form contracts, which were written down according to the three questions in the format. Several members spontaneously mentioned that this was a very helpful exercise because it led to insights about themselves and their frequently "unspoken" or implicit quasi-agreements with others which had led to difficulties in the past.

SESSION 6

I began this session with a didactic presentation of the self theory of J. W. Kinch (1967). This theory postulates connections between the self-concept, what one perceives others think of him, what they actually think of him, and his actual behavior. According to this theory, behavior is held to be a function of self-concept which, in turn, is related to perceived opinions which are related to actual opinions of others. Actual opinions of the actor are also a function of how he actually behaves.[1]

In the context of a training group, I pointed out that the function of feedback is that it makes explicit to the actor what others think of him so that he can correct and refine his perception of their attitudes. Thus, a therapeutic cycle can take place if constructive feedback corrects distortions and helps each member to develop a realistically positive self-concept based on his own behavior and its effect on his fellow group members.

Since the therapeutic corrective cycle for development of a realistic positive self-concept depends on skillful, constructive feedback, I presented the group with the following criteria for promoting this kind of feedback. Constructive feedback (N.T.L., 1969) includes information which is (1) descriptive rather than evaluative; (2) specific rather than general, i.e., is tied to specific, observable behaviors in the group; (3) illustrative of *both* giver and receiver needs of feedback; (4) about behavior that can be changed; (5) given only when solicited; (6) presented as soon as possible after the behavior occurs, if the timing and the group emotion or mood is appropriate; (7) capable of being and often checked for clarity by the giver and receiver; (8) checked for clarity and accuracy with the entire group.

After discussing the criteria for feedback in the group, I offered a definition of anxiety in terms of Kinch's self-theory (1967): "Anxiety in this context is the result of losing control of the perception of what others think of you." The extreme form of this anxiety is what is often meant by the term "paranoid."

Following this presentation I helped the group recall examples of both constructive and nonconstructive feedback taken from our own group experience.

[1] Editors' note: Whether attitudes cause behavior or feedback on behavior causes attitudes, is a heuristic question.

SESSION 7

Prior to this session the staff of the Mental Health Service (psychologist, psychiatrist, chief medical officer, and I) had decided that those members of the group who were ready should be paired as co-leaders and begin working with inmate groups as soon as possible. Each of these staff-led inmate groups were to be observed by a rotating clinical team including me and the psychologist and psychiatrist. The professional staff would then meet with the leaders in a regular supervisory clinic which could also serve as a way of evaluating which group leaders were ready to continue independently.

In this session the members were asked how they felt about beginning inmate groups immediately and many members expressed doubts about their competence. Discussion of these feelings of anxiety and responsibility took up most of this meeting. The members were reassured that their insecurities were understandable and "normal," and that they would have the continued support of the professional staff both in direct observation of their work in inmate groups and the regular clinic sessions after each inmate group meeting.

In my summary of this session I pointed out two useful techniques which had been demonstrated: (1) the taking of turns around the group with each member expressing feelings, thoughts, and opinions; (2) the allowing of free individual expression of anxiety which sets a norm to free others to express their anxieties. It was felt that these techniques or norms would lead to a discussion of the reality of having the members leading inmate groups with minimal interference from partially repressed emotions.

Between sessions 7 and 8 a memo was sent by the clinical psychologist associated with the group training project which indicated that an expansion of the small groups' discussion program was taking place. All inmates were encouraged to volunteer for ten ninety-minute sessions which would be limited to eight members per group. Group leaders were to be staff members who participated in the earlier training sessions.

SESSION 8

At this session, which was our last scheduled leadership training meeting, I disclosed to the group members my experiences in the detailed institutional tour which I had taken between sessions 7 and 8; I noted in particular the loss of a certain apprehensiveness I had about the institution. Many of the group members reacted with pleasure to these disclosures, partly I suspect because I expressed the feeling that I was now even more committed to the group program than previously.

The balance of Session 8 was devoted to evaluation of the series by means of the empathy exercise format described in Session 1. Each participant was asked to list the three most important things he learned about groups in this program and the three most important things to know in order to be an effective group leader, and each was asked to rate the total experience on a five-point rating scale.

The above material was discussed by an inner circle observed by pair-partners in an outer circle, and alter-ego feedback was given in the empathy exercise format. The groups then switched places, different pair-partners were set up, and the process was repeated.

In summary of the total program to date, I stated that in addition to training group leaders our goal was to reduce alienation among inmates and to improve inter-staff and staff-inmate relations. My final statement was, "We would like inmates to feel about themselves and their group leaders the way the members of this group came to feel about each other and their leader."

EVALUATION OF TRAINING SESSIONS

I had a strong impression that the first training series was quite successful. The following tabulation of overall ratings by the participants tended to bear out this subjective impression.

Table 1. Overall Ratings by First (All Staff) Training Group (N=13)

Category	Frequency of Ratings	Overall Mean
1. Very Poor	0	
2. Poor	0	
3. Fair	3	
4. Good	10	3.8
5. Excellent	0	

A mean rating of 3.8 satisfied the criterion that, on the whole, the series was well received. The fact that these ratings were made anonymously would suggest that they would constitute a reasonably valid measure. I have also used this five-point rating scale in many other comparable situations.

Early in this chapter I mentioned that the other three series of leadership training sessions were *essentially* similar on the input side.

However, the increase in the number of sessions as well as inclusion of inmates were significant changes in design.

The decision to include inmates in the training program came as a result of the general success of the program, particularly the initial success of the staff-led inmate groups. It became apparent to the professional staff and the co-leaders that certain inmates were quite sophisticated and able in group situations and that some had had much prior group experience. In addition, several inmates had been trained in transactional analysis at other penal institutions and were, in our opinion, ready for leadership training and co-leader roles in inmate groups. Even so, the inclusion of inmates as potential leaders or co-leaders of inmate therapy groups met with a mixed reception. At least three staff personnel (two correctional officers and one case worker who were signed up to take the leadership training sequence) dropped out of the group because they opposed the presence of inmates. Their reasoning was that they felt that they could not be candid in the presence of inmates, and if they could not be candid, there was no point in entering such a training group. The professional staff guessed (correctly) that this would remain a controversial issue for some time to come. However, those staff people who elected to stay with the training group apparently were very satisfied by their decision, as indicated by subsequent favorable staff evaluations.

Thus, the third series included both inmates (N=7) and staff (N=6) and the number of sessions was extended to twenty due to both the problems and progress of the group. This extension was a joint decision arrived at by the professional staff and the group members. The following highly favorable outcome ratings support this decision. In this case, five categories were rated, each on a five-point scale ranging from 1, "very poor," to 5, "excellent."

The data in Table 2 indicate that staff rated the training experience

Table 2. Ratings by Third Training Group (Staff and Inmates)

Category	Mean Staff Rating N=6	Mean Inmate Rating N=7	Total Group Mean Ratings N=13
Relevance to you as staff or inmate	4.7	4.1	4.4
Learning about self	3.7	3.7	3.7
Learning about others	4.5	4.3	4.4
Stimulation value (emotional, intellectual, spiritual)	4.5	4.0	4.2
Overall Rating	4.7	4.4	4.5

more favorably than did inmates, but that both rated the experience as highly favorable (overall mean 4.5) compared to the first all-staff training group (overall mean 3.8). Percentile scores of the ratings of the third group were also compared to a large number of ratings on the same scales which I have collected on similar workshops over the past three years. In a sample of 188 ratings of the overall value of human relations workshops, the mean was 4.0. The third leadership training group's mean on this scale was 4.5, which is at the 68th percentile of the sample of 188. A t-test for the significance of the difference of these two means was at the .03 level of confidence and, hence, is considered highly significant.

Inspection of the ratings in Table 2 suggests that in this small sample for these particular groups at least, the inmate participation and increase in the length of sessions from eight to twenty may improve the training experience. There is also an indication that the program was probably more effective in the areas of relevance, learning about others, and stimulation value than it was in learning about self. This is consistent with my findings on many other human relations workshops in the past three years, and probably reflects the emphasis on interpersonal relations rather than individual depth psychology in these groups.

INMATE GROUPS

In January of 1970 the staff psychologist began evaluating inmates who had volunteered to participate in the new group counseling program. The first group sessions with inmates began on February 18, 1970. There were three inmate groups, each composed of eight members and two staff co-leaders. The groups met for an hour and a half once a week and each was observed by the rotating professional staff (the institution's psychologist, the psychiatrist and I). Clinics were regularly held after the group meetings and the professional observers were generally impressed with the quality of the leadership and the level of participation by the inmates. The direct observations continued for three sessions, but the post-meeting clinics continued throughout the ten-week duration of the inmate groups. Group members and leaders filled out rating scales at the first and ninth sessions.

At the beginning of the fourth inmate group session, I began training the second group of staff leaders in two-hour sessions as previously, and then met with the ongoing group leaders for the weekly clinic. The entire program continud to operate on a voluntary basis.

At the end of the eighth group session, a student intern conducted structured interviews with the inmates to evaluate their responses to the program.

In May of 1970 three new inmate groups began under the leadership of staff members trained in the leadership training program, and again each of the groups was directly observed by the professional staff for three sessions as in the original three inmate groups. For the first time, a female employee, a clerical worker, began to be a co-leader of one of the inmate groups.

In this manner, inmate groups were initiated and developed over the two-year period of my consultantship. In addition to the leadership training program, the Carkhuff correctional counseling program, a program in transactional analysis, a behavior modification program, and a group therapy program (also run by a woman, a newly appointed psychiatrist), all made therapeutic contributions to the institution.

At its height, the group counseling program—all modalities combined—involved over 110 inmates in some form of group treatment. The greatest number of groups directly spawned by the leadership training program was eight, involving approximately 60 inmates.

It is difficult, and not necessarily desirable, to separate the various groups and mental health interventions made in these various programs. Some groups were combinations of various treatment modalities. The point of major import, in my opinion, is that the programs supplemented one another and did not appear contradictory. On the contrary, more than one inmate participant, inmate leader, or staff leader has remarked about how one program built on the other. This was particularly true of the group leadership training program, the Carkhuff correctional counseling program (Carkhuff, 1968), and the transactional analysis groups (Ernst, 1962).

EVALUATION OF INMATE GROUPS

Three kinds of evaluation were available for measuring the effect of the inmate groups on the participants, the leaders, and the total institutional climate. These were: (1) changes in the pre- and post-attitude tests in the three initial groups; (2) structured individual interview results with the members of the same groups; and (3) a "crisis" anecdote written by one of the correctional officers who was trained in the program.

(1) *Results from attitudinal rating scale pre-test (first session) and post-test (ninth session).*

The leaders and inmates rated their attitudes on a ten-point scale (1=very high, 10=very low) on the following items in Table 3:

Table 3. Item Ranks of Attitude Scales Before and After Group Sessions

Item	Leaders (N=6)		Inmates (N=24)	
	1st Week	9th Week	1st Week	9th Week
1. Yourself	8	5	6	4
2. This Group	1	3	5	6
3. The Institution	9	10	10	10
4. Your Future	4	2	3	2
5. Other Inmates Here	10	8	9 ⟶	3[a]
6. Your Group Leaders	3	7	4	5
7. Your Job	6	9	7	7
8. Your Family	5	1	1	1
9. Your General Health	2	4	2	8
10. Your Housing Unit	7	6	8	9

[a] $p < .05$

Only one of the item changes was statistically significant on an F test, but this item involved inmates' improved feelings about other inmates. This is considered crucial in view of the fact that one of the major missions of the whole group program was to reduce alienation among inmates.

For the staff group leaders, five out of ten items did shift in a positive direction. The largest improvements were in their attitudes toward their own families and their futures. They also felt better about themselves following the group experience, but none of these shifts was statistically significant.

For the inmates also, three items did shift in a positive direction, the most striking upward change being in feelings about other inmates.

Of interest was the finding that initially inmates and leaders were more alike in the rankings of their attitudes (Rho=.75) than at the end of nine weeks (Rho=.59). However, during the nine-week period the leader group changed more than the inmate group (Rho= .59 vs. Rho=.89 respectively). This finding tends to confirm to some extent the higher evaluations given by staff than by inmates to the leadership training program (see Table 2).

(2) *Structured-interview results.*

On April 15, 1970, 21 inmates representing the members of three groups were available to answer the following questions:

1. Of what benefit has this program been to you?
2. Of what benefit has it been to the operation of the institution?
3. What would you change to improve these groups?
4. Do you feel that you accomplished the goals that you set for yourself at the time you entered the group?
5. Are you interested in becoming a group leader?
6. Do you feel that inmates would respond to and respect leaders from their own ranks?

Even though some of the inmates had difficulty answering some of the questions, *all of them* responded positively as to the benefits of the program. For example, five of them stated that they understood themselves better; six said that they were able to communicate more honestly with others; ten indicated that they had become more sensitive toward others, which, in turn, had led to self-help. In addition, twelve inmates expressed an interest in becoming group leaders and five expressed conditional interest (only four were not interested). All of this, plus the fact that only two participants felt that inmates would not respond to peer-group leaders, suggests a strong overall acceptance of the program, subject to the validity and reliability of the interviews. This finding tends to be supported by the impressions of the counseling intern from University of California, Santa Barbara, who conducted the interviews as to the honesty and the interest of the 21 inmates.

(3) *Prison "crisis" report by correctional officer.*

The following report was received from a staff correctional counselor who participated in the third leadership training program with other staff and inmates. A few of the names were omitted to protect confidentiality.

[To Shapiro from Moss]

> Sorry for the delay; but, as you can see from the enclosed report, your training was put to its severest test. Thanks to this incident we seem to have converted some to the merits of group sensitivity.

February 17, 1971

To: Dr. Scott Moss
   Chief Psychologist
From:
   Correctional Counselor

On Monday night, February 1, 1971, a rather explosive situation developed in Unit.3. An Indian man and one of our less stable

Caucasians were involved in a scuffle. While the incident was minor in nature, it almost triggered racial hostilities that had been building up since the unit changeover. The racial minorities felt they were subjected to discrimination and abuse by the Caucasian majority, which was led by the "low riders" who had remained in the unit after the changeover.

Early Tuesday morning, February 2, 1971, I was informed by some of the residents of Unit 3 that a showdown was imminent that evening. The quarters' supervisor was alerted to the impending showdown and informed that weapons had already been brought into the unit.

At 2 p.m. I called in my unit sensitivity group, which I had organized in January. Instead of discussing personal problems, we discussed problems affecting the unit. The group is composed of twelve members, with each ethnic group having two representatives and one alternate. We held a two-hour meeting with Mr. —— in his office in an effort to stop the trouble before it started. It should be noted that this meeting was urgently requested by the more stable inmates who wanted to prevent violence. The main point of dissension appeared to be that the various ethnic groups each felt the others were not showing them even the most basic respect to which they felt they were entitled.

As the dialogue progressed, it was evident which of the men had backgrounds in sensitivity training. It could be compared to a discussion between adults and children. Those with sensitivity training did not feel their manhood would be in jeopardy if a compromise was reached. Those without training feared that a peaceful solution would be a sign of weakness.

At the close of the meeting there was a unanimity of thought among the group that a peaceful settlement was possible if the grievances could be brought out into the open. Each group member gave me his personal assurance that he would help "cool it" in the unit that night. It was further agreed that the meeting be postponed until conditions in the unit allowed a beneficial meeting.

At 4 p.m. I received a call that Mr. —— authorized me to remain on duty until 9:30 p.m. At approximately 6 p.m. I was approached by members of my sensitivity group. They informed me that the men wanted to discuss the unit problems and that there would be no violence. I thereupon authorized the meeting.

About 40 men attended the meeting which was held at the east end of Unit 3. It was evident from the start that it would be a success as the men communicated with each other on an adult level. Each group was allowed ample time to present its grievances.

At the conclusion of the meeting almost 70 unit members were present. The general consensus was that this meeting was one of the most beneficial to take place in this institution. The men all appeared to have been relieved of great pressure and expressed the opinion that Unit 3 was going to be a better place to live in from that time on.

In conclusion, let me state that I realize that what happened in Unit 3 the night of February 2, 1971, is not necessarily the ready-made answer to the problems of penology, but I do feel that it showed the favorable result of our counseling programs. I saw the cool heads of men who had taken the Sensitivity Training, Carkhuff Training, and Transactional Analysis courses prevail with reason over the unit hotheads, who advocated violence. I would urge that every effort be made to expand these programs.

SUMMARY

This chapter attempts to present a detailed description of a group leadership training program at F.C.I., Lompoc, California. The program consisted essentially of four leadership training series with the major purposes of reducing alienation in the prison and training group counseling leaders for inmate groups. The introduction of selected inmates as co-leaders along with staff members from a wide variety of institutional functions represented a major innovation. Various evaluation results are presented, indicating that both the training program and the inmate counseling groups derived from this program were successful in meeting the original objectives.

The author wishes to express his thanks to Burton Kerish, staff psychologist, who contributed much to this program in record keeping and administrative reports.

REFERENCES

Carkhuff, R. R. 1968. *Helping and human relations*. New York: Holt, Rinehart and Winston.
Ernst, F. 1962. The use of transactional analysis in prison therapy groups. *Corr. psychiat. soc. therapy* 8:120–32.
Kinch, J. W. 1967. A formalized theory of the self-concept. In *Symbolic*

Interaction, ed. J. Manis and B. Meltzer. Boston: Allyn and Bacon, pp. 139–52.

N.T.L. Institute for Applied Behavioral Science. 1969. Feedback and the helping relationship. In Reading Book, Laboratories in Human Relations Training (rev.). Washington, D.C., pp. 31–34.

Shapiro, S. B. 1968. Some aspects of a theory of interpersonal contracts. *Psychology Reports* 22: 171–83.

4

The Carkhuff Training Program

Albert G. Thomas

The Carkhuff program received its start at the Federal Correctional Institution at Lompoc in January, 1970, when Charles M. Montgomery, training officer for the institution, was sent to Springfield, Massachusetts, to participate in a correctional counseling institute at the American International College. The institute (cosponsored by the college and the Federal Bureau of Prisons) was a thirty-day total life experience, conducted by Robert R. Carkhuff, Ph.D.

From the beginning, the program had the full support of the bureau and the institution. Indeed, upon Montgomery's selection to attend the first institute, the warden indicated that he would be expected to utilize the skills he acquired as a participant. Thus, upon the training officer's return to Lompoc, he was given the green light to select 12 staff members who were to receive 40 hours of "Carkhuff Training." Since that initial group, 206 staff members and residents have received a minimum of 36 to over 250 hours of training of this type. The essence of the training experience can be only briefly described here.[1]

THE TRAINING EXPERIENCE

THE CARKHUFF RATIONALE

A fundamental premise of the Carkhuff program is that many lay people can, with the proper training, learn to serve as effective coun-

[1] Obviously, limitations of time and space do not allow anymore than these few introductory principles to Carkhuff's method and techniques. For those readers who want to learn more about methodology per se, two books by Dr. Carkhuff will be very helpful, *Helping and Human Relations*, Volumes I (Selection and Training) and II (Practice and Research).

selors, and that counseling which is done by individuals drawn from the subject community is likely to be the most effective, since such individuals are close to the problems at hand and can both see them more clearly and better visualize their solution than could a counselor drawn from the outside.

Although not everyone can be transformed into a counselor (termed by Carkhuff a helper), it is possible to train some people to become more adept at helping others solve their problems. In general, the successful lay counselor is one who can both provide the individual (helpee) with the experience of being understood and, at the same time, serve as a model for him to imitate. He is one who can lead the individual first to explore and then to understand his problem fully, to recognize the different courses of action which are open to him, and finally to act upon what he has come to see. In other words, the goals of a lay counselor are *exploration, understanding,* and *action.*

The Relationship

According to Carkhuff, the helper/helpee relationship involves the following:

1. The helper will be most effective during the early phases when he focuses his attention on the individual and demonstrates a responsiveness toward him, for in that way he can promote self-exploration and then self-understanding on the part of the client. The helper can facilitate such self-examination by showing empathy or understanding for the client (the ability to see the world through the other person's eyes), by demonstrating respect or concern, and by attempting to elicit concrete and specific statements from the individual about his own experiences and feelings.

2. The helper will be most effective during later stages when he initiates action; that is, when, on the basis of what he has learned about the client's problem, the helper shapes the interviews and gives them direction, attempting thereby to help the client undrstand himself more deeply and finally to act upon this understanding. He attempts to deal with the reality of the situation as he perceives it, and there is an immediacy in his ability to understand the feelings and experiences that are going on between him and his client and in his ability to translate this understanding into an honest response.

3. It is important that the responsive and initiative conditions be clearly related to each other. The helper must first respond to the individual's feelings and experiences and then formulate and initiate

his plan of action on the basis of what he has learned by responding to the helpee.

4. At all stages, the helper will be most effective when he aids the client in developing a course of action for handling his own problems. His goal must be to help the individual develop a better way of doing things by helping him to see alternatives and to choose appropriately between them.

To summarize briefly, let me paraphrase Dr. Carkhuff: An individual seeks counseling because he cannot help himself and because the people around him cannot help him. The helper offers him the understanding and encouragement which he needs in order to explore his problem. As the individual explores his problem more fully, the helper offers higher levels of understanding, and, reciprocally, as the helper offers higher levels of understanding, the individual comes to understand his problem more fully. Once the problem has been explored and understood, and once the individual's need to solve it has been defined, the counselor and the client work together to develop courses of action which will give him the best possible chance for dealing with his problem successfully.

The counseling does not end with the solution of a single problem; instead, the cycle of exploration-understanding-action is repeated in many different ways and in many different problem areas so that the individual can eventually learn how to solve his problems by himself. At all times during the period of counseling, he is encouraged to translate his perceptions into action; for when he acts, he learns, he comes to new understanding, and then acts again in a new and more effective way.

In order for this cycle to be successful, the counselor must be responsive to the client and must achieve a genuine understanding of his problem. At the same time, he must serve as a model for the client; he must demonstrate to him that had he found himself in the same position, he would have known what to do. If he cannot demonstrate this, then there is no reason for the client to seek his help. In addition, the counselor must be able to show the individual that there are ways of doing things that are both different from and more effective than the way that he has been doing them. In order to do this, the counselor must himself be involved in a life-long learning and growing process—for that is what helping is: learning and growing. If the counselor is not learning and growing himself, he cannot help others to do so.

CARKHUFF AT LOMPOC

Every attempt has been made to keep the training at the Federal Correctional Institution in Lompoc consistent with that received at the American International College in Springfield. All of the handout materials are the same, and Carkhuff's principles, as presented in his publications, are adhered to as closely as possible. There are, however, several ways in which our "in-house training" differs from that received at the institute, the most important of these being a decrease in the length of the training period from 240 hours to 40.

The first forty-hour class was comprised of eleven correctional officers and one correctional supervisor, selected primarily on Officer Montgomery's personal knowledge of and acquaintance with each.[2] This class was conducted in half-day (four-hour) sessions over a period of two weeks. Subsequent classes were held in a forty-hour week period, because such scheduling was more economically efficient and because it was preferred by the trainees themselves. This limitation has resulted in two other modifications: the extensive use of videotape equipment beginning on the second day and the use of walk-in resident clients during the last two or three days of the session. The videotape equipment is used to record each role-playing situation, which is then evaluated in terms of interaction and counselor performance. Walk-in resident clients are used beginning on the afternoon of the third or fourth day, depending on the progress of the group. These are volunteers drawn from the actual resident population, who submit real-life problems to the counselors in training. At the conclusion of the interaction, the group is polled for their responses, and the client is given the opportunity to choose another helper if he so desires. He is then asked to rate his counselor on a scale from 1 to 5 (from inadequate to excellent).

The training in interpersonal skills is systematic: first, each dimension is thoroughly explained and defined in operational terms; next, each trainee practices the skills in role-playing situations in both large and small groups; finally, on completion of the role-playing situations, the performance of each trainee is evaluated by the group. The dimensions covered are both responsive (empathy, respect, specificity) and initiative (genuineness, confrontation, immediacy) and are directed toward sixteen client stimulus expressions represent-

[2] Mr. Montgomery has since been promoted and transferred to the Staff Training Center in Atlanta, Georgia. His main function is the instruction of correctional counseling techniques at the Staff Training Center. The writer has taken his place as the correctional training specialist at Lompoc.

ing different affect areas—depression, anger, elation, etc.—with different problem situations—social, vocational, marital, etc. Each group member is required to participate actively in the classroom sessions and to submit his developing skills to the scrutiny and evaluation of his fellow members several times each day.

In order to record and measure significant gains in interpersonal skills, Dr. Carkhuff's *Assessing Discrimination Test* has been incorporated both as a pre- and post-test. This has enabled us to accurately record past levels of interpersonal functioning for each trainee. The test consists of standardized problem situations to which each helper is asked to respond with a few selected sentences.

Without exception it has been found that the trainees' ability to discriminate between high and low level responses is initially very poor and that, for the most part, there is a tendency to give the action-oriented solution-type "Ann Landers" response to almost any situation. Thus far, however, every trainee who has completed this program has improved his interpersonal relationship skills, as demonstrated both on the written tests and in the actual role-playing situations. In addition, a majority of those who were tested six months to a year after completion of training demonstrated either continued improvement or maintenance of their previous levels of functioning. This is not to suggest that every trainee has become an instant expert counselor, but it certainly does indicate that this particular type of training and the Carkhuff models can be highly effective in the prison setting. The most impressive indicator of its value is not easily measured. The feeling and the atmosphere of the institution and the communication which takes place between the staff and inmate population are immeasurable.

Table 1 depicts the breakdown of all staff and residents (inmates) trained to date.

Table 1. Breakdown of All Staff and Inmates Trained at Lompoc

	Basic Carkhuff N	Advanced Carkhuff[a] N
Trainees	193	13
Custodial	105	3
Noncustodial	39	5
Inmates	49	5

[a]The advanced Carkhuff training includes any additional instruction of over forty hours.

Residents have been exposed to Carkhuff training, and their functioning level and enthusiasm appear to have been no less than that of the staff. While a systematic follow-up has not at this time been carried out to assess our Carkhuff training program involving residents, it appears to have been very helpful, particularly in strengthening interpersonal relations with both staff and peers, increasing personal involvement in other human relations programs, and in improving overall outlook on life.

CARKHUFF-RELATED CHANGES AT LOMPOC

In addition to the specific achievements in the improvement of interpersonal relationship skills resulting from the training sessions, there have been a number of related changes at Lompoc during the past eighteen months which I feel are a direct result of the Carkhuff program. The following is only a partial list:

1. All new correctional employees are given 40 hours of training in *helping and human relations* during their first year at the facility.

2. All correctional counselors must receive a minimum of 40 hours of Carkhuff training before assignment and an additional 40 hours advanced training after assignment.

3. Counselors have been moved from one central location to the individual units and have been assigned evening and weekend hours in order to allow more immediate contact with the inmate population.

4. Unit officers, primarily on the day watch and evening watch assignments, are given 40 hours of training, thus enabling them to complement the efforts of the counselor and the unit case management system.

5. Caseworkers are scheduled to receive Carkhuff training. At present, we are at 50 percent of this goal.

6. The correctional counselor complement has been increased from 8 to 10, and each is assigned to a separate unit. Two counselors, both of whom have received 80 hours of Carkhuff training, are assigned to the drug abuse unit.

7. One industrial counselor and two correctional officers were selected under merit promotion procedures to attend the second counseling institute in Springfield. Upon completion thereof, each has acted as a master trainer.

8. Inmates who have received various amounts of training have been assigned to one of the master trainers in the capacity of associate trainers.

9. A current program involving "resident helpers" is being taken under consideration at this time and has created a great deal of interest.

10. Carkhuff training has been extended to all departments within the Federal Correctional Institution.

11. "Operation Breakthrough" (see Chapter 7) requires 40 hours of Carkhuff training as a criterion for certification.

12. In the very near future, six deputies from the Los Angeles sheriff's training program will be participating in a 40-hour Carkhuff class. The deputies in turn will be reviewing the program for incorporation into their own training criteria for new deputies at the academy.

13. The mental health service and our Carkhuff training program are interrelated in program development. In addition to the 80 hours of Carkhuff technique required for all correctional counselors, there is now a plan to require 40 hours of Behavioral Approaches to Counseling (initially taught by Ray Hosford with Scott Moss, coordinator of mental health). Also in the planning stage are a series of seminars by Dr. Stewart Shapiro on the structure and dynamics of small-group interaction. In each instance, staff members who are asked to participate will be trained eventually to give the seminars themselves, with the Mental Health people then stepping back into the role as consultants.

14. Drs. Hosford and Moss are preparing a grant proposal to supplement in-service training within the institution, something which will involve all of us on a continuing basis. We hope that graduate students can be assigned to Carkhuff training and in turn that they may be interested in continuing to research the program.

15. Finally, the peer counseling program has been recently included as a specific counseling technique for achievement of a peer counseling certificate.

PERSONAL EVALUATIONS

It is my opinion that Carkhuff training could be the single most meaningful training experience ever offered to staff or inmate personnel. I base this not only on my own personal experiences but also on the improvement demonstrated by each participant, either staff or inmate, who has completed the training, and on the enthusiasm demonstrated—in class assessments—by virtually every student enrolled in the program. Indeed, it has been the consensus that it was the most appropriate training of this type ever received during prison service careers (the length of prison service careers ranges from less than one year to in excess of seventeen years). The following are comments from staff and inmates in regard to what they think of the Carkhuff program:

Case manager: This course has done more to prepare me for a career in corrections than any training I have had in the past. It has been a very rewarding experience. It revealed my ignorance in the area of interpersonal relationships and my need for self-improvement. In a period of five days, this course changed me from a nonfunctional helper to a functional helper.

Dr. Carkhuff's technique provides one with more than the usual "theory" expected in classes such as this; it provides a real and usable tool which can be used by lay workers as well as professionals.

Correctional officer: I have been employed by the Bureau of Prisons for nine years, and up to the present time I have not been exposed to a program that has the validity and merit that this course has. Dr. Carkhuff's model for functional helpers can and will strike home here and anywhere else that it is adequately presented. If this were used to train more of the staff in the immediate future, helping would become a real part of the functional correctional officer in each and every institution within the Bureau of Prisons. If this program reaches each functional helper as deeply as it has in this first class, it is definitely programmed for immediate success, both in our daily and everyday lives and in our chosen life's professions.

Correctional supervisor (lieutenant): I believe this correctional counseling is a good step forward in the prison service, and I think it should be followed through, using as many officers in this class as possible on a full-time counseling basis, coming in two or three hours during the evening.

I definitely believe there are many, many inmates who could be helped through this type of counseling.

Inmate (walk-in resident helper): Today I took part in your program as a helper; now I am almost at a loss for words, as the experience was tremendous. When I walked out of the room, it felt as though a great weight had been lifted from me. Seeing the program actually work, I asked myself why it wasn't started years ago, because for the first time I can see that people do care but they didn't know how to go about it. The communication your program brings about is invaluable in helping return inmates as useful members of society. I am sure the administration will be pleased, as through your program the staff and officers will become more efficient and perform their jobs in a more superlative manner.

Surely not everyone will experience the almost traumatic feeling as I did, but I'm looking forward to entering your class and trying to become a functional helper myself. Inmates receiving this training will be in my opinion, for the first time receiving something of value in helping them become human beings again. Only through understanding can this happen. I certainly recommend your program for both inmates and staff alike. It it a very definite and progressive answer to many problems.

SUMMARY

Let me quote from the 15th chapter of Carkhuff's *Helping and Human Relations*, Volume II:

> We have seen program after program initiated at the federal, state and local levels. Some few succeed, but most fail, becoming bogged down in the follow through and delivery stages. These programs flounder because no functionally meaningful criteria of effectiveness are required. They fail because frequently the best people are not in the key positions. As frequently as not those in key positions do not even have the administrative sense to facilitate the efforts of the more effective individuals among them. Indeed, often they do not have tolerance for those who can deliver, for they themselves become exposed by the contrast in style and outcome.

From our viewpoint, what Carkhuff's training has fully conceptualized and demonstrated is that lay people can be as effective as and oftentimes more effective than the professional helper. In our correctional facilities throughout America today, we have a vast reservoir, a natural resource of line staff members who could be trained to complement the efforts of the professional mental health staff. We have seen at Lompoc just how successful trained line people can be in dealing with inmate problems, and just how effective total employee understanding and cooperation can be in the rehabilitative process. What the Carkhuff method offers the correctional facility is, finally, a more humanitarian and more effective and efficient way of helping an individual return to a successful life in society.

REFERENCES

Carkhuff, R. R. 1969. *Helping and human relations.* Vol. I (Selection and Training) and Vol. II (Practice and Research). New York: Holt, Rinehart and Winston.

5

Peer Counseling

Burton R. Kerish

INTRODUCTION

Inmates in most contemporary correctional facilities are treated, educated, or trained according to traditional medical, educational, and vocational concepts that place them in historically passive roles as patients, students, or apprentices. The weight of rehabilitation and resocialization in such a system rests upon the staff, who are under mandate as part of their jobs to fill in whatever psycho-socioeconomic gaps are presumed responsible for an inmate's past failures according to the current theory of causation. The collection of detailed personal information prior to sentencing by probation personnel and the continuance of such data collection by caseworkers throughout commitment is highly supportive of this claim.

Treatment goals of the staff, shared by the large majority of inmates are: high school completion for the reasonably literate, work skills and habits appropriate to tolerating a minimal 40-hour work week in a specific area of work in which it is hoped the resident has demonstrated some interest and aptitude, and tolerance of the pressures of mass living under an autocratic system which is presumed to be related in some way to the challenge of life in the free society under conditions of parole. Movement through such programs by most inmates is performed in fatalistic fashion, while their more optimistic and alert colleagues may be expected to play "How do I get out of here?" caring little for consideration of events beyond their institutional release.

A blanket indictment of overprotection or suppression of inmate initiative is not herein intended. To be sure, residents are held accountable for many of life's daily demands: personal hygiene, obedience toward reasonable regulation, accountability (being at the right place at the right time), reasonable effort in program assignments, and reasonable respect for authority and colleagues. However, beyond some presumably supportive testing and interviewing during the orientation period, and a minimum of counseling contacts thereafter, the placement and continuance of an inmate in an institution program is frequently governed by factors unrelated to his own personal ambitions or individual tastes. There is a constant aura of "We know what's best for you," the maintenance of a parental position by the institution accompanied by complementary child positions of the inmates, frequently inhibiting growth toward true independence. Thus it is not surprising to hear an inmate relating some aspect of his present situation to what "they" did to him, whether it was negative, such as having his custody increased, or positive, such as having been granted parole. In our desire to produce humane correctional settings, we have developed techniques for mass comfort and a system for fitting young people—at least temporarily—into a rapidly changing society, rather than providing opportunities for exploration of independently selected alternatives. Increased usage of the decision-making model and innovative social learning techniques in correctional treatment would seem to offer promise in the elimination of this serious treatment deficit. It is to this issue that the peer counseling program demonstration was addressed.

PROGRAM DESCRIPTION

Peer counseling is advertised to the institution population as "a program by inmates for inmates." Two certificates and two diplomas are offered in three phases. In addition to the services of its psychologist manager, the program receives consultant services from mental health staff members, personnel specialists, professors from the University of California, Santa Barbara, graduate students, and prominent counseling practitioners from the surrounding community. All inmates may participate.

In the first phase, inmates work toward social control through study and application of basic concepts of transactional analysis in both a classroom and group setting. Emphasis is placed upon motivation analysis and understanding social transactions in a 100-hour program that is split into four separate courses. Upon successful completion of the 100 hours, inmates are deemed qualified both to co-teach classes in transactional analysis fundamentals and co-lead the accompanying groups. The second phase consists of 100 hours of work in communications techniques, counseling theory, specific counseling techniques, and supervised group leading. Upon successful completion of this phase, inmates may independently lead groups and are frequently assigned co-leaders from the first phase. The final phase involves 25 hours of service on the program's executive board and 25 hours service to the prison community. Credit is given for responsible participation in any of the institution service organizations, as well as the cultural or special interest groups. A detailed description of training and activity offered in all phases of the program appears in a mimeographed brochure which is presented to all incoming inmates.

The program has remained, on the whole, a voluntary one. However, residents referred by their treatment teams are also accepted, for example, any resident on psychotropic medication is required by the present staff psychiatrist to participate in a group. Some of these people come and go according to their state of dependency, while others take an interest and remain in the program beyond their initial contracted period.

Each applicant is placed immediately in what has come to be known as a pre-group until the beginning didactic classes have vacancies. Some elect to remain in these groups rather than go on to the more formalized training classes. Characteristically, such groups meet for a maximum of twenty one-and-one-half-hour sessions, generally twice a week, after which they may elect to divide into different groups. With the exception of those who otherwise maintain only limited work and training programs, residents are allowed only two classes at a time following the initial phase. The average amount of time spent in actual groups and class meetings per week is about eight hours for participants and anywhere between eight and forty hours for leaders. Two leaders are assigned full time to the program and one is assigned half time. These men handle administrative chores in addition to their teaching and group-facilitating responsibilities. The program operates during the normal workday and two evenings per week under other staff member sponsorship. A plan is presently being developed for an evening program of individual peer counseling under supervision.

Every effort has been made to achieve maximum accessibility. For example, all didactic classes are taught in the education department, and the program manager's office is located directly off the main corridor in the path of heavy traffic. There is, in addition, an adjoining group room affording much privacy, which at times is shared with the case management section. Both rooms are attractively furnished and decorated. The office seems also to serve as a drop-in center for many who are not directly involved in the program.

Black residents may be found in the program in higher proportion than in the general prison population. Mexican and Mexican-American residents have been less involved until the recent innovation of bilingual groups by a Chicano member of the program executive board. American Indian residents have participated only occasionally. There appears to be no discernible pattern of participation by other ethnic groups with the exception of apparent intellectual appeal to the more highly educated and favorable time structuring for those relatively unoccupied in other formal programs.

It is readily apparent that transactional analysis has the strongest and perhaps most lingering influence in the training program. This approach is a nonmedical model and thus does not have the accompanying stigma of most psychological/psychiatric treatment. Additionally, transactional analysis language and concepts may be grasped at a sixth-grade level of scholastic function.

PROGRAM RESULTS

It is perhaps unfortunate that the gradual development of the peer counseling programs per se, the heavy clinical involvement of the program manager, and the relatively late arrival of outside aid mitigated against any formal evaluative structure. What follows is, in the main, anecdotal.

Reisman's helper principle appears to be operating actively within the program. Inmates who reach counselor status are rarely involved in behavioral difficulty within the institution. They are relied upon for assistance in their respective living units in maintaining unit stability. Indeed, there have been occasions of peer counselors being asked to remain in their regular units rather than transfer to an honor unit (with more personal freedom) because of such valued service. Some have complied and some have exercised their privilege to move on. There is little doubt that peer counselors serve as positive role models for other participants in the program. During a recent disturbance that had racial overtones, not one of the hundred men active in the various stages of the program was reported to have been involved, in spite of the unequal racial balance of the peer groups.

It is characteristic of drug-dependent people to obtain medications whenever they can during incarceration. Peer counselors, in spite of past chronic drug backgrounds on the part of many, project strong anti-drug attitudes. They are rarely seen on sick leave and, to a man, have never appeared before the disciplinary committee. They appear to have high status among their peers, show few traces of dependency upon others for conducting their institutional and personal affairs, and enjoy mature relationships with their correctional supervisors. They are admired and respected by the consultants and graduate students who often remark about the high activity level of the counseling groups in contrast to other groups observed on campus and in the free community.

In addition, inmates who have served as peer counselors have taken an increased interest in academic programs, as evidenced by the fact that every inmate on the executive board of the peer counseling program is presently enrolled in the maximum number of college courses possible (two). Very few of these inmates completed college classes prior to their involvement in the program. Peer counselors may be found among the leadership of almost all other institutional programs. This was true before the introduction of the "community service" requirement in the last phase of the program. The community service category was developed by the writer to give extra credit within the program to those individuals who were, by their own inclination, rendering valuable service to their peers outside of the program.

When the program was first under development, a contract was made between the writer and individual residents who had attained what was then the equivalent of Peer Counselor I status; the terms of the contract called for the residents to write six letters—one every four months for two years—to me following their release. These contracts have not been regularly honored. The first releasee wrote only one letter, and that to another inmate. The second sent a Christmas card with a brief note and a subsequent letter to another peer counselor. The third wrote his first letter, but no other followed. The fourth and fifth have remained in telephone contact with me over a period of six months in lieu of writing. They always call at home rather than at the institution. The sixth releasee recently left to serve a prior sentence at a state institution and has written one letter. I suspected that the maintenance of contact with an institution authority was too aversive to the releasees and they discontinued the contracts.

There have been some curious negative behaviors displayed by residents who had difficulty making a genuine program commitment and who remained a fringe element of the peer counseling group. One of these men is currently following a nomadic existence in the community contrary to the terms of his parole. Another has taken to the use of drugs after having had no previous drug history. Still another became further involved in serious crime while on a bedside visit in the community. On the other hand, of the present executive board, two appear to have impressed the parole board to the point of being considered for imminent release in spite of lengthy prior records and lengthy present sentences for serious crimes. Both have job offers as lay counselors in community service agencies. Another, a previously nonconforming institutional problem child, has received a workshop scholarship from the Esalen Institute in Big Sur, California. He applied for the scholarship on his own initiative and through regular mail contact.

At the time of this writing, five complete-program graduates were in the free community. The first was a youth counselor for a locally administered urban improvement project and has been thus engaged for the past eight months. The second was a full-time student at the University of Hawaii, trying to decide between staying with his original major in business and his newer interests in psychology and sociology. The third, also a full-time student, had been leading encounter groups at a community college while serving as a consultant to urban improvement groups. He worked with a former graduate student intern who was similarly employed in a neighboring area. The fourth was living with a group of students and looking for work in the construction trades to finance school attendance in the fall. He was a volunteer counselor at a community night counseling service. The fifth worked forty hours a week as a counselor at a drug clinic and was taking fourteen units of junior college work majoring in psychology. These five men, all past chronic offenders, had been diagnosed as antisocial personalities during previous incarceration.

IMPLICATIONS FOR PEER PROGRAM DEVELOPMENT

This program is only one of several that suggest that peer influence may be used for positive growth and experience (see bibliography). The existence of an inmate counter-culture within correctional institutions has consistently demonstrated difficulties found in using staff members as role models. Glaser (1964) has pointed out that in corrections the strongest positive staff member impression is made by the job or training supervisor with whom the inmate spends at least six hours a day under normal conditions of institution programming.

Under present staffing procedures, all other contacts are time limited and only minimally effective in changing previously acquired psychosocial behavior patterns. There just aren't enough staff models to go around. Peer counseling seems a viable alternative to increased staffing. It is certainly far less expensive, and it places responsibility for change upon the individual participant in an atmosphere of minimal authoritarian threat. Furthermore, where large age gaps exist between model and imitator, conditions of forced conformity and dependency are too often fostered. Impersonal criticisms of life styles by either age group present serious barriers to communication. Peers have the additional advantage of similar life experiences and seem in many instances more sensitive than outsiders. For one thing, it seems to be more difficult for peers to deceive one another; for another, they are easily accepted by incoming residents looking to learn the life style of the new institution or community. The neophyte assimilates a positive position from those who have previously faced the problem successfully and is in a position to pass the pattern on. Another advantage derives from the fact that the mystique of professional treatment is removed—a peer becomes a knowledgeable participant in his own growth process. His increased communicative abilities and positive assertions with the staff promote rational control over his destiny in a system which he may have otherwise looked upon as overpowering. The promotion of peer counselors within an institution or community implies respect for class, ethnic, age, and other differences, encouraging exploration by removing various old excuses for indifference or nonparticipation so often found with directed programming.

A present concern is the development of staff alienation through independent operation of relatively large resident groups with a minimum of professional supervision. Open invitations to the staff for attendance at peer counseling activities have been received with apparent interest (expressed verbally), but actual attendance has been minimal. The next logical step appears to be the renewal of mixed staff and resident groups to keep open channels of communication and minimize intergroup threat. This same notion was expressed by the two resident peer pioneers two years ago when they wrote the following summary in a paper that was circulated among the inmates, "Lompoc and Resocialization" (Jefferson and Lewis, 1970).

Two hundred years of history in corrections has shown that new and better methods of dealing with the criminal offender are needed.

Some new methods are here in Lompoc and are available to those who are willing to look at them. These concepts and methods are sometimes viewed as threatening by those who do not fully understand the processes involved. It is felt that many of the traditional barriers can be broken down with the cooperation of staff and inmate. It is hoped that communication between staff members and the inmates at Lompoc can be increased through participation in integrated groups, staff and inmate, in the Game sessions. Vigorous encounters of this nature are healthy, both physically and mentally.

This program offers one concrete attempt to answer the problem of resocializing the criminal offender in our society today.

REFERENCES

Berne, E. 1961. *Transactional analysis in psychotherapy*. New York: Grove Press.

Ezell, B. 1970. Justice and the game. *Reality* 2 (3). Marion, Ill.: U.S.P.

Finney, B. C. 1974. The peer group: An experiment in humanistic education. In *Psychological stress in the campus community: Theory, research and action*, ed. B. L. Bloom. New York: Behavioral Publications.

Glaser, D. 1964. *The effectiveness of a prison and parole system*. Kansas City, Mo.: Bobbs-Merrill Co.

Jefferson, H., and Lewis, C. 1970. Lompoc and resocialization. Unpublished paper, Federal Correctional Institution, Lompoc, California.

6

The Drug Abuse Treatment Program
at F.C.I., Lompoc

Kenneth Lebow

In 1971, the Bureau of Prisons inaugurated a "second generation" of treatment programs intended to deal specifically with inmates having histories of drug abuse. Unlike the "first generation," stemming from the Narcotic Addict Rehabilitation Act of 1966, which applied only to narcotics addicts committed primarily for the purpose of treatment, the newer programs included any abuser of restricted or dangerous drugs, regardless of the reason for which he was incarcerated. Treatment teams were authorized at five different federal institutions across the nation: Lompoc, California; El Reno, Oklahoma; Terre Haute, Indiana; Petersburg, Virginia; and Lewisburg, Pennsylvania. Subsequently an additional team was authorized at Fort Worth, Texas, when that facility was transferred into the Federal Bureau of Prisons, and at La Tuna, Texas.

The team at Lompoc consists of a director (clinical psychologist), a correctional treatment specialist (case worker), and two correctional counselors (officers with training in counseling techniques). Initially they were responsible for developing and implementing a systematic approach for the treatment of fifty men identified as drug abusers who volunteered to participate. The program has since been extended to one hundred inmates and additional staff has been added. At present the inmates are housed together in one separate dormitorylike unit. While this practice facilitates the recording of behavioral data, it does have the drawback of imposing group housing rather than the individual cells provided in the rest of the institution.

Because the drug abuse program is designed to offer treatment to individuals who differ from others only by virtue of their histories of drug abuse, the criteria for admission to the program are few in number. The only requirements are a recognition by the individual that drugs have been used detrimentally, a sincere interest in working at modifying some aspect of drug-related behavior, and a willingness to make a commitment to remain in the program for approximately one year. When these three criteria are met and when space becomes available, a person is admitted to the program.

PROGRAM GOALS AND THE DRUG ABUSER

The goals of the drug abuse treatment program are identical to those of the institution as a whole: to help individuals learn to modify their behavior so that they are capable of functioning as productive members of society. The emphasis is upon behavioral change, i.e., upon identifying the specific changes to be made, finding means of effecting those changes, and maintaining those that are achieved. In addition, a specific goal for a drug abuser is abstinence from habit-forming drugs he cannot control. Since it is understood that drug abusers are unlikely to abstain if they continue to follow the same living patterns which eventuated in drug abuse, a significant change in those patterns must, of necessity, occur.

The program is intended to address itself to two different aspects of drug-related problems: first, the need for learning social behaviors that are both rewarding and constructive rather than self-defeating and destructive and second, the need for reducing the reinforcement value of drugs and drug-related material.

There are several factors involved in drug abuse which must be dealt with in an effective treatment program. First, the behavioral assets and deficits of the individual must be taken into consideration. In general, the essentially inadequate and nonadaptive nature of the drug abuser's relationship with other people makes him vulnerable to social pressures with which he cannot cope, and causes him to seek relief from these pressures in any way he can. He readily tries drugs and is easily "hooked" psychologically because they enable him to ignore many troublesome aspects of life by allowing him to focus almost totally upon his own immediate experience. Because he ceases to be concerned with what other people expect he no longer worries about social failure. Instead, he becomes preoccupied with the acquiring and taking of drugs. When his drug needs increase beyond his ability to satisfy them numerous and significant social problems, of which criminal acts are one, usually develop.

A second factor is that of the effect of the social environment—the "drug culture." It is a regrettable fact that strong social pressures encourage and promote the use of drugs in many subcultures. The socially insecure person is particularly susceptible because of his need to conform to peer-group expectations. To expect such an individual to abstain may be unrealistic since peer approval is an extremely powerful reinforcer for him.

A third factor, and one which has seldom been dealt with in the treatment of the drug abuser, is that of the response to the drugs themselves. Even the most casual conversation with a narcotics user will quickly reveal that the initial "rush" and subsequent "high" are pleasurable and intensely reinforcing for him. There is little doubt that to some extent such pleasure is a conditioned response. And, for individuals who have few other sources of reinforcement in their lives, the pleasure they initially receive from drugs is particularly potent. Long ago Rubenstein (1931) and more recently Weil, Zinberg, and Nelsen (1968) demonstrated that many people "feel what they expect to feel" when taking medications or drugs, and that the "conditioned high" response to a placebo may not be distinguishable from the response to a specific drug. As with other conditioned responses, the pleasure becomes anticipatory, that is, it generalizes to stimuli which have previously not evoked pleasure—e.g., the sight or feel of a hypodermic syringe—but which have become associated with obtaining the desired hedonistic experience. Inhibiting the conditioned pleasure response may be essential if abstinence is to be maintained by many drug addicts. Forgoing an intensely pleasurable experience on purely logical grounds requires a clear recognition of need and a great deal of determination. Few drug abusers, however, exhibit these characteristics and at best most are coerced grudgingly into treatment.

TREATMENT

Conventional treatment techniques include individual psychotherapy; various types of group therapy; in-house "therapeutic" communities such as Synanon, Phoenix House, and Daytop Village, and/or the use of opiate substitutes, such as methadone, and opiate antagonists, such as cyclazocine. The relevance of such techniques to the problems of the drug abuser may appear to be self-evident. However, their lack of effectiveness is readily apparent in the extremely high rate of recidivism commonly observed among treated addicts.

At F.C.I., Lompoc, the focus of treatment is on specific behavioral acts and on those ways of thinking which reinforce undesirable behavior. That is, we are concerned not only with modifying the undesirable behavior itself but also with modifying the pattern of behaviors with which the individual customarily responds to situations which are associated with, but which precede the use of, drugs. For some individuals the treatment may be concerned largely with social behaviors in which the goal is to help the inmate learn and practice new ways of responding, including the seemingly simple but in fact very difficult act of saying "no" when opportunities to use drugs arise. For others, treatment may be specifically a private issue, a conflict in which the use of drugs constitutes an attempt to alleviate, if only temporarily, the agony of frustration and despair. Such persons are particularly likely to become addicted psychologically whether or not the drugs are physically addicting. In such cases the treatment goal may be resolution of the personal conflict situation through a methodical exploration of alternative behaviors after the general problem has been clarified. A variety of counseling procedures may then be employed to promote the desired behavioral change. For example, the use of audio and video tape recordings may be used both to model appropriate behaviors which the individual needs to acquire as well as to demonstrate the existence of otherwise unrecognized behavior patterns. In addition, such aids provide immediate and reliable feedback for the observer as he attempts to change his own behavior.

In some selected cases in which psychological addiction has clearly played a major role in maintaining a pattern of behaviors related to drug abuse and for which other treatment modalities have failed, aversive counter-conditioning may be considered as a final phase of treatment. While various means of aversive conditioning might be employed, e.g., electrical, chemical, and symbolic, the usual choice with drug abusers involves presenting a moderate, very brief electric shock and timing this occurrence to coincide with a presentation of some drug-related stimuli. Similarly, termination of shock coincides with removal of the stimuli. This technique has been used successfully in treating many behaviors, e.g., alcoholism, homosexuality, and fetishism (see Rachman and Teasdale, 1969), which are quite resistive to convential therapeutic approaches. (Thus far, aversive counter-conditioning procedures have not been employed at Lompoc.)

EVALUATION OF TREATMENT

When inmates are accepted into the program, active participation is formally stipulated as one of the goals to be accomplished before a recommendation for release on parole is made. Participants in the program are given a battery of psychological tests which are repeated at three-month intervals throughout the program, and a final testing is scheduled immediately preceding their discharge. In addition, several other behavioral measures are taken; these include attendance at and performance in other institutional programs, e.g., work and education. Regular educational and vocational training and work assignments are viewed as therapeutic activities for men in the program. All drug abuse activities are therefore coordinated with these other goal related assignments to avoid overlapping schedules. Further, all inmates participate in small group meetings of eight to ten members scheduled twice weekly for one and one-half hours per session. Sessions are recorded on video tape for replay and evaluation of the group process. Particular attention is focused upon specific acts which negatively influence interpersonal relationships.

STAFF UTILIZATION

All drug abuse treatment staff members function as group leaders and housing unit counselors. The correctional counselors also serve as liaison agents to gather information regarding each inmate's performance on all drug abuse and other institutional assignments. Some member of the drug abuse staff is always in the housing unit during the evening hours seven days a week to provide individual counseling when necessary. Members of the treatment team also attend to inmate disciplinary problems as they arise. In addition to the staff assigned to drug abuse, personnel at all levels show an interest in the program and indicate a willingness to help. For example, a continuing institutional training program has prepared many of the line staff officers to function as effective counselors using the Carkhuff techniques (Carkhuff, 1969). The correctional counselors now on the drug abuse staff have had this training and use it routinely in their contacts with inmates.

FOLLOW-UP PROCEDURES

Legislation has now been enacted to provide aftercare services for individuals released from drug abuse programs. While the emphasis presently at F.C.I., Lompoc, is upon the assistance and guidance needed to stabilize an acceptable adjustment in society, follow-up procedures are only presently being formulated, e.g., provisions such as urinalysis for monitoring drug usage on parole is being contemplated. It is expected that the aftercare contacts will provide significant feedback to the institution regarding the status of parolees. Such data will not only make it possible to evaluate the impact of particular treatments but should also provide the information essential to the continual modification of the program.

SETTING UP THE MODEL

The program began with a careful study of the requirements of both the inmates and the institution, and with a thorough review of available sources of information on drugs and drug abuse. Inmates who either volunteered or were referred by caseworkers or custodial staff members were interviewed to determine their needs. Their feelings were solicited on a whole spectrum of problems surrounding drug abuse and treatment, including the questions of why individuals use drugs and how such individuals can be helped. At the same time, with the assistance of the University of California, Santa Barbara, counseling psychology program, a search was made of the literature in all areas relating to drugs.

The next step was to isolate the kinds of problems which are faced by individuals who are either using or have used drugs, and are problems which might be solved within a drug abuse program having the limitations of an institutional environment. To this end, several fundamental questions were discussed. For example, we were concerned with identifying the kinds of legal and illegal reinforcers which drug abusers have available to them. We were also interested in identifying both alternative behaviors—e.g., saying "no" when asked to "shoot up"—and alternative legal reinforcers which could be as effective within the prison setting as on the outside

The goals of the program were then defined in terms of solving the problems which had been identified and were translated into performance objectives. Ideally the goal would have been to extinguish the use of drugs among all those who were exposed to the program. However, since drugs per se initially are the result rather than the cause of inappropriate behavior patterns, a more realistic goal was established: to help the inmates learn those behaviors needed for them to refrain from using drugs, and to help them develop sufficient self-confidence to do away with their need for drugs. Objectives such as improving socialization skills; engaging in more educational opportunities; developing specific goals in life; and learning to make better educational, personal and vocational decisions became as important as learning about drugs per se. These broad areas are now being rewritten in behavioral terms so that they can be measured.

All of the information collected during the course of these initial steps was processed by the drug abuse committee and then selectively used in setting up the program. Following the processing of relevant data eight inmates were then invited to participate in a small pilot program and from this feedback and other information a systems approach to drug abuse was implemented at F.C.I., Lompoc.

SYSTEMS APPROACH

Figure 1 is a representation of the six basic steps utilized in setting up the program and Figure 2 indicates the total system implemented. The ten functions included were: Study Inmate and Institution Needs (1.0); Define Problem Situations (2.0); Establish Drug Abuse Program (3.0); Design Program Prototype (4.0); Simulate to Test Prototype (5.0); Conduct Pilot Program (6.0); Implement Total Program (7.0); Operate Program (8.0); Evaluate Program (9.0); and Revise or Eliminate Program (10.0).

The program began with a study of the literature in order to identify other programs throughout the nation as well as to learn more about the drug user per se. This information was collected and analyzed and placed into a resource booklet for continual use. The drug abuse committee also met regularly to assess institutional resources in terms of personnel, programs and physical facilities. All of the information was analyzed in terms of the goals and the philosophy of the institution. Finally, the drug abuse program needs were determined in respect to the kinds of inmate drug problems and the goals and limitations of the institution.

DEFINE PROBLEM SITUATIONS

At this point alternative programs which might be used in meeting some of the inmate and institutional needs were defined. This involved a study of drug abuse programs undertaken by the military, by civilian agencies, and by other correctional institutions. In some cases the director and others visited the institution or agency in which pro-

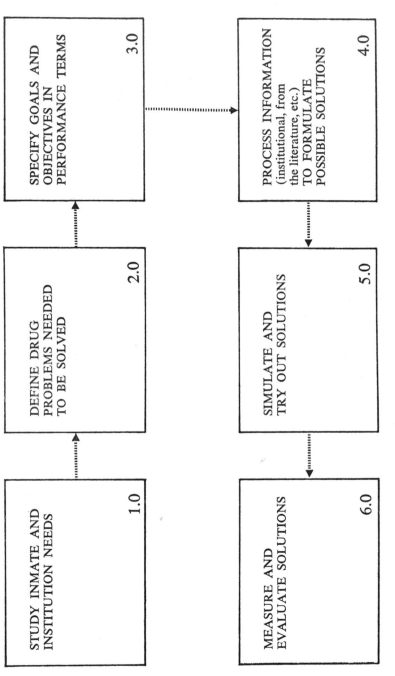

Figure 1. Basic steps in the Drug Abuse Program at the Federal Correctional Institution, Lompoc, California.

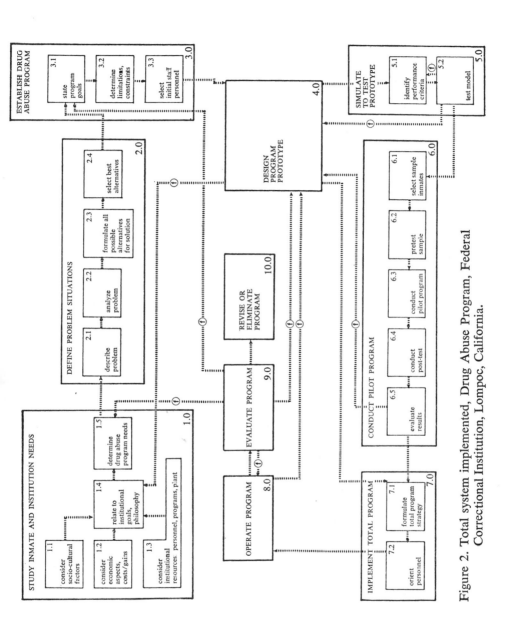

Figure 2. Total system implemented, Drug Abuse Program, Federal
Correctional Institution, Lompoc, California.

grams of special interest were in operation. A variety of programs, treatments, and housing arrangements were considered and after numerous meetings and discussions one alternative was selected. It was decided that the program would involve the following: separate housing for those in the drug abuse program; group and individual counseling; and a major treatment mode based on the principles of contingency management, specifically on token economy.

ESTABLISH DRUG ABUSE PROGRAM

After determining the program goals the drug abuse committee selected the initial staff of two correctional counselors and a secretary, in addition to the director, who was a member of the drug abuse committee. The initial staff was then assigned the task of designing a pilot program for a small number of inmates. (Step 4.0)

SIMULATE TO TEST PROTOTYPE

After considerable study and some additional training of the initial staff a prototype program was created and tested through verbal runthroughs. A consultant from the University of California, Santa Barbara, assisted to a limited degree in assessing the model's efficacy in respect to the program's goals and limitation.

CONDUCT PILOT PROGRAM

A small pilot program of six inmates was conducted for a three months period. Inmates were interviewed and tested on a variety of criteria, e.g., desire to participate, extent of and kind of drug use. The basic treatment mode during this pilot program was that of group therapy with some, but limited, individual counseling. Feedback from staff and inmates was collected and analyzed before the total program was implemented.

IMPLEMENT TOTAL PROGRAM

The first phase of the total program was implemented with 25 individuals. Inmates were oriented to the program and changes in housing were established. The program is presently in operation (8.0) and constant feedback is being sought and collected so that changes in the program can be made where needed. A complete evaluation of the program (9.0) will be conducted at the end of one year. Even now, however, constant modifications are being made as insights are gained and research programs are already planned in which specific treatment interventions will be evaluated empirically. For example, a series of video tape social models are presently being created from which inmates might learn how to assert themselves in situations in which they feel pressured by others to use drugs. Various models, including other inmates, individuals outside the institution, and the inmate himself, are being tried to determine which, if any, is effective in promoting acquisition of the specific behaviors which the drug abuser needs to acquire. Various aspects of the token economy program are being put into research models as are other group and dyadic counseling procedures.

SUMMARY

At this stage the program has been implemented, is ongoing, and is being evaluated. Whether or not the program is successful is yet to be determined. While immediate clinical data are available and suggestive of positive results, the final measurement must be the drug abuser's behavior subsequent to his release.

REFERENCES

Carkhuff, R. R. 1969. Helping and human relations. Vol. I (Selection and Training) and Vol. II (Practice and Research). New York: Holt, Rinehart, and Winston.

Rachman, S., and Teasdale, J. 1969. *Aversion therapy and behavior disorders: An analysis.* Coral Gables, Fla.: University of Miami Press.

Rubenstein, Charles. 1931. The treatment of morphine addiction in tuberculosis by Pavlov's conditioning method. *Amer. Rev. of Tuberculosis* 24:682–85. In *Conditioning techniques in clinical practice and research,* ed. Cyril M. Franks, New York: Springer, 1964.

Weil, Andrew T.; Zinberg, Norman E.; and Nelson, Judith. 1968. Clinical and psychological effects of marijuana in man. *Science* (December 13): 1234–42.

7

Operation Breakthrough

Jake Stoddard

Begun as a service project one year ago with almost exclusive emphasis upon drug-oriented problems, Operation Breakthrough is now attempting to expand into the more controversial areas of prison reform, race relations, and other community problems.[1] Our initial successes were all based upon a simple idea, our concept of drug abuse education. For the most part, we had had no prior experience in public speaking, counseling, or in attempting to run any such operation; however, we did have a desire to communicate our experience to anyone who would listen inside our prison and through trips outside to schools, juvenile halls, Vandenberg Air Force Base, and assorted local service groups. In the beginning, the use of our group as an educational aid for the Vandenberg drug program provided us with experience and undertaking of what we could do for the community, as we used the varied experiences of inmates as a means of describing what drug use, abuse, and other criminal activities were really all about.

Operation Breakthrough is representative of a change taking place within our nation's penal institutions. In the past, prison inmates have been the least effective factor in attempts to improve their own situation, let alone in trying to offer assistance to others. But more and more articulate prisoners are appearing in our institutions, with formal education or extensive "street education." By using their expertise in self-help efforts, panels can enact situations which allow

[1] Editors' note: Jake Stoddard was an inmate when he wrote this article from the viewpoint of his peers. His unusual contribution is included thanks to the approval of the former staff coordinator, Buster Graham, and to the previous associate warden, Gary McCune. Stoddard now attends the University of California, Santa Barbara; his interest in prison reform continues.

outsiders to see the fallacy of having stereotyped images of drug users and convicts. At the same time, some prisoners have gained a more realistic picture of what was previously regarded as an alien and unfriendly society. Descriptions of personal experiences with drugs and crime have served as an educational tool for parents and others with little knowledge of such matters and as a deterrent to children tempted by drugs or criminal behavior.

One result of our program is that, through our presentations to others, we have found that it becomes clearer to us what really brought us here. No matter how easy it is to rationalize to oneself, "putting it out on front street" to someone else requires a high degree of honesty. We are forced to see ourselves as society sees us, and this, in effect, causes us to take a new and broader view of ourselves.

In the beginning, it was difficult to awaken the community to the service we had to offer. Outside groups, especially schools, were very leery about letting convicts work with children, but we found ourselves to be our best publicity men. We raised as many questions as possible on trips out in order to prompt curiosity about our program, and we generally moved our audiences to becoming concerned and interested.

As elementary as this first lessons sounds, we have tried to show that it is imperative to acknowledge that problems actually exist. Too often parents and children proclaim, "It can't happen to me." Parents say, "It can't happen to my family or in my neighborhood"; young people experimenting with drugs say, "I'll never get busted." All of us, coming from every conceivable neighborhood and family, from the best to the worst, stand as proof positive that it can happen and is happening. Working with problems we all face as individuals or as society necessitates maintaining realistic awareness. We have shown young drug users or those contemplating drug use that there are both a good and a bad side to using drugs. Too frequently these individuals are snared between the negative and often misinformed views of local law enforcement personnel and the pictures painted by drug-using friends. We have shown the realistic truth as we have experienced the good and the bad and have come a long way toward promoting communcation through the destruction of stereotypes.[2]

2 Editors' note: We are aware of the current controversy surrounding community drug information programs. Among the most recent reports is a study that found that the majority of drug abuse films may be doing more harm than good (Cohen, et al., 1973). The present article refers to the use of imprisoned drug offenders as community communicators, which is only now being objectively assessed.

The second lesson we have tried to show is that there are no simple solutions. It is counterproductive to apply to drug abuse such "solutions" as total illegality or elimination of availability, without understanding the complexities involved. Proponents of "quick" solutions like the Army's early drive to stamp out marijuana in Vietnam or Operation Intercept did not predict the subsequent rise in heroin use in Vietnam or the increase in barbiturate abuse in this country. A better kind of solution is for all of us to develop a consciousness which allows us to view problems as mutual concerns which are mutually solvable. It is important for all of us to look realistically at drugs, alcohol, cigarettes, and all the assorted products we are tempted to take as magical pills to solve everything troubling society.

As a program to help build community awareness, Breakthrough is only one of many ways of dealing with today's social problems. As an ongoing program within the Federal Correctional Institution at Lompoc, California, started by inmates and to some degree operated by inmates and involving young criminal offenders, the program is unique. The very elements that make for Breakthrough's uniqueness raise special issues and challenging questions, however. Such issues and questions require constant reevaluation of our work and progress by staff and administration and by the inmates involved in order to assure the viability and continued existence of the program.

A fundamental question of penology is "Are inmates sent to an institution *as* punishment or *for* punishment?" Some of the older correctional officers are apparently firm believers of the latter, guarding against extra "privileges" or "freedoms," which are considered to be conducive to future problems. Carrying this attitude to its extreme would simply be to have every man "doing time," lock-up style. As one expression of the new philosophy emphasizing more communication and mutual respect, Breakthrough has shown one way that inmates may offer a service to the community. Like any new program, Breakthrough has been a focal point for occasional staff frustration and prejudice against change. But the program has assisted officers willing to change to the new emphasis on viewing inmates as fellow humans and, more important, as individuals. Idealistically, we would like to think that our program might readjust many penological concepts and eliminate old-line prisons and staffs who think in narrow, "old" terms. At the same time, we would hope to bring about changes in the attitudes of inmates—changes which society and inmates themselves desire.

A basic point of contention between inmate and administration

occurs over allowable inmate responsibility. Frequently young offenders have either never had the chance at or do not know what to
do with responsibility. Prison, as a whole, is a very emasculating experience. Having no choice about what to wear or eat, what work to
perform, or even when to sleep tends to stunt the normal maturation
process or atrophy whatever growth might previously have developed.
Naturally the institution is concerned with fostering responsibility,
but it is more concerned with efficiency, status, and the fear of mis-
representation, and the growth experience in an inmate's existence
is often neglected. Whenever the yoke of responsibility for a prison
program is laid upon staff members rather than program members,
inmates will generally side with their fellows, regardless of the issues
involved. However, when inmates feel they are responsible for their
own program, they will care for it and mature in turn. One could say
the more staff "coordination" is imposed, the less responsibly and less
maturely the inmates act.

It is our belief that immediate supervision which stifles responsibility should be discouraged, and that a more profitable use of staff
time would be the cultivation of community contacts, arranging for
speaking engagements that can specifically help us or through which
we can help others, and locating job opportunities. Consideration
must be given also to flexibility in meeting demands inside and outside the institution, and more important, in working on our role in
relationship to the community.

Our program has clarified the purposes for which correctional line
officers and professional staff people should be used in community
programs. In many situations a correctional officer's viewpoint has
been beneficial, in particular with such groups as the Air Police at
Vandenberg Air Force Base, local law enforcement people, or skepti-
cal audiences. On the other hand, audiences made up of mental
health professionals, drug program administrators, university people,
and political groups appear to respond better to inmate presentations.

Sociologists have long known that inmates determine much of
what goes on within an institution by creating special inmate hierarchies and codes. Operation Breakthrough has been in conflict at
various times with many of these older established unwritten inmate
"laws," partly because of changes in the type of people now going to
prison. Our particular institution is filled with young drug offenders
who have changed the codes simply by bringing their own sophistication into the prison. This culture gap accentuates the problem of
reaching inmates and involving them in our activities. We have found

that men in groups larger than thirty cannot develop camaraderie and do not develop close individual involvement with the program. At the same time, the question remains about what we have to offer the rest of the institution. We hope we can eventually extend to all inmates opportunities for learning counseling techniques, for receiving more choice in liberal arts courses, and for greater interaction with the public.

Something which can't be measured is the degree of "status" our organization, which is neither a club nor a program, has. Many clubs resent the fact that we are allowed more outside guests, that we have an office, that we are allowed more trips, have more publicity, and receive more unofficial attention and funding than other groups. However, we match their resentment with our own sense of frustration at not being a complete program. At a basic level, we frequently lose out on meeting nights because of scheduling conflicts between social clubs and school classes.

Besides occupying a position somewhere between a program and a club, Breakthrough is unique in being a multiracial group. One of our original goals was to try to bring diverse minorities together under one roof. Once a few minority members were introduced into the group, it was much easier to interest others. After some initial success in reaching the outside community, and once we had something to offer to inmate members, our racial balance became more equitable. Unfortunately, the administration attempted to capitalize on this makeup by staging "racially balanced" presentations for public attention. Any artificial use of the group is foreign to the philosophical justification of our program. We want to be inmate-run, to present what we really are, and to talk about what we really have done. For us to attempt to represent anything else is antagonistic to our principles.

We face a lack of interest from many officers and caseworkers. Their ignorance of our goals, their lack of initiative to learn about what we are attempting to accomplish, and our inability to interest them are discouraging problems for all of us, but especially for those who have, possibly for the first time, tried to help not only themselves but others. It is clearly up to us to integrate our presentations into the lives and training of our staff. Problems like drug abuse are important to all families, and if what we have to offer could be utilized by the staff, the benefits would be obvious. First, we would have more association with the people who work here. More important, many staff members would share something of their personal lives. For inmates to see beyond the "official" job front and begin to view staff members as interested human beings could not help but widen their perspective toward society.

A stumbling block to progress has been the lack of coordination between our efforts and other work within the institution. It would seem obvious that integration of our program with programs like the drug abuse treatment program and peer counseling would allow a natural development in helping inmates to realize their responsibilities to others and the community, but rather than complementing each other, we have too often ignored or ended up at odds with each other.[3] Many of us in Breakthrough see our activity as the final stage of the rehabilitation process begun by these other programs, all designed to lead the "together" person into community-conscious channels. The academic aspects of our program—our attempts to get psychology, sociology, and similar courses—would appear to mandate a coordination and rapport between ourselves and the education department. This coordination has been largely lacking so far. Our only integration into other institutional programs has been achieved so far by involving our members in other programs. As our position and achievements become more accepted within these other programs and departments, we feel we will have more success in gaining access to their services as we move toward our common goals.

Since we do not have official recognition as a program or receive an official budget or have a professional staff, we lack the status necessary to achieve recognition among counseling professionals outside the institution. Many of us hope that being certified through our program can have some benefit to us in our reentry into society. Ideally, such a certification should be academic, in order to offer real

---

[3] Editors' note: What Stoddard has to say about the initial organization of Operation Breakthrough has considerable historical validity. However, since the time this was written, certain changes have come about; Operation Breakthrough has been incorporated into a group activity program which now includes over a dozen different type inmate social activities (e.g., the Puma, Nordic-Celtic, Jaycees, Afro-American, Your Pal groups) under the direction of an officer-coordinator. Many of these organizations have extensive relationships with outside contacts, and hence Operation Breakthrough no longer has the major share of community associations. It is true that Operation Breakthrough still retains independence from the formal drug abuse treatment program as well as the mental health service, although some of its training is through the peer counseling program. Correctional institutions everywhere have been forced to recognize that they share with society a lack of racial harmony, and perusal of the names of many of the social groups indicates one way in which F.C.I., Lompoc, is attempting to handle this difficult situation.

assistance in obtaining higher educational goals. Also, such a certificate must have real meaning for those who go into community counseling work, either on a voluntary or paid basis. It should even help those who enter jobs where there is contact with people. We see that our nonprofessional status and lack of academic accreditation contribute to our sense of frustration, but the more support we can count on the more we can hope for success in extending our operations.

Despite the frustrations, none of us anticipated the success we have enjoyed up to the present. It has been a warm and enlightening experience to have been allowed to present ourselves to so many, but we have suffered somewhat in not having had the foresight to realize what we were getting into. It is essential now for us to take a collective long-range view of where we can go and where we want to go. However, most prisoners view the present only in terms of how much longer they will be imprisoned and what will work or suffice within that period. For us it is important not to ignore the need for building a foundation for our program which will let it become not dated or inoperable but will let it change to accommodate the future needs of the community and prisoners. Our program is a channel of awareness between the "outside" society and the "inside" society. Ideally we must not only increase the community's awareness of prisons and their responsibility to them, but we must also increase the prisoner's awareness of the community and his responsibility to it. We believe that opening the gates and encouraging people to find out about prisons will go a long way toward bringing about a reevaluation of correctional institutions and their functions and such legal matters as prisoners' rights. We believe we can be a force on a personal level, by reaching individuals and helping them achieve an additional commitment, and on a legislative level by showing the direction in which changes are necessary.

Another area in which such changes are needed is in opportunities for inmates after release. We hope to let individuals begin to see convicts as people and to influence those prejudices which result in fewer opportunities for ex-cons. We are attempting to do away with many of our archaic laws concerning voting rights, jury duty, and limits on jobs. It is a slow process, but it is most certainly one that we are in a unique position of helping to change.

To accomplish our ends both collectively and personally we need others. What we want is the opportunity to participate in a self-help approach to community problems and to be allowed to work with these community problems. Our most basic goal is to turn what has always been a deficit in the community—the prison—into a positive force, a resource of experience and commitment that can be used in helping others.

REFERENCES

Cohen, A. Y.; Harvey, W. M.; Nichols, E.; Nowlis, H. H.; and Winick, C. 1973. *Drug abuse films.* Washington, D.C.: National Coordinating Council on Drug Education.

8

A Thousand Men and I

Barbara E. Bliss

"If you are determin'd, Madam, to raise a disturbance in the prison,
I shall be obliged to send for the Turnkey to shew you the door."
John Gay, *The Beggar's Opera*, II, xiii

A thousand men—and I—walk that corridor. A friendly secretary is sometimes obliged to scuttle through it under escort, and female consultants or bright groups of visitors make their brief appearance and vanish. It's an unusual and exhilarating experience to be a woman in a prison of almost a thousand young men. Add to this that the woman is twenty to thirty years older than the men, is more extensively educated than any of them in a culture where the male is presumed more educated than his counterpart, and also, that the female, being salaried by "the Establishment," becomes more or less identified with "the enemy," and the situation becomes fraught with tragicomedy potential.

On "the other side" are the several hundred staff members from the Establishment who have spent a varying portion of their lives in an exclusively male environment where their roles, although slowly changing, have been relatively immutable, and who have had experiences of mental health personnel treating them with indifference, contempt, or frank opposition. They, too, have many mixed feelings about the sudden appearance of a female psychiatrist in their midst.

When I was starting to describe what it is like to be a woman working in a man's prison, I gradually realized that the prison is only one part of a complex relationship, and that I could only write about what it is like to be one particular woman, *me*, in *this* particular prison. Certainly, there are aspects of a woman working in a prison that are probably common to all adult correctional settings. But it quickly becomes evident that after the initial contact, the multiple interactions that develop depend on the personality and orientation of the therapist. No less important is the setting. In this institution, the age range is such that there is no inmate who could not be my son. I have to assume that the interaction between myself and inmates might be altered if there were a different age group. Certainly, *I* would react differently to a thousand men who were the age of my father or even men of my own age. If nothing else, the Depression and World War II would be shared experiences for us; in this institution, I have to understand that the inmates have all experienced a different world in their lifetime.

Taking into consideration all of these variables, there still appear to be certain facets of my position which are linked to my gender. For example, the open toilet and shower facilities limit my movement out of consideration for the men. Even in the industrial area, where I quickly learned to ask someone to check the latrines before I walk through, my femininity is accentuated so that I am not and cannot be seen as only a physician but have to remember, myself, that I am a female physician. The first area in which I became aware of this accentuation of my gender role was when I was informed that I would be escorted whenever I was out of the hospital or office area. I had, of course, been escorted when I first was shown around the institution, but it had not occurred to me that this escort would continue once I was employed. Although I had been in private practice for many years, I had continued to teach in a state hospital residency program; I had worked for two years in a juvenile correctional setting, which included some youths in their late teens. In all of these settings, I had been labeled only "doctor" and moved as freely as those women labeled "nurse" or "aide" or "social worker." Thus, I met the news that I could not move freely because of my sex with shock and irritation. At the same time, I felt that I had to recognize that I was *not* in a state hospital nor a juvenile setting but in a prison, and that the custodial staff was experienced in penal institutions and undoubtedly had a rationale for thus limiting my movements. Even the inmates seemed to expect me to be accompanied by an officer. Nevertheless, I chafed under the escort rule and hounded the warden almost daily to let me move freely.

After two weeks, over the objections of the Captain, the warden removed the escort requirement, and I have moved freely throughout the institution, with the exception of the housing units where, as stated above, the principal consideration is for the men. The inmate reaction to my freedom was one of surprise and pleasure.

Today, I no longer question the advisability of having a woman employee escorted initially. Many women do come to the institution for varying periods (secretaries, consultants, graduate students, visitors), and they present themselves in various ways. There are women who present themselves in a seductive manner and others who obviously fear inmates or are supercilious. There have been occasions when some have been openly contemptuous of the prison staff, reinforcing the inmates' feelings of being unjustly treated. Fortunately, almost all of the permanent female staff are mature women, whatever their chronological age, who truly like both the inmates and the staff and come to the prison to do a job. All do come into contact with a greater or lesser number of inmates, although it is sometimes across the grill of a door behind which some secretaries are locked.

I was originally unaware of how quickly a prison environment could become tension laden, even explosive. I have since learned that there is at least one difference between a mental hospital setting and that of a prison: in the former, outside of the adolescent unit, the patients seldom act in concert; one or two may become upset, but it is an unorganized eruption from which the other patients abstain. In a prison milieu, the outburst frequently involves a large group and is more or less planned and organized, increasing the danger a hundredfold. During these times, both staff and inmates tend to lose their *human* labels and become symbols to be attacked or used. (Hence, the constant worry about the occurrence of interracial outbursts where normal interracial friendships will dissolve, and it will become "Blacks vs. Chicanos" or "Whites vs. Indians.") At these times, it becomes the primary responsibility of the custodial department to keep or to restore order, and any woman in the area is generally seen as an additional liability in an already tight situation. Knowing how quickly these eruptions can occur and spread, one can understand why the staff wants to know how any female employee is going to handle herself in the institution, both with the staff and with the inmates.

One of my most gratifying moments occurred approximately a year after I came to the institution. On a sun-filled Sunday morning, a riot alarm sounded, and, well before it stopped, cars were pouring from the nearby housing area. Although I was not the medical officer on duty, I was the only physician living in the prison housing, so I, too, sped to the prison. There, everything was being handled much like a well-rehearsed ballet, quietly but efficiently. At the door to the main compound, I saw the warden, the two associate wardens, the captain, and several other officers calmly discussing the situation. For a moment, I feared that they would not let me enter, and, indeed, several of the officers seemed to question my presence until the warden waved a hello and went on talking. Later, I told one of the associate wardens of my gratification at not being stopped, and he, surprised, said, "Why should you be? You're one of the staff." I felt I had won my keys.

This protectiveness does not come exclusively from the custodial staff. Intermittently, inmates caution me. This past week, one of the tougher and more potentially dangerous inmates confided in me that he thought I should leave the prison "because it's just too dangerous for a woman." Other inmates repeatedly tell me, "You're having games run on you," or that I am too softhearted, or they tell me of a fresh rumor that is going around and indicate their concern.

Like any institution, a prison is a rumor factory. Originally, many of these rumors appeared to center around the question of why any woman would want to work in a prison, particularly when it meant a loss in income. Inmates were the first openly to question my presence, except for the warden, who asked me this kind of question in my initial interview. I realized that my responses would be discussed widely and that much of my interaction with inmates would depend on the answers. Second, it was apparent that the men had some fantasies about my reasons for working here that could be most detrimental if acted upon. Finally, I practice on a cornerstone belief that psychotherapy is an interaction between two basically equal human beings; that it may be, and often is, one of the most intimate interactions that we can experience. Thus, once I had been able to overcome what I later saw as fallacies of my original analytical training, I have felt that any patient has the right to ask me questions about who I am as a person, and that I have the obligation to give truthful answers. The answer to why I have wanted to work in a prison is not a simple one, having dendritic roots that spread into many areas of my life. The earliest factor was probably being taken into the confidence of a schoolmate whom I had grown to like. One day, she told me that she had done time in the State Industrial School for Girls. Because I felt very close to her and because the delinquent label seemed so incongruous with what I knew of her, I was more interested than repulsed, and we spent long hours talking about her life. As I remember, she was a very intelligent girl of about fifteen, and, as we talked, she was able to present a picture of herself reacting to a series of traumatic home situations which led her repeatedly to run away and, finally, to be declared "incorrigible." Often, I think that it was these discussions which propelled me into psychiatry.

Later, in Paris, I lived across the hall from a man who had spent time in the French penal colony in French Guinea after he had been sentenced for killing a policeman whom he had found having an affair with his mistress. During World War II, he had volunteered to fight with the Free French Forces and had been amnestied. Although he never talked of his family background, he spoke often with me of his experiences in the penal colony (which, interestingly, he saw as a far superior way to do time than in a penitentiary, as he had been able to work on the mainland, have his own hut, a mistress, etc.)

When I arrived in my residency at the Menninger Foundation, my first case was a man referred for attacking women and, finally, asking one of them to give his name to the police. At that time, the Menninger Foundation was the leading psychiatric residency center in the United States, and the training was rigorous. Our initial study cases were almost microscopically evaluated, with many hours of interviews with the patient, exciting hours of joint sessions with the social workers (who interviewed families), psychologists (who did extensive testing), and ward personnel. Our psychiatric supervisors asked us seemingly interminable questions that we had to return to the patient to answer. Again, I became fascinated by the question of what leads one person to choose, often repeatedly, a criminal solution to his problems. By the time I had finished my residency, I had determined to work in a prison.

In 1959, however, I was in a buyer's market, and no one was buying a woman psychiatrist for a man's prison. Several facilities wanted me to work in a woman's correctional setting, but, having sought out during residency several female patients who had committed crimes, I was then of the opinion that women felons tended to fall into two categories: those who were involved only because of their attachment to a man, or those who were basically neurotic. (Today, I might respond differently.)

Therefore, I took employment in a juvenile diagnostic and treatment center where, being the only psychiatrist available to the institution, I was assigned principally to the care of psychotic children. (Two of these boys I met again in my first week in this prison. Twelve years ago, these men were pre-teenagers receiving intensive treatment under my guidance! Should I ever get an exaggerated opinion of my own importance, remembering my meeting with them in the halls of Lompoc should return me to perspective. Neither of them, incidentally, is or was psychotic, but both appear to have become habitual criminals.)

After two years, I entered private practice and became more and more a specialist in communication and family therapy, heavily influenced by Virginia Satir and, later, by Fritz Perls and his gestalt theories. Encounter groups, sensitivity, and marathons became a way of life. Finally, just before I came to the prison, I was able to do some intensive work with Harvey Jackins and I have continued a definite enthusiasm for his reevaluation counseling techniques. (We are just finishing an eight-week introductory class in reevalution counseling at the prison under the guidance of an experienced counselor. It is too soon to state how effectively this technique can be used in this setting other than in individual therapy, where I find it valuable.) Throughout the time that I was in private practice, I took every opportunity to work with the courts and with the parole and probation departments. While I felt that I continued to learn a great deal about criminal behavior, I met the classical problems of treating these people on an outpatient basis and was seldom really satisfied with the results.

Finally, there was a mundane reason for my decision to leave private practice: I had grown progressively more wearied of the ever-increasing nonprofessional complications of running an office practice. The business side of such practice had changed from being a simple bore to being an ever heavier weight.

All or part of the above, I explained when asked why I had come to work in a prison, sometimes more succinctly, sometimes elaborating on one or another aspect. In spite of this, fantasies continued to be turned into rumors as facts. A few of these centered around power; i.e., I wanted to have power over males. Fortunately, I strongly believe *vive la différence,* and I believe these rumors have had little credence.

More persistent and disruptive have been the sexual rumors. In spite of being at least nineteen years older than the oldest inmates, I am frequently seen as a sexual object. To my surprise, a fair number of men tell of prolonged affairs with women twenty years older and more. (Although I have no statistics, I suspect that this is unusual behavior in the general American population.) From these fantasies, it is only a step to bizarre stories that I am working in this setting for sexual reasons, and that a great deal of sexual activity takes place in my office.

One of the more unpleasant occurrences took place in my first group meeting. A real "duck" (inexperienced person), I assumed that I was offered the most comfortable chair out of gentlemanly deference. I was intent on organizing the group and only later was I told that I had been maneuvered into a low-chair position where I couldn't help exposing my underclothing. (Without question, pantyhose are a must.) Remarks have also been made about my "seethrough" dresses. It took me some time to discover that this means dresses of cloth that permit anything under the garment to be seen, such as polyesters and the more sheer cottons. Again, it is assumed by a few inmates that I am wearing such clothing to seduce them into my fantasied seraglio.

Much of this could be eradicated by uncovering the window in my door. However, this would, I believe, also eradicate any therapeutic effect which I may have in many cases. Even with the window covered with a venetian blind, inmates attempt to peer in or eavesdrop. Furthermore, no patient could feel free to express his feelings if he felt that a staff member might look in at any moment. Because I feel that discharge of feelings in a nonharmful manner is important, I have also discovered that there is really more hurt and grief on the compound than anger (although, living up to the culturally accepted male image, the men usually translate the hurt into anger), and many tears have been shed in my office. In the ingrown atmosphere of the prison, scapegoating is a way of life for many men, and feelings expressed openly with me could become sources of painful ridicule if it were not for my insistence on privacy. Thus, I made the decision that the rumors are the price I have to pay for the privacy I require to be effective.

On only one occasion have the rumors been acted upon. A large but borderline-retarded man suddenly pulled me to him and made an obscene proposition. Taking into consideration his limited intellectual functioning and the emotional tension he was under from other sources, I pulled away and gently told him that that was a most improper suggestion, reminding him that I was there as a doctor. He then said something about having heard that I did such things. I continued to tell him that I was there as a doctor, and that people make up all sorts of stories. A few moments after he left, he came back and apologized with what I felt was genuine contrition.

Partly to counteract these problems, I have accentuated my maternal features, and this, in turn, has created some classical difficulties.

As one of the psychologists said, "You're one of the best things that happened to me here. I used to see all the dependent and/or immature personality problems. Now, they all go to you." Several inmates refer to me as "Mom," more or less seriously. It is evident that in some cases, I am the only caring mother-figure that they have known. I attempt to be both caring and realistic. In a few instances where sibling rivalry has developed to a serious degree, I have seen the men together, and, to date, I know of no instance where these relationships have led to harm, although there have been several occasions when I was apprehensive for several days. Perhaps surprising to those who have never worked in a prison, I have also met some of the most mature, sensitive, and courageous humans of my experience among these relatively young inmates. Some men have entered the prison with these qualities; some have gained them here. Some of these also call me "Mom." Most inmates, like people on the streets, are somewhere in between personality extremes. They react in an appropriate way to most of the moment-to-moment situations which they face but occasionally fall into patterns that are either destructive of themselves or others—or, all too often, both.

Relationships with the staff present as many problems as do relationships with inmates. After all, they, too, wonder why a woman would want to work here, and they, too, have their fantasies and their resentments.

During the first weeks, I often felt like the pivot arm of a delicately adjusted balance. Prisons tend to be fields on which life games of cops-and-robbers are played; any new element entering the arena is carefully weighed by each side. I was a new participant, and the rules weren't clear to me. Rather, the official, codified regulations were understandable, relatively simple, and generally made easy sense but, like all written policy, were superficial. In many ways, the rules of the other side—the inmate code—I could only sense. I had to learn a new vocabulary, as if I had been working at Harvard and transferred to an office in the heart of cockney London. (What does *bon-et-roué* mean? And "snake" . . . used as a compliment? Someone was upset because I "shined him on"? What does it mean that a dime commissary is equal to a nickel green?) [1] Nor is this difference only in words

[1] Editors' note: *Snake* refers to an insidious manipulator; *shined on* means that one affected a false sense of cordiality to someone but in essence ignored him; the *nickle-dime* indicates that it takes $10 in commissary privileges to equal $5 direct currency; *bon et roué* means giving particular care and time to one's type

but, also, in physical communication and the value or lack of value placed, by general consensus, on acts or words or objects quite at variance with the value generally given these acts, words, or objects outside the prison.

In some ways, I perhaps found myself more disoriented than would someone who was not accustomed to working in equally large institutions labeled "mental hospitals." All psychiatric hospitals of a certain size and of a certain quality have many things in common; one develops a "feel" for them after a while, so that one can be aware of the unwritten rules within a day or two. Because the prison seemed in some ways like a hospital, it was tempting to assume that the same mechanisms were functioning. However, there were subtle shocks, like small sparks of static electricity, that didn't fit the patterns to which I was accustomed, and I consciously reminded myself that this was a prison and not a hospital. Even so, for several weeks, I found myself jumping to assumptions which were not valid. It was almost two months before I could say that I truly had the feel of the institution. (Prison personnel describe the same semi-sensory learning about prisons and the same sense of something askew in a different type of institution.) During this time, I, like every newcomer, was particularly vulnerable to being manipulated.

Although I was not aware of it at the time, looking back, the fact that I was a woman—and one who walked freely about—was as disconcerting to the protagonists as the rumblings of their subterranean codes were to me. *Then*, I still thought of myself as "doctor" first. After all, on the streets, there are women everywhere, and while an occasional patient might object to a woman *doctor*, the accent remained on the profession. In prison, the accent has been heavily on my sex. (I believe that this is almost universally true for women employees. The only exception of which I'm aware is one surgeon who comes to the prison for special consultations, enters brusquely, fulfills her obligation with sharp efficiency, and leaves.) One evidence of this accentuation of my gender role is the frequency with which I am called "Miss" or "Mrs." in the prison and the paucity of times that this occurred in either private practice or in a hospital. Then, when a patient persisted in calling me "Mrs. Bliss," I felt that it in-

---

of dress. Those interested in colloquialisms in the prison setting are directed to *A Dictionary of Criminal Language* by W. L. Barkdull, L. A. Bennett, and M. L. O'Malley (Sacramento: California Board of Corrections, 1962). Unfortunately, none of the above words is defined in it, a fact which points out the transitory nature of the idioms of prison talk.

dicated a difficulty in our professional relationship. In the prison, the use of "Miss" or "Mrs." *may* indicate an interpersonal problem; for example, there are patients who call me that only when angry. However, I now believe that the usual reason is that my outstanding trait, for the inmates, is my feminity rather than my profession.

From the staff's side, the fact that I am a woman physician was more evenly balanced, but the concern that they had for my safety *as a woman* led them, too, to stress this. Interestingly, I have never been addressed as "Miss" or "Mrs." by any member of the staff, but always as "Doctor" or, as they grew more comfortable with me, "Barbara."

The often unrecognized but profound importance of how one human addresses another and the relationship message thereby given is nowhere more in relief than in a prison, where relationship messages have exquisite importance. The use of the first name implies equality and friendliness. Between inmate and personnel, it is seldom heard except by mental health staff. Most employees routinely address an inmate by his last name; when an inmate addresses a staff member by his last name alone, this generally is an indication of a positive relationship. That is, when staff has particularly good feelings for an inmate, they call him by his first name; when an inmate has friendly feelings toward a staff member, he drops the title and uses the last name only. Occasionally, well-liked members of the staff have well-known, accepted nicknames that are used. As women, we have to find another way. In my experience, almost no woman is comfortable calling others or being called by family names, and men share this discomfort in relationship to us. There is a scratchiness in calling Penny MacIntosh "MacIntosh" that disappears in saying "Penny." Hence, secretaries are usually called by their first names or accorded the title of Miss or Mrs.

For many years, I have called patients by their first names, whatever their age, because I feel that this addresses them as a total person rather than some aspect of their lives; i.e., "Gloria" includes all that she is, whereas "Mrs. Brown" labels her only as the wife of her husband. In many situations, the latter is preferable; in psychotherapy, I believe it presents a barrier. Because I use the given name, I encourage patients to reciprocate if they feel comfortable in so doing.

The use of my given name, which has the same therapeutic value here as it does in any practice, has led to some complications. As a few officers predicted, some inmates do not know how to handle the implied equality. Some seem to see it as evidence that I don't respect myself. Others have used it in a pathetic attempt to "prove" that they are someone set apart. Fortunately, most use it in the sense of human equality and many, outside my office, will refer to me as "Doctor."

Thus, many of the facets that joined together to make me into the psychiatrist that I am and which led to only minor comments in my former practice, appeared startling in this environment. They, as myself, were outside the unwritten "rules." As such, they could not be easily evaluated by the protagonists, and, because they aroused anxiety in both staff and inmates, a definite pressure was brought to bear on me to be different than I am, to fit more closely into custom. In some instances, these pressures made good sense; in some, it was truly a question of precedence.

It would be incorrect to assume that the personnel do not have an unwritten code, as well as the inmates. Policy can describe corridors of action. It cannot dictate the emotional reactions of two or more persons at a given moment nor the exact choice of words or posture. Especially for the staff who see their job as rehabilitative through interpersonal relationships, policy sets guidelines in which small cracks must be anticipated in carefully selected situations.

Contrary to the media presentation of prison life, in my experience almost all of the staff wish to have human-to-human relationships with the inmates and refer to officers who do not with expressions ranging from concern that the rigid officer may get harmed to outright contempt. At the same time, experience has taught them to be careful. I suspect that there is no one on the prison payroll who has not been manipulated at least once—and the price for falling into such a trap may go as high as death for oneself and others or imprisonment for oneself. Looking the other way in an incipient riot situation, allowing a violent felon to get in a position where he can escape, or granting special, hard-to-get favors to one man or one group can lead to overwhelming disaster, but fortunately, occur with great rarity. In such major cases when even a tiny crack can suddenly become a major crumbling, regulations are clear and almost always followed to the letter.

It is in the more intimate, day-to-day experiences that a staff member may be manipulated—or may actually reach and help an inmate. There is no one working with prisoners who doesn't make this choice a hundred times daily, although it may have become so routine that he is no longer aware of the decision process. Do I give this inmate a cigarette and spend some quiet time talking? Do I let this other man make a phone call? Do I give this inmate convalescence for his headache, or is he malingering to avoid handling a problem at work? Do I write up a disciplinary report in this borderline situation, or can I work it out with the man myself? Etc., etc., hour after hour. Can I trust this man's reactions, and, in so doing, have a relationship which will help—which will lead to one of those Christmas cards saying that our relationship was a turning point in his now happy life? Or am I being used? If so, where is the trap?

It is little wonder that some staff members opt for the simplicity of rigidity. My wonder is that so many continue to try, continue to leave themselves open to the possibility of humiliation, hurt, or worse. Throughout the institution, security is the most basic concern, and different staff contribute to this in different ways. Some consciously establish good relationships with inmates to have an information line into the population. As "snitching" is a cardinal crime in the inmate code, for which retribution will probably be exacted, many inmates try to avoid any appearance of close communication with an officer. I was tested initially by both sides, as I suspect is any mental health person who is the recipient of confidences. The first time that I was told that a knifing was imminent, I was in a quandary. It was evident that I was told to see my reaction but what if it were true? If it were and I said nothing to the custodial staff, I not only would have failed in my primary role as a physician, but I would alienate the officers; if it were not true and I reported it, I would alienate the inmate population. I fell back—and continue to do so—on a clear statement that everything is confidential *except* information that someone is going to hurt someone or themselves. I have since been told, on a few occasions, something of this nature, and if I felt that I had not been able to dissuade the person I have consistently reported it at once. I have been equally consistent in not reporting information that doesn't fall into these catagories, with the result that staff members have, very occasionally, become irritated with me. Interestingly, if I reported too much, I would lose the respect of the staff.

Writing this, I become aware that it has been much more difficult to discover the custodial "code" than that of the inmates, because it is hidden so much better from neophytes. I cannot explain why hospital personnel, teachers, or industrial workers will discuss their relationships with inmates readily, whereas officers remain behind a cool wall of impeccable politeness for a much longer period. I cannot say how much of this had to do with my femaleness. Certainly, a lot had to do with the unfortunate manner in which some mental health personnel have related to the custodial staff, so that few officers have not had the experience of being treated as less than human by some of us. Apparently unrecognized by these professionals is not only the true humanity of the officers, but the fact that close ties *do* exist between the custodial and inmate populations. One can have the dislike of one officer here and another there, but if one earns the resentment of the majority, one's professional relationships with the inmates may be totally destroyed. The multiplicity of ways in which the staff can undermine a mental health professional—in small remarks, in not sending patients on schedule, etc.—is almost unlimited. And while the relationship between inmates and custodians may appear superficially distant, there is an interdependency that throws a klieg light on each side's reactions, as if a basketball suddenly replaced the classic pigskin in a bowl game, and each team evaluated the other team's response. The fundamental rule of never interfering in a marital battle unless you intimately know the "rules" that the spouses have set for themselves is nowhere better followed than in a prison.

Rereading the above, I am aware that my picture of what it is like to be a woman working in a man's prison may be discouraging for many. If it seems so to a woman reading this, perhaps such employment is not for her, or perhaps she might handle herself differently, or the institution might have substantial differences so that her experience would be totally different. If, on the other hand, the total experience sounds as fascinating to her as it has proven to be for me, I should like to suggest several guidelines which may make the experience more rewarding and help her to avoid some of the pitfalls inherent in the meeting of a woman and a prison. First, she must examine her own motives closely. No matter how thoroughly one does this, the inmates and staff will be even more thorough and will test their theories either by direct questioning or by subtle suggestions. Remember that the degree of suspicion is high and that at least some of the men will be unable to believe that one's reasons can have a positive base.

Undoubtedly, the most helpful suggestion that I can make is to approach the prison with a totally open mind. Because we each have heard of prisons all of our lives, we each have a mental picture of what they are like and of the men who inhabit them; thus, it is necessary for most of us to remind ourselves that our fantasies are just that and that we are in a here-and-now reality once we step inside the institution. Particularly, we are not interacting with a symbolic guard or an equally symbolic convict but with individual human beings, each doing the best he knows how at the moment—as we are.

During the first weeks, at least, I would suggest that a woman let herself "float"; as she exposes herself to the setting, chatting with this one and that, she will begin to be seen as a person and will start the long process of removing the mystery of "that woman." As she drifts around the institution, it will be like sitting down before a gigantic jigsaw puzzle, turning up pieces one by one. Here, a bright color or an unfamiliar word will catch her eye or ear. Little by little, she will find several pieces that fit together to form a picture within the total frame, although it may be months before she learns just how the mini-sections fit together to form the whole. Personally I am still learning and still being surprised.

Because of one's femininity one is already outside the "rules," and should expect to feel pressures from all sides. At first, official policy provides comfortable guidelines to follow until one gets the true feel of the prison. Still, because prisons have rules that apply nowhere else in society, such as stringent control of phone calls or the need to count at specific times, one will probably find oneself being gently (or brusquely) reprimanded for offending against some policy that one had not imagined could exist. Before becoming too incensed, ask for an explanation. One will be surprised how often the explanations fit.

Especially during the first weeks, when a new person is being turned under the microscope and each vein is being examined, she should try to anticipate *any* interpretations that can be put on her responses. At first, someone will be misinterpreting each thing she does or says, and it is only after weeks or months that her consistency will be accepted. Second to this, she should remain aware of any possible consequences of each thing she does or says. If she does, she will avoid most unpleasant encounters before they start. Unfortunately, it is impossible to avoid all unpleasantness in such a highly charged atmosphere, so that one needs always to have an emotional —or real—escape hatch for the times that these do occur. My own formula is to attempt truly to understand the point at which the other person finds himself and accept him as he is at that moment.

Above all, one has to try not to get caught in the game of "cops and robbers." While this may sound simple to accomplish, the pressures to take sides can only be imagined until they are experienced. If one does get caught up in this game, it is evident that one has to take sides. In my opinion, when that happens to a mental health worker, his abilities to do his work are massively diminished, if not shattered. Inching along the tightrope while remaining genuine and relating to each person on a human-to-human level is tremendously challenging; it can also be exhausting. Possibly because of this, apparently many of us have fled the scene. We have either worked the least number of hours possible and then sped to the golf course, or we have holed up in our offices like shadow-frightened groundhogs. This behavior does not go unnoticed and has apparently been so common that it is expected. When, instead, one of us does put in an extra hour occasionally or comes to the prison in time of trouble or takes time to chat with the staff or acts as a sponsor to an evening inmate group or comes with one's family to a special event, we counteract the old image of health personnel who come to a prison job as to a sinecure and who, like so many of the people in most inmates' backgrounds, have only mouthed interest in them.

The list of do's and don'ts that I have garnered for myself might be capped with an admonition about language. A woman shouldn't come to a prison if vulgarity disturbs her—but she shouldn't join in it herself. Nowhere in our society, in my experience, is the double standard so strong as in a prison, and nowhere is it more imperative to "act like a lady." If one doesn't respect one's own femininity, one can be sure that it will not be respected by many of the men. Another tightrope to walk: preserving one's own dignity without disapproval of the language and acts of the men around one.

If a woman succeeds in avoiding *most* of the traps inherent in the situation, particularly the big ones that lead to disaster, and if she does not run from the myriad human encounters that she meets each day; if she can look past the uniforms or the language or the games that are constantly being played to the men behind them, she will find herself interacting with some of the finest human beings it is possible to meet.

Because a prison is remarkably alive and pulsating, she will never have one day like another nor an hour of boredom. And, always, her femininity will make of her someone special in that environment. In fact, it is temptingly easy to fall into what inmates call "an ego trip." A person will have no time to plan encounters and little time to think about them afterwards but will be living them, second by second. It is no place for a neophyte, but, once one has one's therapeutic skills sufficiently engrained so that they are a part of one, a way of *being*, then one can come to the prison.

One day I entered the hospital, and a group of inmates began singing to the tune of the Miss America song, "Here she comes, Mrs. F.C.I." A little stream of bubbles issued forth in the glass of champagne that every workday offers.

COMMENT: R. E. HOSFORD AND C. S. MOSS

There are several points we feel should be added to Dr. Bliss's personalized account. Dr. Bliss takes more than her share of seriously disturbed inmates, freeing the psychologists to work with those who are essentially more socially than emotionally inadequate. She has taken it upon herself to work dyadically and in groups with homosexuals who feel discriminated against and who wish to modify some aspects of their behavior and attitudes. She has also been active in in-service training for other staff members, as well as in sponsoring training in reevaluation counseling for the peer counseling and Operation Breakthrough inmate programs. She is presently becoming involved in the supervision of female psychology graduate students enrolled in counseling internships at F.C.I., while Dr. Moss supervises the males.

While she has quite vividly presented her role as a woman therapist in a prison setting, we feel that her impact has been greater than she has implied. This impact has been felt by inmates and staff alike and is due not only to her competency as a therapist, but also to the fact that she has demonstrated that a woman can function professionally in an all-male prison.

However, we differ with Dr. Bliss's perception of what types of women can be successful in a men's prison setting. Despite the strong emphasis she places on being a maternal woman and a physician, our experience has been that there is also merit in exposing inmates to younger female professional counselors. Discussion of sex is not out of place if handled in a mature, nontitillating fashion, of course with the safeguard of constant vigil by a male staff member. The chapter by Boulette, as well as referenced cases by Dechant and Forssell are examples in point (see Chapter 9). We are in grave danger of succumbing to the conventional model of an asexual prison which means the elimination of heterosexuality, not only in practice but in conceptualization as well. One of the real kinds of isolation faced by an inmate is isolation from women. How can he go back into society and behave "normally" toward women if he has not been able to even communicate with a woman for months or years? Is it then any wonder that homosexuality is such a major problem in prisons?

II

Illustrative Counseling Cases in the Treatment of Social Offenders

In addition to a discussion on counselor training and a concluding chapter which elaborates in some detail the editors' views on prison mental health programs and needed changes for the future, Section II also contains a collection of selected counseling cases in which inmates were the actual clients. While these cases might be viewed as being most germane and useful to practicing counseling and clinical psychologists, they are intended also to provide information about the kinds of problems for which incarcerated individuals need help and the therapeutic programs which were effective in helping inmates achieve the behavioral changes necessary for the solution of their problems. Above all, the examples serve to illustrate some of the counseling techniques that can be easily taught to intelligent lay and non-psychologically trained staff.

For the most part, the theoretical approach represented by the counseling techniques employed by the therapist is perhaps best described as that of behavior therapy. That is, the counselor proceeds by (1) identifying the maladaptive behavior and determining with the client whether that behavior needs to be increased or decreased, (2) identifying the environmental contingencies maintaining the undesirable behavior or reducing the probability of the client's performing a more desired behavior, and (3) identifying those types of environmental changes, usually reinforcing stimuli, within *and* without the client which might be modified in order to alter his behavior. The key principle is consistency of application.

Two of the cases presented, those by George and Boulette, represent the effective use of this approach by students in training. Both of these counselors were enrolled, along with six other students and two institutional case managers, in a counseling seminar and practicum conducted at F.C.I., Lompoc (see Moss, Chapter 2, for a detailed description of the training). From the several cases conducted and written up during this training session, those of George and Boulette were selected for inclusion as chapters in Section II because they represent some departure from those cases most often found in the literature. The former consists of a White counselor working effectively with a Black client and using desensitization techniques to modify a stuttering behavior. In this case the difference in race between the inmate and counselor did not seem to make any observable difference. The Boulette chapter was chosen because it illustrates once again that female workers, even young ones, can function effectively in an all-male prison setting. And the fact that both the client and the counselor were Chicanos makes it possible for the reader to gain additional knowledge concerning the ethnic variable in counseling. An interesting aspect of this case, apart from the overall counseling per se, is that the therapist utilized the speaking of Spanish as a reinforcer for the client contingent upon his verbalization habits, i.e., when the client voiced positive statements the counselor spoke to him in Spanish, but when he resorted to complaining and talking about self-destructive behaviors, she immediately switched to speaking English.

The other five case studies were conducted by the human resources staff. When an acute or difficult case comes to the attention of the correctional officers, they might well refer it to the mental health staff; the alternative in the past would be to place the offender in segregation (the "hole"—a prison within the prison). But even segregation—relabeled the Intensive Treatment Unit (ITU) in this facility—is now used sparingly; for example, ITU now houses only .01 percent of the total prison population, dealing mostly with the chronic violent cases. As was stated earlier, we are attempting through continuous in-service training to enable the officers to deal more effectively with enhanced therapeutic skills. We hope that in the near future they will be able to reduce or even prevent the occurrence of some such cases by alleviating the stresses or tensions in prison life.

It should also be pointed out that the proportion of highly disturbed individuals that become the concern of human resources constitutes only a small segment of prisoners; however, they do represent a disproportionate amount of time and interest from mental health counselors, and hence are presented here primarily for instructional purposes and particularly for the advanced student.

9

Counseling in the Prison: Implications for Counselor Training

Ray E. Hosford and C. Scott Moss

Traditionally, counselor training programs have been university based and have included only minimal practicum and field experience, generally confined to eductional and/or hospital settings. Such programs often have little articulation between training and on-the-job counseling in correctional settings. Even the traditional types of counseling procedures frequently prove to be ineffective, if not irrelevant, when applied to the problems of individuals confined to prisons.

In an effort to develop a more effective counselor training program, the University of California, Santa Barbara, and the Federal Correctional Institution, Lompoc, have decided to bring together the university and the employing institution in the planning, implementing, and evaluating stages of a joint program in which the resources and personnel of both institutions are utilized. We hope that in this way a relevant and efficient program can be developed which can be empirically tested and used by these two institutions, and which can be exported as a program to other correctional and university settings.

While the project differs considerably from other counselor training programs in that it is a competency-based program, i.e., students must demonstrate proficiency in the acquisition of certain knowledge and in the performance of specified counseling skills rather than the accumulation of a number of course units, perhaps its most innovative aspect lies in the combination of the training of graduate students in counseling psychology with ongoing in-service training programs for correctional officers, case management staff, administrative officials, and selected inmates, so that all of the participants are both teachers and learners. In addition to their participation in practicums and internships at the correctional facility, students will meet with prison staff and inmates in seminars both at the university and prison locations. The proposed program is specifically designed to improve the overall rehabilitation of inmates by equipping counselors and other correctional staff members, as well as inmates themselves, with the knowledge and skills for establishing the types of external and internal environmental contingencies which bring about attitude and behavioral changes. Performance objectives are being developed for each trainee group and for each aspect of the total program. Each training unit will be produced, tested, and modified so that it can be utilized for continuing in-service programs at both the correctional institution and university, and so that it can be exported to other institutions.

Development of the program began with a three-year period of informal discussions between university and correctional institution personnel. It was from these discussions and a pilot study, as well as from our own experience and review of the literature, that we defined and established our position. Basically, it was our conclusion that the medical approach which most psychologists and psychiatrists practice outside the correctional setting to change behavior tends to be both inefficient and ineffective in the prison situation. In the first place, the high ratio of inmates to professional staff makes such one-to-one therapy nearly impossible and the questionable effectiveness of this approach in changing behavior makes it of doubtful value for clients in general, and inmates in particular. Therefore, we wanted to identify and test existing procedures, as well as develop new techniques which would be both practical within the limitations of the prison setting and suited to the special goals of rehabilitation. At the same time we wanted to provide training and experience for the counselors in working *with* and involving others in the rehabilitative process. Too often those of us involved in mental health separate ourselves from other staff members and from other programs. Just to be familiar with the jobs of other staff members is not enough. If we are to rehabilitate the inmate, we must establish programs within the prison which promote collaborative working relationships among all staff members having some impact on that inmate's life. In addition, these relationships must include people, agencies, and organizations within and without the institution, and these resources must be actively included in the counseling process. In other words, we needed a much broader definition of counseling than is generally perceived and we wanted a program which would train counselors to work as consultants and trainers of those who act as change agents for the inmate. Rather than becoming experts at "talk therapy," we wanted our counselors to become skilled in teaching line officers, inmate families, and inmates themselves more effective and time-saving methods of behavioral change.

To this end, considerable time was devoted initially to the development of the specific performance outcomes which we wanted counselors to accomplish as a result of completing the program. Basically, these competencies fell into three areas: preventing problems, teaching decision-making, and modifying behavior.

PREVENTING PROBLEMS

Much of what is done in the name of rehabilitation, by society and by the correctional institutions, may at times constitute a far greater crime than anything perpetrated by the inmates. Consider, for example, the question of the diagnoses and placement of inmates. Too often, an individual is placed in a given group for convenience, for ease of management, rather than because a given group is suited to his rehabilitation needs. Instead of helping an individual acquire the types of behaviors he will need in order to succeed in society, we teach him to behave in abnormal ways; these are the models to which we expose him, and all too often it is the deviant behavior that we reward by our attention. Thus, when, as is all too often the case, we group hardcore criminals with first offenders we, in fact, provide models from whom the new inmates learn more, and more sophisticated, methods of criminal behavior. In effect, the very practices which we, as society, have designed to reduce aggression and alienation serve instead to promote, rather than eliminate, these behaviors. Much of what we have learned through research in learning indicates that imitation is a potent source of attitude and behavior change. To separate from society the inmate who is capable of being rehabilitated and thus separate him from those individuals who demonstrate normal behavior is antithetical to any program which supposedly is designed to bring about appropriate behavior. Even mental hospitals are realizing that placing mildly neurotic individuals with those who demonstrate severe psychotic behaviors serves to promote "psychotic behavior" rather than to help these persons act normally.

Commitment to preventing problems is crucial. Thus we felt that a major part of our counselor training program should focus on helping counselors develop competencies in assessing the various types of individual, organizational, and institutional behaviors—both inside and outside the prison setting—which serve to promote problems of aggression and alienation, or which in other ways retard the rehabilitative process. Dealing with individuals after criminal-type behaviors are already well established is far more difficult and much more costly than is modifying those environmental practices which promote the very behaviors which prisons were designed to alleviate. In essence, this part of the program may be seen as a "subversive activity," one which seeks to modify institutional and societal practices which produce human problems.

Shapiro's chapter on group leadership training describes the use of one kind of intervention procedure in problem prevention which counselors might employ to improve staff-inmate relationships at all levels. Several other programs also concerned with modifying individual, organizational and institutional behaviors, which might serve to prevent subsequent problems of aggression and alienation, are presently in operation at F.C.I., Lompoc. Among these is the creation of training packages in behavioral approaches to counseling for correctional counselors and case managers. These packages include video tapes, films, and selected readings which accompany a self-administered step-by-step training manual on behavioral counseling (see Chapter 2).

TEACHING DECISION-MAKING

One of the major problems for which inmates seek counseling and which led directly or indirectly to their incarceration is that of poor decision-making. These individuals never learned to make decisions in a wise and rational way; instead, many act impulsively and without any thought to alternatives or consequences. Many inmates have dropped out of school and have entered and failed in vocations because they went about the process of vocational decision-making without any systematic plan or procedure. Still others are in constant states of anxiety because they cannot make for themselves the decisions which will affect their lives. Because they are unable to assert themselves, these individuals often allow others to make their decisions for them. This part of the counselors' training program will focus on developing, testing, and implementing with inmates a variety of counseling procedures e.g., self-teaching kits, social models which demonstrate appropriate behaviors, etc., to help inmates acquire knowledge and facts of their own values along with the consideration of possible alternative courses of action and the consequences of each.

Examples of recently utilized counselor interventions designed to help inmates acquire the behaviors necessary for making good decisions, are found in he discussions by Kerish (1972) and Dechant (1972). Kerish worked with an inmate whose anxiety related to making decisions prevented him from formulating for himself an acceptable plan for parole release. However, after the inmate received systematic training in decision-making in a method described by Gelatt (1962) and positive reinforcement for performing the appropriate relevant behaviors, Kerish reports that in response to the counselor's inquiry, "What did you get out of these counseling sessions?" the inmate replied: "I understand more how to make decisions. Before I could look only at one aspect. Now I bring everything in that could happen if I did something and don't decide until I've looked everything over. I feel I have gotten on my feet and am accomplishing things."

Dechant worked with an inmate who sought counseling because of his concern about returning to heroin after release from prison. She used both systematic practice in decision-making and assertive training (Wolpe, 1969) to help the inmate learn to say "no" to his addict friends if and when they offered him drugs. Besides learning a variety of verbal responses to invitations to use heroin, and increasing his confidence about his ability to say "no," the client also began making and carrying out decisions related to continuing his education upon release from the institution.

MODIFYING BEHAVIOR

Our view, and that which guided most of the cases in this book, is that antisocial (i.e., criminal) behaviors are learned the *same way* socially acceptable behaviors are. This conceptualization, of course, has several implications for counseling inmates as well as for therapy in general. It implies, for example, that behaviors, whether appropriate or inappropriate, are acquired through experience. Neurotic reactions, evident in many of the cases presented below, are acquired like any other behavior, and as such can be altered by changing the contingencies which maintain and control that behavior. Thus, while most of the cases presented in this section are those treated by one-to-one therapy sessions, this approach does not in itself necessarily offer the most effective means for rehabilitating the inmate. Counseling must be viewed in a much broader sense. Warden Kenton, while addressing himself to the role of the unit officer says ". . . when we conceptualize rehabilitation as a total process involving all of those who have an effect on the inmate's total environment, then and only then can we help him gain the vocational, educational, and social skills needed for him to be successful in society" (1973, personal communication). This view closely parallels that of our own. Indeed, as Ford and Urban (1967) suggest, the day of therapy as a one-to-one kind of verbal interaction to the exclusion of other learning situations may be passed. They state:

> The picture of psychotherapy as a condition in which two people sit privately in an office and talk about the thoughts and feelings of one of them with the expectation that changes in these will automatically produce changes in overt behavior outside the office has been shattered. . . .
> Simple understanding is not considered enough. The primary emphasis seems to be on *behavior* as it presently occurs, present behavior defined to include feelings, thoughts, and images; physiological responses; interpersonal relationships; and motor behavior. [pp. 366–67]

The counselor's role must involve much more than that one-to-one or even group counseling procedures. It must consistently involve working with those significant persons and those institutional and societal practices which have control over and shape the inmate's behavior.

Central to this goal is that counselors begin to conceptualize inmate behavior in terms of learning principles rather than disease-oriented internal constructs and that they only view inmates as individuals brought up in environments in which they have learned to seek satisfaction of their needs through illegal means. They are not perceived as psychotic or abnormal, but as individuals who have learned different behaviors. Many criminals, for example, are proud of being "good" criminals because there are so few other behaviors they have learned in life for which they receive any reinforcement. When individuals do learn the various personal, education, and vocational behaviors which receive attention from society, they seldom seek deviant means of gaining reinforcement. Counseling an inmate back into society means helping that individual to learn to do the type of behaviors reinforced by that society.

Cases by Forssell (1972a, b), Day (1972), and deVisser (1972) are illustrative of some of the kinds of techniques counselors might employ to help inmates achieve changes in their behavior so that they can function more effectively in society upon their release. Forssell (1972a, b) reports having achieved considerable success with two inmates experiencing severe anxiety when dealing with interpersonal relationships. In the first case she used graduated role-playing situations with an inmate who had learned to withdraw from any social situation in which talking with females was a possibility. Forssell relates that she interacted with the inmate on a "boy-girl" rather than a counselor-client model. As the client increased his ability to relate interpersonally with her, his success appeared to generalize to other areas as well. For example, by charting the frequencies of positive and negative self statements emitted by the inmate during five tape recorded sessions, she found that his number of negative self statements decreased from 25 per hour to 5, while his positive self references increased in frequency from 2 to 28. In the second case, Forssell found that of the several therapeutic techniques she used, social modeling (Bandura, 1969) and systematic instruction in decision-making (Gelatt, 1962) were the most effective in helping a client improve his ability to interact interpersonally with others and subsequently to achieve a more positive self concept.

Day used behavior rehearsal (Wolpe, 1969) in helping an inmate learn how to communicate more effectively with his parents. This problem had led him before his incarceration to resort to using drugs and to living with others involved in the drug culture, because he had found that in doing so he could "communicate his feelings without experiencing the anxiety he felt when he could not assert himself . . . with his parents." According to Day, practice in assertive behavior helped the inmate to relate to his parents upon their first visit to the institution in over a year some of the feelings he had experienced in the past but had been unable to verbalize with them. After their visit and after the inmate subsequently initiated a renewed correspondence with them, his parents indicated that they would help financially and would allow him to return home during the four-week period between his release on parole and the start of a vocational training program elsewhere in the state, something which they had previously been unwilling to do.

Another example of what a counselor might do to help an inmate change his own behavior is a case reported by deVisser. DeVisser used thought-stopping and desensitization (Wolpe, 1969) to help an inmate who complained of recurrent insomnia. Using client self-report, validated by observations from the unit officer on duty during evening hours, to evaluate the success of counseling, deVisser reports that after only five sessions the inmate's number of weekly nonsleeping hours between 10 P.M. and 1 A.M. decreased from a base rate of six taken over a three-week period to that of less than one.

If prisons are truly to become rehabilitative rather than custodial agents, then, upon completion of a period of time in prison, an individual should have acquired the behaviors necessary to function effectively within the constraints of society. That is, he should be able to perform the types of behaviors which can elicit sufficient reinforcement so that he will not need or desire to resort to criminal-type behaviors to achieve these same aims. Rather than spending time learning how to diagnose and classify inmates in terms of some nosological categories (which does little to bring about positive change and often serves to promote the very behavior that the diagnosis suggests), we wanted our counselors to become competent in behavioral change strategies which would help inmates acquire the specific knowledge and skills they need in order to be successful in life. These behaviors could include any of a variety of outcomes ranging from learning how to apply for a job to a goal such as learning to respond in a relaxed way to situations which previously elicited severe anxiety. This aspect of the program not only requires that the counselor demonstrate his competency in working individually with inmates and with a variety of counseling techniques, e.g., desensitization, social modeling, dyadic and group counseling, but that he be successful in involving other staff members, inmates, and individuals outside the institution in the change process. Specific skills to be developed by the counselor during this phase of the program include learning how to (1) define problems in terms of behaviors, (2) observe and record behaviors, (3) modify behavior, and (4) evaluate behavior change.

While the program incorporates many of the principles and techniques utilized in behavior therapy and community psychology (see Chapter 2) it was not designed to follow any one theoretical point of view. Rather than relying on one theory or one method, the program seeks to train counselors whose efforts can be evaluated relative to what an inmate can do as a result of receiving counseling service. In some cases, the counselor's success must be determined relative to the extent he can teach and motivate others to become involved in the change process. In others, success might be evaluated in terms of positive changes in institutional practices which the counselor identified and helped to modify. In any event, it is not allegiance to any one theory or adherence to any method, but what happens to the individual inmate as a result of our efforts which determines rightfully the success of counseling and of rehabilitation per se.

IMPLICATIONS FOR TRAINING

In the Afterword, ". . . and the Walls Came Tumbling Down," we discuss in detail a model for prison mental health services. We feel that implementation of the model is necessary not only to improve correctional institutions generally, but also to improve the effectiveness of the total correctional counseling program within the institution. Basically, the model presents mental health services in the prison setting as involving four types of interventions: in-service training, consultation, applied demonstration and research, and direct therapeutic counseling. Clearly if these types of intervention are to become a reality, closer cooperation between university clinical training programs and correctional institutions is needed so that trainees can get needed instruction and practice in each of these areas. Counselors-in-training, for example, can and should be given supervised practice in conducting in-service training for prison staff members. Such in-service training becomes particularly important when we recall that helping staff members acquire more effective ways of communicating positively with inmates may be more effective than, for example, one-to-one counseling in helping inmates learn to deal with hostility and a host of other problem behaviors. Much of the research in helping individuals learn how to control their own thoughts and behavior (see Krasner, 1971; Cautela, 1969; Patterson, 1970; Kanfer and Phillips, 1970) indicates that modifying the behavior of those significant others who interact with the client not only "pays off" in terms of achieving the desired goals for the client, but also in modifying the behavior of that staff member. In effect, he becomes a more effective change agent for others in other situations. The importance of incorporating this aspect into counseling and counselor training is brought out well by Kanfer and Phillips (1970) who suggest that:

> Therapeutic agents who are a natural part of the patient's environment can enhance immediate effect, assure the maintenance of

change, and provide generalization of newly acquired behaviors. Since the therapeutic agent is often part and parcel of the problem behavior or problematic system of behavior interaction, as when family members reinforce each other's undesirable behavior, intervention by people who are actually on the spot involves Reissman's "helper" principle in a very direct way. [p. 560]

Training others to be change agents or at least to become involved in the change process is, then, an important intervention procedure, and one in which counselors need training, especially if they are to work in the prison setting.

Some have said (e.g., Krasner, 1971) that counseling is research and research is counseling. Nowhere is this principle more applicable than in the correctional setting. The prison environment is unlike any other. Upon incarceration, an individual is exposed to a completely different system of pressures, restraints and reinforcers than any he has heretofore experienced. When an individual is deprived, as he is in the prison setting, of the normal valued reinforcers—social, sexual, etc.—which most of us receive in our daily lives, he will resort to the most bizarre behaviors in order to obtain them, or some resemblance of them. For example, it is not rare for the therapist to counsel inmates who are active homosexuals, who masturbate ten to fifteen times a day, who hear voices, who have delusions, or who demonstrate an array of other atypical behaviors, but who, on the outside, are complete heterosexuals, do not hear voices, and do not have delusions or exhibit other inappropriate reactions. An inmate with whom we recently worked intentionally did things that caused him to be placed in isolation. When we discussed the reasons why he did this, he replied, "I like to see those bastards work for me. They have to bring me food, carry my trays." Because he had so few other reinforcements in his life, even this was highly reinforcing. He knew what he was doing and why he was doing it. Staff members, on the other hand, perceived his behavior as symptomatic of some mental illness. Moss's "Dealing with a Drug-Induced Psychosis" and Hosford and Rifkin's "A Case of Chronic Schizophrenia" in this book are rather detailed examples of other bizarre behaviors which are frequent in the prison setting.

Research is badly needed not only to find more effective means for ameliorating such behaviors, but for preventing their occurrence in the first place. Much of a counselor's training should be devoted to determining ways in which modification in correctional practices increases or decreases particular types of inmate problems and behaviors. If the correctional institution is to be a rehabilitative agency of society, we must discover more effective ways for helping it achieve this goal. As Menninger points out in *The Crime of Punishment*, much of what we do to "rehabilitate" the criminal is a crime in itself, not because our practices are criminal but because incarcerating the individual defeats its own purpose: "The crime of punishment is that punishment aggravates crime."

Perhaps part of the reason why our rehabilitative attempts have not been very successful is that we have engaged in very little systematic research which prisons in general and counselors in particular can use to support major changes in policies and practices. On the other hand, much of the research that has been carried out has been mutually exclusive to practice. We who counsel in correctional institutions are going to have to do "our homework." We need to return to the basics of observing, recording, and analyzing our data so that we know *what happens when* and what the conditions are— before and after—that are controlling that individual's behavior.

A part of a mental health program in correctional settings, of course, is that of direct therapeutic interventions; most of the cases in this section are examples of counselors using specific techniques to help inmates modify some particular behavior. These cases represent brief, crisis-oriented psychotherapy, which is perhaps more typical of correctional counseling than would be the long-term therapy often employed outside the prison setting. Most of the therapeutic procedures employed in these cases emanate from social learning concepts. Detailed discussions of each technique are readily available elsewhere (see Krasner, 1971; Hosford, 1969; Ullmann and Krasner, 1969; Bandura, 1969; Kanfer and Phillips, 1970) and therefore are not covered here. The degree to which they were successful in these cases, however, strongly supports their application to counseling in the prison setting. It soon becomes apparent, even to the most naive counselor, that the therapeutic relationship per se, although important, is far from sufficient in itself for helping inmates solve the problems for which they seek counseling. Nor is the relationship sufficient to help the inmate acquire the specific social, educational, and vocational competencies he will need if he is to be successful and refrain from criminal behavior on the outside.

Another area in which correctional counselors should have expertise is that of group counseling. In the past few years we have witnessed a tremendous increase in the use of groups as therapeutic technique. Within the counseling profession we now have Gestalt groups, TA groups, self-help groups, encounter groups, sensitivity groups, and a host of others from which one may choose. As with any new procedure, extremes occur and practices develop quite independently of any evidence of success or worth. Group procedures, however, have much to offer in correctional counseling, and we personally feel that for some individuals groups can offer much more than individual counseling in achieving certain types of goals. More important than saving the counselor's time, although this is an important by-product, the group setting often increases the individual's ability to modify his behavior. In effect, individuals learn from and serve as models for each other. In many cases, particularly for inmates, peers rather than therapists serve as effective models and reinforcers. Quite often a counselor helping group members learn to help each other is more successful than that counselor working directly with each inmate. Shapiro's chapter on the establishment of groups at F.C.I., Lompoc and Kerish's on peer counseling are excellent examples. Inmates as well as nonprofessional staff members not only became involved in groups as members but later became leaders of other groups.

Many of the same techniques a counselor uses in one-to-one counseling can be used effectively in groups. Social modeling procedures (Bandura, 1969), for example, offer great potentialities for group counseling in correctional settings in particular. Films and audio and video tapes can have tremendous effect on observer behavior. For example, through imitation, inmates can learn how to apply for a job or how to respond to statements of being an "ex-con" as well as the whole process of learning how to make decisions, how to reduce anxiety, and a host of other behaviors.

IMPORTANCE OF UNIVERSITY AND CORRECTIONAL INSTITUTION COOPERATION

We have suggested some major areas for which counselors need training if they are to function effectively in the correctional setting. These areas, however, represent only a beginning. The counseling practitioner often complains, and justifiably, that the research in counseling is often irrelevant to practice. Similarly, we feel that the training procedures as well as the specific competencies we try to produce in counselor training are often equally irrelevant to counseling in the prison setting, if not to counseling in general. We strongly support Warden Kenton's view that we must promote closer cooperation between the institutions which society has created if each institution is to accomplish the goal for which it was created. Counselor educators and others concerned with applied programs at the university level must get out of the ivory towers and into the field if they are to understand fully the types of jobs and the competencies required of those we are training as practitioners.

Correctional counseling can have a bright future and can play an important role in bringing about change in the whole correctional process—not change for change's sake, but change which evidence shows will benefit both society and the individual presently labeled "criminal." We hope that reports like the ones in this book will help those planning on, or presently working in, correctional institutions to reevaluate their own conceptualization of the whole correctional process, and to begin to monitor and modify practices which have little to do with truly rehabilitating the inmate.

REFERENCES

Bandura, A. 1969. *Principles of behavior modification.* New York: Holt, Rinehart and Winston.

Cautela, J. R. 1969. Behavior therapy and self control: technique and implications. In *Behavior therapy: appraisal and status,* ed. Cyril M. Franks. New York: McGraw-Hill.

Day, John. 1972. The case of Rick. Mimeo. Lompoc: Federal Correctional Institution.

Dechant, Valerie. 1972. The case of Frank. Mimeo. Santa Barbara: University of California.

deVisser, Louis. 1972. The use of relaxation and thought stopping techniques with a case of insomnia. Mimeo. Santa Barbara: University of California.

Ford, D., and Urban, H. 1967. Psychotherapy. *Annual Review of Psychology* 19: 333–72.

Forssell, Cherri. 1972a. The use of role playing as a behavior modification technique in a case of a male inmate learning appropriate behavior in situations dealing with females. Mimeo. Santa Barbara: University of California.

————. 1972b. The use of behavior modification techniques with an inmate resistant to therapy. Mimeo. Santa Barbara: University of California.

Gelatt, H. B. 1962. Decision making: A conceptual frame of reference for counseling. *Journal of Counseling Psychology* 9: 240–45.

Hosford, R. E. 1969. Behavioral counseling—A contemporary overview. *The Counseling Psychologist* 1:1–33.

Kanfer, F. H., and Phillips, J. S. 1970. *Learning foundations of behavior therapy*. New York: Wiley and Sons.

Kerish, Burt. 1972. A case in decision making. Mimeo. Lompoc: Federal Correctional Institution.

Krasner, L. 1971. Behavior therapy. *Annual Rev. of Psychology* 22: 483–532.

Menninger, Karl. 1968. *The crime of punishment*. New York: The Viking Press.

Patterson, G. R. 1970. Behavioral intervention procedures in the classroom and in the home. In *Handbook of psychotherapy and behavior change*, ed. A. E. Bergin and S. L. Garfield. New York: Wiley and Sons.

Reisman, F. 1965. The helper therapy principle. *Social Work* 10: 27–31.

Ullmann, L., and Krasner, L. 1969. *A psychological approach to abnormal behavior*. Englewood Cliffs, N.J.: Prentice-Hall.

Wolpe, J. 1969. *The practice of behavior therapy*. New York: Pergamon Press.

10

An Empirical Case Study of the Systematic Desensitization of Stuttering Behavior

Gary O. George

The following is a case study of an inmate who volunteered for counseling to overcome his stuttering problem. The objective of the counselor and the client was to reduce the frequency of the client's stuttering to a negligible level so that he might communicate more effectively with others. Systematic desensitization therapy was employed with the hierarchy items being role-played. The client's stuttering was reduced from 3.93 stutters per minute to 0.83 stutters per minute within a nine-week period of seven sessions of sixty minutes each. All sessions were tape recorded.

PERSONAL HISTORY

The client was a twenty-two-year-old Black male who was incarcerated in the Federal Correctional Institution at Lompoc, California. At the time of counseling, Jim had served one year of his sentence and had two years to serve before he would be eligible for parole.

Jim was the oldest of four children who were all deserted by their father and were raised primarily by their mother. He reported that he did not finish high school because of his stuttering and his inability to give speeches and participate in class discussions. Jim appeared to be of average or above average intelligence. He related that he felt he was controlled by his mother and siblings and tried to spend as much time as possible away from home. He left home at eighteen and had lived in Hawaii, Oregon, Washington, and finally, California, before his incarceration. During this period he said he was a "con man" and held several menial jobs that he got through friends. He reported using heroin, LSD, cocaine, marijuana, and various other drugs in this period.

At the time of counseling, Jim was taking correspondence courses from a local junior college and undergoing vocational training at the institution. I became his counselor through the counseling seminar and practicum there. He reported that his stuttering had been impairing his ability to communicate his ideas and emotions and had singled him out as a "different type person." He related that both consequences of this behavior made him unhappy and frustrated. According to him, his stuttering was a break in the flow of his speech and therefore of his ideas, a distraction of the listener's attention, and a waste of time. He had been unsuccessfully treated for this problem before, but he wanted to try again to see if his problem could be "cured."

COUNSELING THE BLACK INMATE

Because the client in this case was Black, we might take a moment, before turning to a consideration of his stuttering, to examine the problems involved when a White counselor works with a Black client, an area of considerable concern in the field today. Advocates of the "segregation policy" hypothesize that a White cannot understand and work with Black clients since the counselor's "White background" serves to influence the counseling sessions in a negative manner. The logic of this hypothesis seems at first glance to have some validity since most traditional therapies depend upon interpretation, transference and/or guided insight. Williams (1970), for example, says "White mental health workers cannot successfully treat the Black psyche" and that he "cannot see the White mental health professional comfortably dealing with the fantasy material coming out of the world of the Black psyche." Similarly Mitchell (1970) states: "For the counselor to dwell only in the early childhood experience often turns off Black students. . . ." However, techniques based on learning theory, it would seem, would not depend on culturally biased constructs nearly to the same extent. Indeed, in numerous sessions in which I have counseled Blacks, Indians, and Chicanos, using behavioral techniques, I have yet to find any technique-related problems.

It should be pointed out, however, that some Blacks, as well as other minority members may, for their own personal reasons, refuse to come to a White counselor. There are perhaps several reasons to explain why this situation may occur. First, many minority individuals are afraid of being labeled "Oreos," "Red Apples," and the like if they were seen going to a White counselor. Another reason, according to Mitchell (1970), may be that "To most Black students, a White counselor already has one strike against him because of the student's previous experience with Whites . . ." or, in other words, "The client rejects him on sight simply because of the fact that he is White" (Vontress, 1969). Too, the Black client may have "a background of guidance experience [in relation to Whites] that have been demeaning, debilitating, patronizing and dehumanizing" (Russell, 1970). Thus, there may well be a natural selection process which excludes a prejudiced Black inmate from seeking counseling unless he is referred or it is part of the requirements for parole.

As is true in any therapy, behavioral counseling relies upon a positive relationship between the counselor and the client. Mitchell (1970) says of Whites attempting to counsel Blacks that "the basic ingredient is the counseling relationship, for it is there that the counselor builds trust with the student." This may be one overriding variable in cross-cultural counseling that applies to all Blacks. In dealing with any member of a minority group, the building of an effective counseling relationship may be difficult. First, if the White counselor is not known and vouched for by at least some significant Black members of the community (in this case the prison community), he will have to go through a period of being "checked out" (in my case, this took several months as rumor had it—because of my tie and short hair—I was an undercover F.B.I. agent). There seem to be two main questions for which minorities want answers. A crucial one is: Does the White counselor act, verbally or nonverbally, as if he were prejudiced? Vontress (1970), for example, believes that counselors who bring their own personal racial and ethnic biases into the counseling relationship will not be able to empathize with inner-city clients and that the counselors' racial hang-ups will directly or indirectly prevent them from using their professional skills effectively with minority clients. An inmate may resort to a variety of behaviors to gain an answer for the question. He may "game" the counselor by challenging someone as being prejudiced and then generalizing to all Whites. This is one way to detect racial bias since "the counselor must fully accept his own Whiteness since an apologetic or uncertain air often signals unconscious racism" (Wolpe, 1971). Another way for the Black to have this question answered is by directly accusing the counselor of racial prejudice during the first session when the client has no objective evidence that the counselor is in fact biased. The counselor's response also gives such an individual information about the counselor's feeling of security in working with Blacks.

Another related question is: Will the counselor do what he says he will do or is he a hypocrite? This is an important question for the counselor to consider since many members of minorities have experienced the White "do gooder" who will make grandiose promises and then not follow through. Thus, the minority inmate will often ask the counselor to bring him something or to talk to someone in his behalf. This request is different from that of the usual "con game" run on newcomers to correctional institutions since the requests, e.g., books, applications for school, or talking with his case manager, are often within the rules. The inmate con game would involve something illegitimate, e.g., bringing cigarettes, taking out mail, or signing a pass with a false time written on it. The checking out then, is to find if the White counselor is willing to do something for the Black (besides talk with them)—" 'Words are nice, but action is better' has become the force that hustles Afro-Americans . . ." (Thomas, 1970). According to Proctor (1970), promising only what can be delivered is a key to success in dealing with Blacks (or any other client regardless of skin color, I might add).

Once he has been "checked out" for prejudice, the counselor can get on with the business at hand, i.e., helping the client solve the problems for which he sought counseling. There are several things he can do to facilitate his interaction with the Black client. First, he can become familiar with "Black jargon." In many cases, of course, Black jargon is synonymous with prison vocabulary. Thus one of the most effective ways for a counselor to acquaint himself with it is by spending some time working within the prison. Along these lines, it is wiser for the counselor to ask what unfamiliar terms mean rather than to pretend a knowledge of them. For one thing, in doing so he lets the client know that he is willing to let him know his ignorance and at the same time, promotes a feeling of equality between the client and himself. For another, there is always the danger that if the counselor pretends, he may get caught in this game and trust will be lost. Learning "Black jargon," then, is one step toward achieving the "high degree of positive regard for people who are different" which is so important if a White is to counsel a Black (Vontress, 1970).

There are other ways in which a White counselor can have a better relationship with a Black client. For example, he can "learn more about his way of life and his ethnic and social values" and can develop an "understanding of the socio-psychological background of the client" (Vontress, 1969). Proctor (1970) says that to achieve these goals the White counselor should know the lives of Malcolm X, Eldridge Cleaver, Martin Luther King, and Nat Turner, among others. In addition, he feels that the counselor should interact with as many Black counselors as possible on a wide range of Black problems so that by becoming familiar with the worries, frustrations, and fears of Blacks in general, the White counselor will be more able to empathize (in the Rogerian sense) with his Black clients. Proctor is right when he states that "It is not asking too much to expect student personnel staff people to get informed on the Black experience," as is Cobbs (1970) when he says that we must not kill blackness but that we must try to relate to it.

Finally, in working with Black clients, White counselors must, as Mitchell (1970) puts it, "know themselves. They need to know their own prejudices and fears and seek solutions to their own hang-ups, they need to get themselves together first." Vontress (1969) says that to achieve this goal (and others) prospective counselors need to have in-service training in counseling blacks in the ghetto (or in the prison setting, since this is another kind of ghetto) and to talk with as many Blacks as possible. Only through experience can a counselor overcome (unlearn or relearn) his biases to the extent that solid positive relationships can be generated between the White counselor and the Black client.

According to some authors (Thomas, 1970; Peek, 1970; Williams, 1970; and Ward, 1970) the White counselor can never work with a Black client as effectively as can a Black counselor. However such a view advocates a "segregationist policy" which I feel to be misguided. For one thing, it discounts the question of counseling skills. Mitchell (1970) points out the importance of "the counselor's repertoire of skills and understanding of human behavior. To be just a 'nice guy' who listens is not enough in counseling Black clients; the counselor must help the client to develop tools for dealing with his problems." Vontress (1969) puts it a little more explicitly when he says "In some cases, the Black counselor may be accepted completely, simply because he is Black; but if he is unable to assist the client with the problems he experiences, then his Blackness will be of fleeting value. Thus, race and resultant attitudes are *initial* barriers in the counseling relationship" [emphasis added]. Russell (1970) goes on to add, "There is no special mystique involved in relating to the Black client; hence the counselor need not assume any kind of unusual posture or resort to tactics, techniques, or approaches he would not use with other clients." Therefore, it does not seem that a Black counselor would, in the long run, be any more effective than a White counselor provided that the White counselor is willing to spend some time getting to know Blacks in general, and his client in particular.

In this era of emphasis on individual differences, variables such as skin color, sexual identification, age, etc., are factors that must be taken into account in the counseling situation, but certainly they should not be factors that are used to limit the counselor's functioning or to provide excuses for failure. Vontress (1969) said of cross-racial counseling that "Often, their [Black] colleagues tell them [Whites] that they don't understand' or 'can't understand' simply because they are White. Unfortunately, some White counselors are beginning to believe it."

DESCRIPTION OF CLIENT'S PROBLEM

Jim first remembered stuttering while in the third grade. He said he used his stuttering to evade answering questions and talking in class. His stuttering became a problem to him in the sixth grade when peers began to tease him and he could no longer control it. He had stuttered continuously from age nine until the time of counseling.

The stuttering behavior consisted of repeating the initial sounds of words; he used too much air outflow on explosive consonants, elongating the "S" sounds, and dropping initial-voiced sounds. During the initial interview, he had an average rate of stuttering of 3.93 stutters per minute taken over a period of fifty-five minutes.

During the initial interview, Jim reported that he did not stutter in all situations or when talking about certain topics. Further questioning revealed that he felt tense and anxious when in situations where he was controlled (e.g., talking to his parole officer or answering a question in class) and when talking about topics he knew relatively little about (talking about applying for a job or discussing sexual arousal). When asked if certain situations and topics elicited more anxiety than others, he replied that they did; there seemed to be a hierarchy of situations and topics which brought about varying amounts of anxiety. Some of the general categories the client described initially can be seen in Table 1.

Table 1. General Categories Used to Construct Anxiety Hierarchy Items

1. Counseling another inmate (low anxiety)
2. Giving a stranger information (high anxiety)
3. Being in a hurry to leave and having to talk (high anxiety)
4. Doing something his own way (low anxiety)
5. Having to do something with another person, telling him how (high anxiety)
6. Being in a classroom (high anxiety)
7. Being in the "hot seat" in an encounter group (high anxiety)
8. "Hustling" (playing social games and winning) (low anxiety)
9. Meeting a girl for the first time (high anxiety)
10. Talking with a girl he likes (low anxiety)

In carefully observing his behavior, I noted that when he was talking about non-anxiety–producing topics, his stuttering stopped completely and when talking about threatening situations and/or topics, the stuttering became readily apparent. When the stuttering started, he would drum his fingers on the desk making thumping noises, twist in his chair, break eye contact, and even perspire after prolonged discussion. These behaviors ceased almost immediately when the topic was changed. Several situations and topics were role played to determine what effect they had on the client. I noted, for example, that Jim did react with different amounts of anxiety (as determined by frequency of finger drumming, restlessness, and stuttering) to the different roles he played.

OBJECTIVES AND PROCEDURES

Many techniques have been employed in therapy for stutterers: operant conditioning with positive reinforcement for fluent speech (Shames et al., 1963; Browning, 1967; Russell, 1970), operant conditioning with negative reinforcement for disfluent speech (Siegel, 1966; Martin and Siegel, 1966), satiation therapy (Jakobovitz, 1966), carbon dioxide therapy (Kent, 1961), drug therapy (Aron, 1965), and time out, a technique in which the removal of a positive stimulus serves as the aversive stimulus (Haroldson et al., 1968;

Martin and Haroldson, 1969). Reports are also available, starting in 1960, of behavioral research on the anxiety component of stuttering (e.g., Santostefano, 1960; Adler, 1961; Vlasova, 1962, Aron, 1965). The success of systematic desensitization therapy (SDT) with stutterers has also been shown effective in some cases (e.g., Rosenthal, 1968; Lanyon, 1969; Reynolds, 1969).

Operant conditioning did not seem practical due to the variety and kinds of reinforcing agents at the institution. Carbon dioxide and drug therapy could not be used since these treatments can only be utilized under the direction of a medical doctor. Time out and satiation were considered, but I decided on systematic desensitization therapy due to the observed anxiety contingency of Jim's stuttering behavior and the hierarchy of anxiety-producing stimuli which I obtained from the role-playing procedures. The client had previously used a method of satiation by repeating a word over and over that he had stuttered on and had had little or no success. Time out, as a procedure, was not considered because of Jim's anxiety level. Further, he indicated that having to wait for anyone or anything raised his anxiety level.

INITIATION OF TREATMENT

The first objective was to explain systematic desensitization therapy (SDT) to Jim and to form a contract for the remaining counseling sessions. During session one, I explained that his stuttering was a learned behavior and could be unlearned. The process of counter-conditioning and specifically SDT (Wolpe, 1969) was explained in detail. The construction of an anxiety hierarchy and the process of gradually conditioning relaxation to each item was explained. I related that by gradually learning to relax in situations which used to give him anxiety, he should be able to converse without stuttering in all of the situations desensitized and probably others as well. Because of earlier speech therapy, he asked a few questions like "Shouldn't I practice specific words?" and "How does relaxing help my speech?" After I explained to him that he did not always stutter and that he had reported feeling "up-tight" when he did stutter, he agreed to try the desensitization treatment. I then explained that other treatments would be utilized if we did not achieve the progress we should. Jim related that this plan seemed good and that he hoped it would work. Throughout the counseling sessions, I could consistently show Jim how well he was progressing by using Table 4 with its change in average stutters per minute.

The second objective, after agreeing on the goals of the counseling and the specific intervention procedures to be used, was to take a baseline of his stuttering behavior. This was accomplished during the second and sixth sessions by conversing with him and dividing the total number of stutters by the number of minutes during which the conversation occurred (giving a measurement of average number of stutters per minute). Two baselines were taken, one before any type of therapy began and one after the anxiety hierachy had been constructed and role-played, to see if Jim's stuttering had decreased due to the relaxation practice and/or his familiarity with me. The topics of conversation specifically used in both sessions were: (1) life in prison, (2) relationships with his family, (3) job opportunities, (4) educational background, (5) the onset of stuttering, (6) need to control his environment, (7) feelings about self, (8) aspects of life situations he would like to change, (9) sex life, and (10) life after getting out of prison.

The third objective was to construct and rate the anxiety hierarchy. This was accomplished during the second through fifth sessions. First, Jim made a general list of categories (Table 1) from which specific items were constructed. He was given "homework" of thinking of specific items during the week between the second and third counseling sessions. I always verbally reinforced him for completing his "homework" by saying: "That's great. You really must have worked hard this last week," or something similar.

After the anxiety hierarchy items had been constructed (Table 2), Jim subjectively rated them on a 0 to 100 scale of amount of anxiety he felt while in these situations or when discussing these topics. I told him the 0 represented no anxiety, while 100 designated extreme anxiety (Wolpe, 1969). All of the items were rated in this manner. Then, each of the items was rated behavioristically as Jim and I role-played each behavior for a period of three minutes. The number of stutters for each item was then divided by the number of minutes to obtain an average stutters per minute rating for each item. This was accomplished during the third, fourth, and fifth sessions. There were several instances during the third session in which Jim kept getting off the subject in role-playing the items by talking about other situations or talking about why he felt anxious in this particular situation. I asked him to stay on the subject so that as much as possible could be done in the limited time available. He agreed and I consistently reinforced him at fifteen-minute intervals for staying on the subject thereafter. Several new items were formulated during these digressions, however.

Table 2. Anxiety Hierarchy Items with Objective and Subjective Anxiety Ratings

Subjective Rating[a] (0–100)	Objective Rating[b] (stutters per minute)	
0	0.00	1. talking about not being able to drive
60	1.50	2. a friend telling me how to program my time
15	1.55	3. person in adjacent bed asking me for food
40	1.84	4. meeting a new person
10	2.00	5. teaching a girl something she does not know
65	2.77	6. counseling another inmate about his offense
20	3.00	7. being questioned by someone I don't know
NR[c]	3.33	8. talking about physical sex
NR	4.36	9. talking about how I have used sex
50	4.80	10. talking to parole officer about parole
NR	5.33	11. describing how to seduce a girl
50	5.60	12. being in the "hot seat" and talking about my size
NR	5.73	13. how a relationship ended with a girl I loved
65–80	6.00	14. talking about drugs in relation to anxiety
30–50	6.00	15. talking about being emotionally involved with a girl
NR	7.50	16. talking about anxiety and how it feels
60–70	9.42	17. school instructor asks me a question about Neanderthal man
50	10.10	18. reading out of a text book
50	11.08	19. reading poetry out of Negro magazine
50	14.00	20. reading a newspaper article aloud

a Subjective rating is the 0 to 100 scale used by Wolpe (1969). Jim rated each of the items on this scale.

b Objective rating consisted of the number of times Jim stuttered during the role-playing of the items divided by the number of minutes the role-playing took. Therefore, this is a rating of average stutters per minute of the role-played item.

c NR means not rated; these items were added after the subjective rating had been made.

The fourth objective was to teach Jim how to relax. During the second session, he was instructed on deep muscle relaxation (Jacobson, 1938). He reported being able to relax and agreed to practice this procedure twice daily during the week. During the third session, Jim reported that he could not practice the relaxation due to peer pressure; he was kidded about it since he lived in an open dorm. We then switched to relaxation by imagining an outline of his body filled with water and slowly draining out. The different parts of his body were to be subvocally named as he visualized the water draining out (suggested by Hosford, 1971, personal communication). Jim reported that he could relax using this method and promised to practice it twice daily (he did this each of the weeks between the third and eighth sessions). Each week, I praised him for practicing the relaxation. Jim reported that he had no problem with his peers or problems with being unable to relax after switching to the new procedure. He did report that as time progressed he was able to stay relaxed for longer periods after he had completed this exercise (from two minutes during the first week to fifteen minutes during the seventh week).

The fifth objective was to desensitize Jim to the items on the anxiety hierarchy (SDT itself). The procedure I used was to have him relax deeply at the beginning of the session and then role-play the hierarchy item. When Jim role-played the item for two consecutive two-minute periods without stuttering, we would then proceed to the next item up the hierarchy. After each two-minute role-play, he would then relax using the visual imagery of a warm hillside with soft clouds and a bubbling brook. During the seventh session, it became apparent that Jim was unable to maintain a relaxed state. He related that his mind kept wandering and he could not concentrate on the hillside scene. These factors raised his anxiety level so that he was stuttering on the first item (during the rating of the items, he had scored this item zero). We then tried thought-stopping to keep his mind on the scene. He would vocalize his thoughts and when he would start wandering, I would say "stop." This did not work, so I asked him how he thought he could maintain relaxation while role-playing the item. He replied that walking around the room would help. We then role-played the first two items, while Jim walked around the room, with success.

The structure of each counseling session then became that of (1) relaxing using visual image of body with water draining out (2) role-playing the item while he walked about the room and, (3) sitting and visualizing the body without water before role-playing again. This method was used during the latter part of the seventh session and all of the eight session. Six items were successfully desensitized.

I told Jim of his progress on the items (Fig. 1) and verbally praised him for each success. Whenever he stuttered while role-playing an item, I would say, "That's O.K., let's try again." The main influence other than Jim's knowing of his own success was my constant praise for each success ("There goes another down, you're really doing great!"). At the same time, sessions seven and eight, I asked Jim to

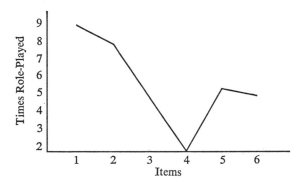

Figure 1. Number of times an item was role-played before two consecutive role-plays with no stuttering.

gradually stop using defensive behaviors such as word substitution, evasion of anxiety-producing situations, and keeping quiet to cover up his stuttering behavior. He agreed to try this with the stipulation that he was to withdraw from the situation if he started stuttering. During the eighth session, Jim reported that he had found that he did not stutter in some situations that he had previously stuttered in. I concluded that the SDT was generalizing, at least in part, to situations outside of counseling.

Due to the fact that the seminar I was enrolled in ended at the end of the eighth session, my part in the counseling was terminated. However, continuation was to be maintained by another counselor.

DISCUSSION

During the course of counseling, several other behavior areas were uncovered and Jim expressed a desire to work on these problems as well. One problem was discovered while role-playing item number 5. Jim was asked to teach a girl (played by me) how to apply for a job. He started talking about how to hustle and how to get friends to get her jobs. When questioned about this, Jim explained that he did not know how to apply for a job. If time permits, role-playing different situations after the behavior had been modeled by a counselor may help him gain this behavioral ability.

Another problem area discovered was that Jim was unable to assert himself while role-playing various items (2, 4, 9, 14, and 18). He would say, "Oh, is that right." "Oh, yeah." "Look, man. . . ." This would be in response to my prodding him by saying, "You're crazy." "How do you know?" "Come on, you're just trying to put me down," etc. An assertive hierarchy could be constructed and role-played to teach Jim assertive behaviors he could use when confronted with these types of pressures.

Although Jim reported in the initial interview that he had no sexual problems, during the role-playing of some items (8, 10, 12, 14, and 16) various problems were observed. He was unable to describe actual sexual intercourse as he had always found a way to evade this behavior ("I'm too tired." "I'm too uptight." "I don't feel like it.") These evasions were used by him, although he reported having been naked and in bed with a woman. This area would need more investigation before a specific program could be designed.

Although the systematic desensitization program was not completed, Jim's stuttering rate was lowered from 3.93 stutters per minute to 0.83 stutters per minute (Figure 2). Since the actual desensitization was not initiated until the seventh session, the second baseline reading was taken during the sixth session. There was a significant decrease in stutters per minute, from 3.93 to 1.72 (Figure 2), but one cannot conclude that either relaxation or rapport were the causal factors. One conclusion was that systematic desensitization did help decrease his stuttering from 1.72 stutters per minute to 0.83 stutters per minute (Figure 2) during the seventh and eighth sessions. It appears that systematic desensitization therapy is useful in significantly decreasing stuttering where there is no physiological factor involved.

An interesting outcome of rating the hierarchy both subjectively and objectively is that the two ratings did not correlate (Table 2). I used the objective rating (as determined by average stutters per minute) in the desensitization program. As only six of the items were desensitized I could not determine whether or not the hierarchy would

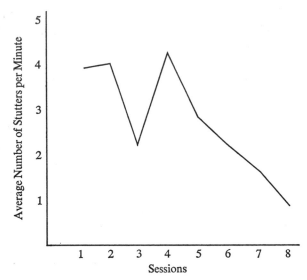

Figure 2. Average number of stutters per minute for each session.

be completed as constructed (without adding new items or switching the order to successfully complete the desensitization). It would be interesting to desensitize two groups so that each would construct the two hierarchies, but one group would use the subjectively rated hierarchy and the other the objective hierarchy. My hypothesis would be that there would be fewer changes in the hierarchies that had been objectively rated.

REFERENCES

Adler, R. 1961. An integration of some research studies in stuttering. *Rehabilitation Literature* 22:34–31, 53.

Aron, M. L. 1965. The effects of the combination of trefluoperazine and amylobartuton on adult stutterers. *Medical Proceedings* 11 (10): 227–33.

Browning, R. M. 1967. Behavior therapy for stuttering in schizophrenic children. *Behavior Research and Therapy* 5 (1): 27–35.

Cobbs, Price M. 1970. "White Mis-Education of the Black Experience." *The Counseling Psychologist* 2 (1): 23–27.

Haroldson, S. K., et al. 1968. Time out as a punishment for stuttering. *Journal of Speech and Hearing Research* 11 (3): 560–66.

Jacobson, E. 1938. *Progressive relaxation.* Chicago: University of Chicago Press.

Jakobovitz, L. A. 1966. Utilization of semantic satiation in stuttering: A Theoretical Analysis. *Journal of Speech and Hearing Disorders* 31: 105–14.

Kent, L. R. 1961. Carbon dioxide therapy as a mental treatment for stuttering. *Journal of Speech and Hearing Disorders* 26:268–71.

Lanyon, R. I. 1969. Behavior change in stuttering through systematic desensitization therapy. *Journal of Speech and Hearing Disorders* 34: 253–60.

Martin, R R., and Haroldson, S. K. 1969. The effects of two treatment procedures on stuttering. *Journal of Communication Disorders* 2 (12): 115–25.

Martin, R. R., and Siegal, G. M. 1966. The effects of response contingent shock on stuttering. *Journal of Speech and Hearing Research* 9:340.

Mitchell, Horace. 1970. The black experience in higher education. *The Counseling Psychologist* 2 (1): 30–36.

Peek, V. Lonnie. 1970. The black student in a white university. *The Counseling Psychologist.* 2 (1): 11–16.

Proctor, Samuel A. 1970. Reversing the spiral toward futility. *Personnel and Guidance Journal* 48 (9): 707–12.

Reynolds, D. S. 1969. The effects of systematic desensitization on stuttering in a standardized interview situation. *Dissertation Abstracts* 29 (10–13): 3920.

Rosenthal, T. L. 1968. Severe stuttering and maladjustment treated by systematic desensitization and social influence. *Behavior Research and Therapy* 6:125–30.

Russell, R. D. 1970. Black perceptions of guidance. *Personnel and Guidance Journal* 49 (9): 711–28.

Santostefano, S. 1960. Anxiety and hostility in stuttering. *Journal of Speech and Hearing Research* 3:373–77.

Shames, G. H., et al. 1963. A discussion of nonfluency and stuttering as operant behavior. *Journal of Speech and Hearing Disorders* 28:3–18.

Siegal, G., et al. 1966. Punishment of disfluencies in normal speakers. *Journal of Speech and Hearing Research* 9:208–18.

Thomas, Charles W. 1970. Something borrowed, something black. *The Counseling Psychologist* 2 (1): 6–10.

Vlasova, N. A. 1962. Prevention and treatment of children's stuttering in the U.S.S.R. *Cakaslovenska Otaluripiegal* 11:30–32.

Vontress, Clemmont E. 1969. Cultural barriers in the counseling relationship. *Personnel and Guidance Journal,* 48 (1): 11–17.

———. 1970. Counseling blacks. *Personnel and Guidance Journal* 49 (9): 713–19.

Ward, Eric J. 1970. A gift from the ghetto. *Personnel and Guidance Journal* 48 (9): 753–56.

Williams, Robert L. 1970. Black pride, academic relevance and individual achievement. *The Counseling Psychologist* 2 (1): 18–22.

Wolpe, J. 1969. *The practice of behavior therapy*. New York: Pergamon Press.

————. 1971. Counseling black college students in special programs. *Personnel and Guidance Journal* 50 (1): 29–36.

11

Some Effects of Operant Conditioning with a Mexican-American Male

Teresa R. Boulette

The present empirical case study describes some effects of operant conditioning methods on a twenty-three year old, unmarried, Texas born, first generation Chicano[1] incarcerated in a federal correctional facility. Although limitations of the case study method in social research prevent undue certainty and generalization of any findings, it is hoped that this case will serve in some way to stimulate scholarly endeavors and pertinent research in the neglected area of the mental-health care of low-income Mexican-Americans in general, incarcerated Mexican-Americans in particular.

THE STUDY

Investigation of this client's history was undertaken to determine areas of similarity with reported Chicano characteristics, to demonstrate my interest and concern, and to make inferences concerning the probable efficacy of various behavioral strategies.

Mr. R. is the youngest of eight children in an impoverished family deserted by the father shortly after his birth. In order to live, the family worked at harvesting seasonal crops in the states of Texas, Arizona, and California. As a result, Mr. R. attended many schools for relatively short periods of time. He reported having behavioral as well as academic problems in school, and by the age of sixteen had reached only the seventh grade. Shortly thereafter he became a

[1] For the purpose of this paper the term Chicano is used interchangeably with Mexican-American. It should be noted that these terms differ greatly in their connotations.

school dropout. His use of glue fumes, pills, and alcoholic beverages brought him to the attention of the juvenile probation department. He spent time in juvenile halls and later was sent to a Job Corps Center, where he received academic as well as occupational training. He responded enthusiastically to this center and was disappointed that his 192 hours of training as a warehouse attendant did not result in a job. He returned home discouraged.

His failures and disappointments bothered him, but his position of *coyotito*[2] within his family provided him with much maternal and sibling affection. However, his position as favorite shifted when his mother became seriously ill. Although his mother had had a history of illness—in addition to having been hospitalized for three years with tuberculosis, she was a diabetic who had lost both her sight and her hearing, and had had one leg amputated—the family blamed her latest illness on the constant worry caused by Mr. R. Her condition deteriorated, and she asked to see her favorite son. Because Mr. R. did not realize the severity of his mother's illness, and because he had mixed feelings about her life-long suffering, he decided to go out with some *chavalas*[3] and to visit her at a later time. His mother died that night, and his brothers and sisters angrily accused him of causing her death.

Shortly after his mother's death, Mr. R. related that he underwent a severe personality change. He no longer felt docile and happy-go-lucky. He frequently felt angry and physically aggressive toward his brothers and sisters. He would ride around aimlessly, stopping to "beat up sailors" and torture and kill cats and dogs. He drank heavily and drove recklessly, and was repeatedly arrested for drunken driving. His behavior so concerned his family that they hospitalized him on two occasions for a psychiatric evaluation. The outcome of these evaluations is not known. Shortly afterwards, he was arrested for mail theft and was subsequently convicted and sentenced to a federal prison.

Mr. R.'s prison adjustment was stormy. In a period of eight months he was placed in solitary confinement twelve times. He made few friends. He refused to follow his diabetic diet, and at times, refused to take his insulin injections. He frequently went to the medical unit, accusing the inmate medical technicians of being incompetent and

---

[2] An affectionate term given to the youngest in a family. It means, literally, "Little Coyote."

[3] A slang term meaning chicks or girls.

not caring enough about his problems. He was experiencing some discomfort and drainage from his penis, and he insisted that he needed to be circumcised. His request was refused, because it was apparently not in his best medical interest. He reported that he mixed some dandruff medicine with some foot medicine and some other ointment and applied this to his penis. He boasted that he knew how to medicate himself and he was now cured. A few days later, he was alarmed because of some bleeding from the same area.

He expressed considerable anti-Anglo feeling. He repeatedly verbalized the injustice of his incarceration and his plans for vengence. He reported frequently feeling angry and purposely looking for provocations to violence. He refused to make plans for his release. In fact, on one occasion in which he was to meet the parole board, he behaved very negatively, as if to promote a negative disposition toward his case. For example, when asked his name, he replied, "Can't you read, it's right in front of you." Thus, his angry, insolent manner influenced the board to turn down any request for parole at the time.

TREATMENT

Mr. R. had had diagnostic interviews with two male Anglo psychologists who expressed concern and desire to help him. When he was offered counseling with a Chicano doctoral student (myself), he guardedly accepted. By his own preference he spoke Spanish during all of our sessions. During the first three sessions, he quickly exchanged courtesies with me and then spoke incessantly and angrily about his unjust incarceration, his plans for revenge toward Anglos, his feeling of hopelessness, his physical symptoms and the refusal of the prison staff to treat him, his guilt for being a bad son to his mother and a bad brother to his siblings, and how he deserved everything that had occurred. The intensity with which he discussed these areas of concern plus the loudness of his voice made it difficult for me to raise questions which would elicit specific responses as to what he might like to change about himself. When I did manage to speak, he would say "un momento" or "todavia no acabo."[4] Throughout these three sessions, I kept encouraging him to specify treatment goals, and he kept talking in the same repetitive manner about the above-mentioned areas of concern. All three of these sessions were essentially the same except for one incident in the second session.

[4] These Spanish phrases mean "wait a minute" and "I'm not through."

Before the start of the second session, the prison psychologist stated that Mr. R. no longer wanted counseling because it was sexually too arousing. He had told Mr. R. to personally discuss this with me. To my amazement, Mr. R. did not even mention this incident. When I brought it up, he quickly dismissed it by stating he had said that because he was angry with this psychologist for implying that he wanted a circumcision in order to engage in homosexuality.

The client's refusal to set treatment goals made the task of establishing a behavioral diagnosis essential. The components of such a diagnosis are well illustrated by Kanfer and Saslow (1969, p. 419). The value of a behavioral diagnosis lies not in the classification of the client's problems but in collecting precise and comprehensive data which would pinpoint the nature of the problem and strategies which might be effective in dealing with it.

The structure of Kanfer and Saslow's behavior diagnosis consists of seven different parts. The first part is the "Initial Analysis of the Problem Situation" and consists of behavioral excesses, deficits, and assets.

Mr. R.'s behavioral excesses were: (1) generalized angry verbalizations (excessive frequency and duration), (2) Anglo-focused angry verbalizations (excessive in frequency and duration), (3) verbal complaints of physical illness (excessive in frequency and duration), (4) self-persecutory verbalizations (excessive in frequency and duration), (5) pessimistic verbalizations (excessive in frequency and duration), (6) angry verbalizations regarding the injustice of his incarceration (excessive in frequency and duration), (7) verbalization concerned with his belief that everyone was out to "put him down," "to burn his mind" and "to play with him" (excessive in frequency and duration), (8) verbalizations concerned with threats of physical violence (excessive in frequency), (9) excessive assignment to solitary confinement (excessive in frequency and duration— twelve times in eight months, usual stay of one week), (10) excessive eating (excessive between meals and at meal times; refuses to keep diabetic diet).

His behavioral deficits were: (1) insufficient concern about maintaining habits important to controlling his diabetic condition, (2) infrequent and insufficiently intense verbalizations indicating personal assets, (3) infrequent and insufficiently intense verbalizations indicating plans for out-of-prison adjustment, (4) infrequent and insufficiently intense verbal efforts aimed at achieving desired goal,

(5) infrequent and insufficient verbalization concerned with affection for others.

His behavioral assets were: (1) completion of 192 hours of training as a warehouse attendant, (2) completion of basic course in auto mechanics, (3) ability to read and write in English and Spanish, (4) absence of serious convictions, (5) interest in working, (6) interest in owning a car, (7) ability to play a guitar, (8) absence of drug involvement while in prison, (9) apparent emotional support of him by his brothers and sisters, (10) existence of an apparently interested girl friend, (11) some social skills, (12) desire on the part of several staff members to help him.

The second part of the Kanfer and Saslow structure is the "Clarification of the Problem Situation." In Mr. R.'s case it was noted that his undesirable behaviors seemed to occur randomly with other inmates and with staff. Specific environmental conditions which reinforce this behavior were not determined.

"Motivational Analysis" constitutes the third part of the structure. Based on my judgment, the following events were ranked from most powerful to least powerful in effectively initiating or maintaining desired behavior: car ownership; acceptable employment and work satisfaction; food; cigarettes; sibling approval; social approval from his ethnic group; girl friend; guitar; reading material (western paperbacks); money. At the same time the following aversive stimuli were ranked from most powerful to less powerful in discouraging needed behavior changes: feelings of guilt—reduced by external punishment; fear of failure in the nonprison community; fear of out-of-prison temptations: (a) liquor, (b) drugs, (c) crime, and (d) involvement in violent anti-Anglo groups; fear of closeness in interpersonal relations; fear of close relations with women; fear of homosexuality; fear of responsibility of success.

Part four includes "a developmental analysis." This includes a biological analysis, and an analysis of social changes and behavioral changes. The findings in Mr. R.'s case are as follows:

1. The primary biological limitation was his diabetic condition, which was aggravated by his failure to take insulin and to follow proper diet and rest routine. Intellectually he was average. He seemed fairly strong and was said to be a good worker. His obesity should be controlled. There were no biological limitations to impede his needed behavior change.

2. Mr. R.'s attitudes and verbal excess were not, in my opinion,

in harmony with the prison's milieu. He had a poor image with other prisoners and with the staff. He presented himself to others as a surly, chronic complainer and constant threat maker. He was seen as a "pest" and as a "spoiled little kid" rather than as a man. These conclusions were drawn after talking to several prisoners and staff members.

3. The client's upbringing in a large impoverished family disrupted by parental desertion resulted in many early deprivations. The harsh and frequently hostile environment of the migrant field worker probably further aggravated his family's difficulties. The mother's illness and early demise also contributed further stress. Mr. R.'s adolescent conduct difficulties seemed relevant to his family's deprivations. His post-adolescent behavior changes seemed related to his feelings of guilt, sadness, and anger over his mother's death.

"Analysis of Self-Control" was done as part five. This area was very significant for Mr. R., who seemed to use assignment to isolation as a means of self-control. He frequently feared losing control of his violent impulses. He seemed to use his frequent arrests and current imprisonment as a means of reducing his guilt feelings. He may also have been attempting to control his self-destructive impulses by provoking his imprisonment. His current level of self-control could be increased with behavioral interventions.

"Analysis of Social Relationship" is the sixth part of the structure. For Mr. R., it revealed that the most significant people in this client's current environment were one inmate friend who expected transfer to another prison, a Mexican-American staff member, his caseworker, his liaison officer, this therapist, and a psychologist. He responded differently to staff and inmates, demonstrating his undesired behavior primarily to staff. His response to inmates was one of defensiveness in regard to his fear of being controlled and being put down. He tended to respond more courteously and in a less tough manner with professional females (the psychiatrist and this investigator).

The last section is the "Analysis of the Socio-Cultural-Physical Environment." This analysis revealed that the undesired behaviors are not part of the norm in this client's ethnic group nor in the prison population. He maintains these behaviors in all parts of the prison institution with the exception of his work area, where the supervisor is said to "take very little nonsense." Mr. R. is said to work well and to say little. The complexity and the largeness of the prison institution makes it difficult to control the reinforcement that this client received via his undesired behavior. His liaison worker and caseworker were kept informed of the behavioral strategies by the investigator.

Because of the client's persistent refusal to define treatment goals, I was forced to select the following: (1) decrease in frequency of those behaviors labeled as behavioral excesses and (2) increase in frequency of those behaviors labeled as behavioral deficits. With the exception of two items (prompting of assignment to isolation and eating), the behavioral excesses are verbal behaviors. These excessive verbal behaviors are labeled as "sick talk." All of the behaviors labeled as behavior deficits except one (poor diabetic care habits) were verbal. These verbal behaviors are referred to as "healthy talk." No attempts were made to control his poor diabetic habits. "Healthy talk" is defined by Ullmann and others (1964) as ". . . verbalizations relating to comfort liking, good physical or mental health, personal assets, presence of motivation, enthusiasm, etc." (p. 238). "Sick talk" is defined as the opposite of "healthy talk." Thus, three specific changes in behavior were specified as the treatment goals: (1) decrease frequency of "sick talk," (2) increase frequency of "healthy talk," and (3) decrease frequency of assignment to isolation.

BEHAVIOR STRATEGIES

Guilt seems to impel Mr. R. to make "sick talk" responses to cues in the stimulus situation. This response is reinforced by staff attention and by punishment (assignment to isolation); the reinforcements reduce the guilt. Thus, in order to reduce "sick talk," reinforcement must be eliminated. This process is referred to as extinction (Wolpe, 1969; Miller and Dollard, 1961). During treatment, for example, whenever "sick talk" was demonstrated within the counseling situation, the investigator stopped smiling, head nodding, eye contact, and talking. When words were necessary, only English was used. When "healthy talk" was demonstrated, the response was reinforced with attention, smiling, head nodding, and Spanish phrases indicating approval. The approving behavior was paired with more substantial reinforcers such as Mexican song books and western paperback novels. These additional reinforcers were given at the end of each interview, contingent on the client's making two or more "healthy talk" responses.

In using extinction and reinforcement, the following principles guided my actions. Intermittent reinforcement can sustain the undesired response. Cessation of reinforcers must be complete to insure that extinction will take place. Reinforcement must be given immediately after the desired response is made. Verbal reinforcers are conditioned reinforcers which have been associated in early childhood with primary reinforcers. Thus, verbal reinforcers must be ethnic and class focused. The client's environment should be manipulated to prevent reinforcement of undesired responses and to facilitate reinforcement of desired responses. Several staff members were contacted for this purpose.

It should be also noted that Mr. R. received additional reinforcement from fellow Mexican-American inmates. Receiving special attention by a relatively young Mexican-American female professional placed him in a position of importance. Several inmates approached him and requested that he attempt to get counseling for them. Several others asked his opinion in personal matters. Also on several occasions he allowed one or two Mexican-American inmates to use ten to fifteen minutes of his interview time.

RESULTS

Figure 1 demonstrates the successful outcomes of these methods. Sick talk was decreased by 70 percent. Healthy talk was increased by

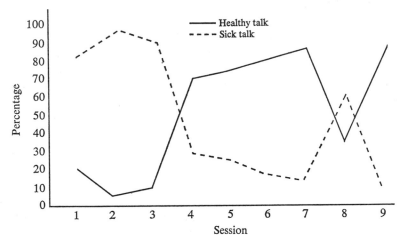

NOTE: This graph is based on two 5-minute base-rate measurements of "sick" talk and "healthy" talk during each therapy session.

Figure 1. Percentages of session used for healthy talk and for sick talk.

70 percent. Assignment to isolation decreased in frequency. Whereas before treatment, Mr. R. had been placed in isolation twelve times within a period of eight months, during the counseling treatment he had spent two months without being placed in isolation. Several staff members sought me out to comment very favorably on Mr. R.'s improved behavior. Particularly, they described him as being more friendly and more cooperative. Of perhaps greater importances was the fact that he was credited with preventing serious bodily harm to an Anglo inmate when heretofore he had stated his hatred for all Anglos. He also approached the prison psychologist and the university supervising professor to thank them for their interest and efforts to help him. In addition, he requested and maintained a new job assignment at the furniture repair shop. He mentioned being commended by the foreman for being such a good worker. Still further, he accepted referral to an inmate discussion group which a bilingual officer whom he admired was to lead.

DISCUSSION

One of the most important things to keep in mind in connection with this case is the fact that Mr. R. was not simply an inmate but that he was a Chicano inmate, and that he therefore brought with him to the correctional facility a heritage that was different in significant ways from that of the Anglo majority, a heritage that had affected and shaped his attitudes and behaviors all of his life. Like all Chicanos who seek counseling, Mr. R. needed to be responded to as a Mexican-American; that is, it was necessary to respect and understand Mr. R. in terms of his own background and at the same time use that background to help him. Indeed, it is evident, I think, that an understanding of the Chicano's cultural identity is an essential prerequisite for those who purport to serve him. Yet ignorance of his culture is widespread among "highly placed government officials, social scientists, and the proverbial intelligent laymen" (Mittlebach and Marshall, 1966). Many social scientists who have studied this population have perpetuated the existing ignorance by failure to differentiate between (1) culturally specific characteristics, (2) characteristics specific to poverty conditions regardless of ethnicity, (3) characteristics specific to social pathology, i.e., mental illness, and (4) characteristics arising from victimization, i.e., economic exploitation and prejudice.

Just what are Chicano-specific characteristics? Several factors make this question very difficult to answer. Some of these factors are:

1. *The heterogeneity of this population.* Peñalosa (1967), Romano (1969) and Grebler et al. (1970) clearly emphasize this important aspect. Chicanos come in all sizes and all colors. There are *queritos* (blond ones), *prietitos* (dark ones), *triquenitos* (light brown ones), *negritos* (black ones), and even *pecositos* (freckled ones). This heterogeneity also exists in the Chicano's occupational, educational, economic, political, and acculturational attainments. For example, the degree of the Chicano's identification with Mexico, his motherland, varies greatly and is usually associated with his geographic and generational proximity. His Spanish fluency also varies, as does the type of Spanish he speaks; he may speak flawless Castillian, traditional and correct Mexican-Spanish, *pochismo*, Tex-Mex, or *pachuquismo*.[5] His ethnic presence may differ greatly, depending on such factors as his socio-economic status, his geographic location, his generational nativity, the ethnic population density of his locality, the presence of kinship in Mexico, the frequency of his visits to Mexico, and his desire to assimilate or accommodate to the dominant culture.

2. *Lack of systematic scientific research.* The majority of the existing studies are seriously lacking in scientific methodology. Many were guided by stereotypes perpetuated by earlier studies. The investigators frequently did not speak Spanish and had limited experience with their target population. Overgeneralizations were frequently made. Cultural ideals were often interpreted as cultural norms. Indeed, many of these studies could be described as cultural litter because of their polluting effects on the Chicano culture.

3. *Prejudice toward this population.* For the most part studies concerning the Chicano have been conducted by members of the dominant race. Allport (1954) states that ". . . four-fifths of the American population harbor enough antagonism toward minority groups to influence their daily conduct." Brody (1959) mentions the impaired reality-testing of the prejudiced individual who ignores, selectively uses, or modifies information which is not compatible to his prejudices. Westie (1964) comments that few people are neutral in their biases, and that the biases of the professional are as intense and pervasive as those of the nonprofessional, except that they are concealed with more sophistication in scientific terminology and sta-

---

[5] *Pochismo* and *pachuquismo* are dialects which are mixtures of correct and incorrect Spanish with words of other languages and present cultures tossed in.

tistical tables. Close scrutiny of current studies reveals degrading and insulting statements, camouflaged racism, and pathological descriptions of the Chicano culture and of the Chicano's family structure.

The paramount difficulty in describing Chicano-specific characteristics does not excuse continued cultural pollution, and vague generalities made by Chicano professionals are of no higher merit than those made by Anglo professionals. Specificity, clarity, and comprehensiveness are important and sorely lacking goals, and these goals cannot be achieved without professional collaboration and sustained support effort.

The following comments are intended as guidelines which may merit further scholarly consideration in regard to service for the Chicano.

1. *Demography.* Chicanos, according to Barrett (1966), are young. Their median age is 19 years compared to the Anglos' 28 years. They are urban based; 79.1 percent live in urban centers. They are native born; 85 out of 100 are natives. They have a high fertility rate which they have controlled since 1950. They are frequently educationally inferior to white and nonwhites. Chicanos are economically deprived; high percentages receive less than $3,000 per family per year and unemployment rates are high. Their families shown a high degree of disruption by divorce, separation, desertion, or death of the male spouse (40 to 50 percent). They usually live in Texas or California (82.1 percent) but they can also live in Arizona, New Mexico and Colorado. Los Angeles, California, and San Antonio, Texas, are two cities with the highest Chicano concentration.

2. *La Familia.* The Chicano attributes to himself extraordinary familism, but this is unsupported by the U.S. Census (1960) and by comprehensive research (Grebler et al., 1970), both of which indicated an extraordinary degree of family disruption by divorce, separation, and desertion. Extended family as a current practice is very minimal (Grebler et al.) and as a current cultural ideal is a myth. It is possible that the extended family was never a cultural ideal but that it was a necessity to survive the burdens of poverty. Visiting patterns do differ among the Chicanos and these may maintain the belief in extraordinary familism.

3. *Patriarchy* is also attributed to the Chicano family. In the traditional patriarchal family, the male head makes all important decisions. His authority is unilateral, while the wife is seen as submissive and childlike (Madsen, 1964; Thurston, 1959; Griffith, 1948;

Woods, 1956). Grebler and others question whether this practice was ever a behavioral norm either in the United States or in Mexico, and they present considerable evidence in support of their position. Patriarchy may have been and, perhaps still is, a cultural ideal held by Chicano men but it is doubtful that it is a viable practice. The social studies which perpetuate this myth, e.g., Madsen (1964), fail to differentiate cultural ideals from cultural norms and cultural specific characteristics. Grebler and others (1970) state, "We might suggest, in fact, that the patriarchal values as well as the belief in the stable family became cultural ideals of the Mexican American at least in part because of the weakness of both the family structure and the male role" (p. 360). The pervasive importance of the mother is supported by the literature (Grebler et al., 1970) and by this writer's experience. The mother is the subject of extensive poetry, literature, songs, and movies. The respect that Chicanos have for their mothers is demonstrated by observable behavior, affectionate reference terms (*mamacita*), and by the male's willingness to fight when the term "your mother" is used in a derogatory manner.

4. *Machismo* is an ethnic concept of masculinity which is attributed to a Chicano by social scientists. This cult of masculine superiority is also accepted by many Chicanos. Machismo is described by Madsen (1964) as manly strength, sexual virility and bravado, manly honor defended by physical aggressiveness, tolerance for heavy alcoholic consumption, ability to participate in verbal dueling, conquest and domination of women, and marital unfaithfulness. The wife or the *hembra* plays the perfect counterpart of the *macho*.

The ethnic concept of *hembrisma*,[6] the cult of female inferiority, implies that the Chicano woman is weak, submissive, respectful, subdued, in need of protection from her man, pure, unresentful of her subordinate role or of her man's unfaithfulness, and grateful and accepting of physical abuse. The concepts of *machismo* and *hembrisma* are unsupported by empirical evidence. Evidence does exist, however, that attributes these characteristics to the culture of poverty regardless of ethnicity (Lewis, 1965; Thomas, 1967; de Jesus, 1962). Minuchin and others state: "Interacting variables such as economic discrimination, the ghetto subculture, a pattern of migration, and family disorganization (mother-centered families, divorce, desertion, separation, illegitimacy) result in confused masculine

---

[6] The term *hembrisma* has not been officially accepted; nevertheless, it suits this author's fancy.

identity and a subsequent drive toward exaggerated masculinity"
(p. 23).

It is important to consider that even though it is very unlikely that
machismo is a cultural norm for Chicanos, it may be a cultural ideal;
therefore, the destructive effects that this cultural ideal may have on
the stability of the family should be considered. Also considered
should be the built-in resistance to behavior modification that this
cultural ideal implies. The immature Chicano male who may be con-
tributing to the instability and ultimate disruption of his family by his
heavy drinking, his unfaithfulness, and/or his domination and physical abuse of his wife, may dismiss efforts to help him control these behaviors with "that's part of my culture" or "that's part of my
machismo."

5. *Compadrazgo*, or co-parenthood, is a kinship prototype specific
to the relationship of the child's godparents to his parents. The required witnesses at a wedding are referred to as *compadres*. Also,
close friends are at times also affectionately referred to as *compadres*
and *comadres*. This kinship prototype is still viable in varying degrees
among Chicanos.

6. *Carnalismo* is a term which implies close blood ties or sameness
of flesh; it is used to refer to close friends of the same ethnicity. Chicanos, according to this writer's experience, demonstrate preference
for close friendship characterized by affectionate and animated verbal exchanges, physical touching and fairly close body to body proximity. Evidence in support of these observations has not been found.

7. *Personal Observations.* These comments are unsupported by
empirical evidence but are based on this writer's experience. Chicanos
seem to be more demonstrative in their affection, more animated in
their friendships, more courteous, more generous and more humor-
ous than members of other ethnic groups. In working with Chicano
clients, folksy, down to earth, friendly, and authoritative approaches
seem to be very well received. The clients are usually on time for ap-
pointments when the importance of doing this is explained and when
the client's realistic home situation is taken into consideration. No difference of time perspective has been noted. They seem to appreciate
being addressed in friendly but respectful terms. Interestingly, their
address to this writer varies from respectful "doctora," "Senora
Boulette," "Estita" (short for "senorita") to "Teresita." The clients
respond well when the professional takes time to explain his or her
understanding of their problems, and explains in clear terminology

the professional area of experience and how this expertise will benefit the clients.

In general, the Chicano client is a very perceptive individual who is an expert in surviving in a hostile and difficult environment. His strengths and his past coping experiences can be used as a framework for the professional-client interaction, and his current beliefs to enhance the therapeutic process. For example, if the client expresses belief in God, in prayers, special saints, or even in *curanderas* (faith healers), the professional can effectively respond to and work with these beliefs in order to maximize the client's motivation for improvement.

Edward Joseph Shoben, Jr., has stated that "it seems unlikely that we can fully respect another person—that is, react to him as a person and not a thing—without approximating in some imperfect but significant degree an understanding of his identity" (Shoben, 1966). It is hoped that this case will contribute to such an understanding and that that understanding in turn will contribute to more effective counseling of Chicanos, whether they be inmates like Mr. R. or members of the outside community.

REFERENCES

Allport, Gordon W. 1954. *The nature of prejudice*. Cambridge, Mass.: Addison-Wesley.

Barrett, Donald. 1966. Demographic characteristics. In *La Raza: Forgotten Americans*, ed. Julian Samora. Indiana: Univ. of Notre Dame Press.

Brody, Eugene B. 1959. Psychiatry and prejudice. In *American Handbook of Psychiatry*, ed. Silvano Ariti, vol. III. New York: Basic Books.

de Jesus, Carolina Maria. 1962. *Child of the dark*. New York: Signet Books.

Franks, Cyril M., ed. 1969. *Behavior therapy: appraisal and status*. New York: McGraw-Hill Series in Psychology.

Grebler, Leo; Moore, Joan W.; and Guzman, Ralph C. 1970. *The Mexican-American people—the nation's second largest minority*. New York: The Free Press.

Griffith, Beatrice. 1948. *American me*. Boston: Houghton-Mifflin Co.

Kanfer, Frederick H., and Saslow, George. 1969. Behavioral Diagnosis. In *Behavior therapy: Appraisal and status*, ed. Cyril M. Franks. New York: McGraw-Hill, pp. 57–71.

Lewis, Oscar. 1965. The culture of poverty. In *Poverty in affluence*, ed.

Robert E. Will and Harold G. Vatter. New York: Harcourt, Brace, and World, pp. 129–35.

Madsen, William. 1964. *The Mexican-American of South Texas*. New York: Holt, Rinehart, and Winston.

Miller, N. E., and Dollard, John. 1961. Reward. In *Reinforcement*, ed. Robert C. Birney and Richard C. Teevan. New Jersey: D. Van Nostrand Co., pp. 33–38.

Minuchin, Salvador, et al. 1967. *Families of the slums*. New York: Basic Books.

Mittlebach, Frank, and Marshall, Grace. 1966. The burden of poverty. In *Mexican-American study project advance report, no. 5*. Los Angeles: University of California.

Peñalosa, Fernando. 1967. The changing Mexican-American in southern California. *Sociology and Social Research* 51:405–17.

Rickard, H. C.; Dignam, P. J.; and Horner, R. F. 1960. Verbal manipulation in a psychotherapeutic relationship. *Journal of Clinical Psychology* 16:364–7.

Romano, Octavio I. 1969. The historical and intellectual presence of Mexican-Americans. *El Grito*, Winter, pp. 49–77.

Shoben, Edward Joseph, Jr. 1966. Personal worth in education and counseling. In *Revolution in counseling*, ed. John D. Krumboltz. Boston: Houghton, Mifflin.

Thomas, Piri. 1967. *Down these mean streets*. New York: Signet Books.

Thurston, Richard. 1959. Urbanization and sociocultural change in a Mexican-American enclave. Ph.D. dissertation, University of California at Los Angeles.

Ullmann, L. P.; Krasner, L.; and Edinger, R. L. 1964. Verbal conditioning of common associations in long-term schizophrenic patients. *Behavior Research and Therapy* 62:128–32.

Westie, Frank. 1964. Race and ethnic relations. In *Handbook of American ethnic groups*. New York: Harper Brothers.

Wolpe, Joseph. 1969. *The practice of behavior therapy*. New York: Pergamon Press.

Woods, Sister Francis Jerome. 1956. *Cultural values of American ethnic groups*. New York: Harper Brothers.

12

Application of Behavior Therapy to Compulsive Exhibitionism and Homosexuality

Ray E. Hosford and Harvey B. Rifkin

Problems of sexual perversion resulting from the deprivation of female partners are not uncommon in prison settings, and the majority of heterosexual inmates who engage in homosexual relationships because of this deprivation usually return to heterosexual behavior upon release from the institution. Other acts of perversion, however, are not necessarily related to sexual deprivation per se, but may simply be behaviors which have been learned in the same way as any other behavior is learned. Exhibitionism, i.e., the act of intentionally exposing the genitals, often accompanied by masturbation, is a case in point. Whereas Freudians regard the act of exhibiting oneself as a defense against the specific fear of castration (see Lorand and Balint, 1956), behaviorists consider the practice a learned behavior, a conditional inhibitor of many kinds of anxiety (see Wolpe, 1969; Bond and Hutchinson, 1960; Dengrove, 1967).

The view that exhibitionism and other psychophysical sexual reactions are maintained by anxiety reduction has considerable support from actual case studies, including those conducted by Masters and Johnson (1966). Research and clinical cases have also demonstrated that sexual arousal and anxiety are antithetical (see, for example, Wolpe, 1958, 1969). In fact, sexual arousal has been used as a therapeutic technique to counteract the emergence of nonsexual anxiety (Wolpe, 1969). That is, if an individual experiences inappropriate anxiety in a given situation, and if he or she can become sexually aroused in the same situation, the sexual arousal will impede and often halt the arousal of anxiety. Similarly, self-exposure can be viewed as an act which an individual has acquired in order to reduce an anxiety response cued by certain classes of stimuli (Bond and Hutchinson, 1960).

Exposing oneself can be reinforcing for a variety of reasons. For example, since sexual arousal lowers anxiety, such behavior will be very reinforcing to an anxious or fearful individual. Then too, because exhibitionism is accompanied by high levels of sexual excitement, the individual is able to concentrate on the act and to cut out all competing stimuli—in this case his worries and concerns—which is, in itself, highly reinforcing for someone who is depressed and/or anxious. In addition, the reactions of persons viewing the act can often be a potent reinforcer to an individual who receives few other reinforcements in life. Furthermore, so long as the behavior is reinforcing to the individual—for whatever reason—it will tend to be repeated with increasing frequency.

THE CASE OF DON

The following case study represents an example of the use of a variety of behavioral techniques with a 22-year-old man who, though committed to a federal correctional facility for other reasons, was seeking help for compulsive exhibitionism. At the time of counseling the client was undergoing treatment for a beating he had received in the prison yard a short time previously. The beating had been sufficiently severe to require both medical assistance and extensive dental surgery; for this reason he had been committed to the prison hospital.

During the initial interviews Don related that at the age of thirteen he had been caught by his father lifting up the dress of a younger girl who lived next door. He recalled that his father had spanked him and had threatened to "beat him to a pulp" if he ever heard of his doing such a thing again. It was "not too long" after this incident that Don attempted to expose himself for the first time. Although he said he would like to, he had never had, or tried to have, sexual intercourse with a girl.

Don's behavior in prison was one of compulsive sexuality, specifically homosexuality. He also had an increasingly severe problem with exposing himself, something which he claimed he had been able to control during the year of his imprisonment until pressures in the yard got to be such that he could not control himself. Because of his small stature and his homosexual behavior, some inmates would threaten him for being "a queer" while others would threaten him if he refused to have homosexual relations with them. Although his claim may have been exaggerated, Don estimated that he had had sexual relations with at least 300 inmates in the institution. Reports from the staff indicated that he kept to himself almost exclusively, and that he had few, if any, relationships, other than sexual with other inmates.

Don freely discussed both his homosexual experiences, which he indicated that he was able to continue even though confined to the prison hospital, and his compulsive exhibitionism. His emphasis when describing exposure incidents tended to center more on the reactions of the observers than on his own responses. However, he did relate that orgasm was stronger during times of exhibition than when he masturbated alone.

During our first interview, Don was extremely agitated and flighty, very withdrawn, and highly suspicious. He appeared to be unable to respond to those about him in any but a very superficial manner. In addition, his speech was very rapid and staccatolike, and occasionally he stuttered. He spoke in a monotone, and was concerned primarily with his fears of being beaten again in the yard. According to Don, the beating was the result of his refusal to perform fellatio with a particular inmate whom he disliked. In retaliation the inmate had recruited a number of friends who had joined him in taking turns in beating Don for being "a queer." While attacks of this severity are not frequent, the case is not atypical. Many inmates will pressure known homosexuals or weaker men, particularly if they are young and small, to perform fellatio on them at night while during the day, in the presence of other inmates, these same individuals ridicule the homosexual or the person whom they forced to perform a homosexual act.

Although an analysis of his reports concerning his behavior before incarceration indicated that Don had been quite anxious and fearful for most of his life, his anxiety was particularly intense during the period of counseling and psychiatric exaluation which took place at the time of his hospitalization. An observation written by a male inmate nurse vividly illustrates the extent of this anxiety: "Patient was locked in strip cell . . . at his own request. He is very afraid to come out without an officer around and thinks he will be beaten up by other patients. Many times other inmates would upset him by shouting things at him, throwing water in his cell. During the first week of being locked in, the patient was observed at least once daily exposing himself by masturbating in doorway facing the hall."

Additional observations, substantiated by feedback from the staff, indicated that Don was anything but truthful. He would consistently model his responses on what he believed his listener wanted to hear. For the most part he limited discussions to those topics which he wished to dwell on; and, at the same time, he would respond only to his own suggestions, remaining impervious to those which others might attempt to give him.

Don was seen weekly for a period of three and a half months in interviews conducted jointly by the authors. The first four or five sessions were used to gather information from which to set up goals for therapy.

Don's primary concern was his compulsive exposure. Although he would frequently state that it was the prison which caused his behavior and that he knew that he could stop once he was released, he indicated that he wanted to work on this particular problem during our counseling sessions. We noted that the anxiety-producing events occurred within the prison—the incident in the yard is a good example—or in his own personal life—bad news from home, etc.—and the frequency of exposing himself had increased greatly. He would stand in a doorway or a window until someone passed or looked his way, and then perform the act.

He also indicated that being a homosexual was, as he put it, "a bad trip," in that he felt he was always being used. For example, he was consistently the one to perform fellatio, he did not receive it. Thus, in addition to stopping the incidents of exposing himself, he wanted to become bisexual. He did not want to give up homosexuality but he did want to be able to become aroused heterosexually, which at present he could not do.

GOALS

After determining what Don wanted to accomplish we set up some tentative, but, given his incarceration, realistic goals. Because many of his problems, e.g., anxiety, compulsive exposure, homosexuality, and withdrawal, were interrelated, more than one behavior was worked on at the same time. Although he stated that he wanted to work on his problem of exposing himself, we were not at all sure that he was committed to stopping the behavior. Thus, contrary to usual practices in behavior therapy, several goals, rather than one, were set up for the counseling. These included a reduction in the frequency of exhibitionism, a development of the ability to relax, an initiation of sexual arousal to symbols of heterosexual stimuli, and an increase in interpersonal relationships with others.

TECHNIQUES

A variety of techniques were employed. During the interviews we verbally reinforced Don contingent upon his relating that he had performed, or was going to perform, a certain behavior related to accomplishing his goals. In addition, inmate nurses in the hospital were instructed how and when to reinforce Don both verbally and with pats-on-the-back for playing cards and otherwise relating interpersonally with other inmates. At first Don was asked to keep track of what he had done during the week to help alleviate his problem. Later he was asked to keep a written diary of his efforts. We used both the nurses' reports and the diary to gain responses for which we could reinforce him for appropriate behavior.

To reduce his general anxiety state Don was given relaxation training similar to that developed by Jacobsen (1938). In addition to going through the procedures weekly, he was given a sheet of instructions which he was to follow during the week. One inmate nurse also read the relaxation instructions to him two or three times a week. After his practice in relaxation, the process of desensitization (Wolpe, 1958, 1969) was explained to him. He was instructed to keep track of both those situations which occurred during the week and those which he recalled from past experiences in which anxiety usually developed and which were later followed by his exposing himself.

Don constructed a hierarchy which had to be modified several times due to events which occurred within the institution and his own personal life. This hierarchy included:
Writing to parents
Talking with a female from the University who was on an internship at the prison
Thinking of being hospitalized
Going to the Parole Board
Getting parole

Failing to get parole
Being out of prison and getting turned down for a job
Asking a girl for a date
Being turned down for a date

In addition to the desensitization procedures per se, conditioning procedures were devised to promote sexual arousal to heterosexual stimuli. Because his sexual experiences had all been male oriented, including most of his exhibitionism, he could not relate verbally how he would feel in a variety of heterosexual situations. He was instructed in relaxation procedures, and with his eyes closed, was asked to imagine, one at a time, various sexually oriented scenes, e.g., male rubbing his hair, female performing fellatio on him, male performing fellatio on him, male inserting penis into his rectum, himself inserting into a female, male exposing himself, male in underwear, girl naked sitting on him, girl naked, and girl in underwear. As each scene was described, he was to indicate the extent, if any, of sexual arousal. He indicated arousal to all five male-only oriented scenes and no arousal to female-only scenes. However, when heterosexual acts with individuals other than himself were presented with emphasis on male behavior, some arousal occurred. He indicated, for example, a male inserting into the female and a female sitting on the male produced some sexual reaction. On the other hand, a female performing fellatio on a male with emphasis on the female did not produce any effect.

After determining which scenes elicited some arousal, we developed situations involving heterosexual stimuli with which we attempted to help Don learn to associate sexual arousal. This hierarchy ranged from seeing a pretty girl fully clothed to that of performing heterosexual intercourse with the same girl. Descriptions of male physique and behavior were vividly described in close contiguity to descriptions of female physical attributes and sexual performance. To promote the desired outcome, Don was also requested to imagine, during any act of masturbation, a particular heterosexual scene which elicited some arousal. In addition, he was given instructions in thought stopping (Wolpe, 1969) to perform if, in those incidents of masturbation, scenes of male eroticism intruded. Thought stopping usually involves having the client close his eyes and verbalize a typical thought pattern which is unproductive or in some way a problem to the individual and then having the therapist shout "Stop!" This is repeated until the client learns to do it for himself.

The objective is to stop the unwanted thought at its beginning and to replace it with a desired response. In this case, we instructed Don to stop his male-only thoughts during masturbation by saying to himself silently, "Stop," and then thinking of a sexually arousing scene in which a female was involved. During the weekly interviews he was given relaxation training, and was asked to imagine vividly particular heterosexual scenes until he began to experience arousal. A fifteen-minute film was then used to promote greater generalization to the heterosexual stimuli. The therapeutic film showed heterosexual behavior including foreplay and actual intercourse. Don was shown the whole film first. This produced some sexual arousal on his part as evidenced by self report and penile movement. After that he was only shown a small portion of the film, and asked to describe how he felt, what came next, and so forth. Relaxation training always preceded the conditioning exercises.

RESULTS

Two types of evaluations of Don's behavior were made. Inmate nurses kept written notes of observations taken six times daily, one hour apart. (Due to problems involved with using inmate nurses, the observations did not begin until five weeks after treatment began.) In addition to written descriptions, graphs were made showing the number of times Don exposed himself, engaged in homosexual activities, socialized with others, and watched television. Tallies were made relative to the particular behavior the client was engaged in during the observation time. These graphs were turned in each week just prior to Don's scheduled interview and were used both to assess the status of his behavior and to determine the accuracy of his own statements. Don knew that the nurses kept medical reports for all hospitalized inmates, but he did not know that they were recording the specific behaviors which he engaged in or that they were making frequency counts of those behaviors.

Because systematic observations were not made to determine base rates during the initial stages of the counseling, client statements jotted down during the interviews had to be used as a base rate. Don related that he often had the urge to expose himself many times during the course of a day and that he had exposed himself as many as six times in a single day. His self report of over 300 homosexual experiences was somewhat supported in part by reports from inmate nurses and staff members. Observations of his withdrawal behavior were made by the authors several times during the early stages of the counseling. Before, during, and after the interviews for approximately a two-hour period each we observed that at no time did he talk with or interact in any way with the inmate nurses or the other hospitalized inmates.

Figures 1, 2, and 3 present the data for the nurses' observations. On the two occasions in the third month of treatment in which he exposed himself three times within a six-day period, he was experiencing considerable anxiety because of a severe beating one inmate received from another inmate; Don was afraid he would be next. The homosexual activities decreased markedly only to increase during the fourth month of treatment. Nurses' notes and notes taken during the interviews indicate that Don was being pressured again to engage in homosexual activities. Rather than risk another experience of being beaten up, he would reluctantly go along. However, his socializing, such as playing cards and talking with other inmates, increased considerably and consistently. In addition, although far from being heterosexual, he was able to become aroused when exposed to heterosexual stimuli. This was evidenced not only by self report but by penile movement (movement of trousers in the genital area) observed by us after exposure to various heterosexual stimuli.

CASE CONFERENCE

At the time counseling had to be terminated due to both authors leaving the area, a case conference was held to assess the extent of Don's progress. Excerpts from the tape-recorded session follow:

... still consider him flighty but there are occasions when he seems more relaxed and will listen, will kind of let the other guy in. [He will] pause a bit and he seems to have a greater capacity to listen [and] demonstrates a decrease in the pressure of speech, though he still basically is kind of flighty, self-centered, and shows poor concentration. But . . . these are improved over the period of time. . . .

He does participate in the limited recreation that we have in the hospital and has established some friendships—talking friendships—which are nonsexual. He remains, however, basically very hostile toward authority. . . .

Still staccato speech. Still stutters. Can't really say clinically if there

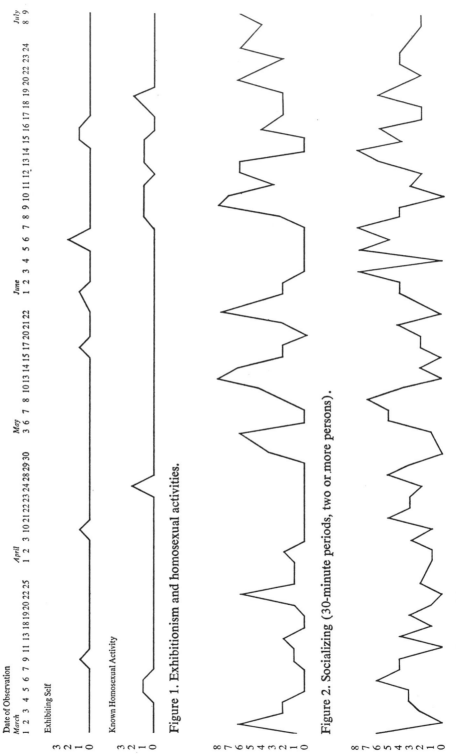

Figure 1. Exhibitionism and homosexual activities.

Figure 2. Socializing (30-minute periods, two or more persons).

Figure 3. Watching television (30-minute periods).

has been a difference. He still shows considerable pressure in his speech. He is able, however, to stop and relax himself somewhat and continue the speech without the stuttering.

DISCUSSION

This case was described not to demonstrate the effectiveness or lack of effectiveness of behavioral techniques with chronic exhibitionism, but to present an example of some kinds of techniques and procedures therapists might try with cases of this kind. At times we thought the counseling was proceeding well only to find out that Don had exhibited himself again. Upon following this up we would learn of some incident in the prison or in his own family which elicited higher levels of anxiety than he could now handle. Thus, he would resort to the only behavior he had learned which would reduce, if only temporarily, the distressing effects of anxiety. Conversely, during periods of less strain and anxiety, we noticed that Don's frequency of exhibitionism attenuated greatly.

COMMENT: C. S. MOSS

This is the classic manner of treatment by behaviorists with an acute (or chronic) acting-out sexual offender or psychopath. It dispenses with psychoanalytic theory or therapy, including only a token gesture as to how exhibitionism and homosexuality were formed or developed; nor does it make any pretense about treating with such sacred mystiques as transference. These are all considered to be Freudian "mumbo-jumbo," devised to confuse rather than to clarify. The psychiatrist, Dr. Rifkin, is to be congratulated for allowing what must have seemed to him as treatment by such an unconventional method.

Although treatment did not result in a "cure," as the authors point out it did result in a demonstration of the effectiveness of a variety of behavioral techniques. Absolutely the whole treatment procedure consisted of varying the environmental contingencies in the here-and-now to remove undesirable behavior and to replace it with acceptable conduct (see Chapter 9, page 95). The single, biggest obstacle was to apply the principles of behavioral change in any consistent manner.

The case is self-explanatory and needs little elaboration, except for pointing out once again that behavioral counseling does lend itself to greater objective verification than do traditional methods, perhaps because (1) it is time-limited, (2) it is concerned only with present behavior, and (3) many of the adherents are relatively recently trained psychologists sophisticated in research, meaning that *overt* behavior, not subjective client "feelings," id, ego, etc., is used as the criterion for assessing the effects of therapy.

REFERENCES

Bond, I. K., and Hutchinson, H. C. 1960. Application of reciprocal inhibition therapy to exhibitionism. *Canadian Medical Association Journal* 83:23–25.

Dengrove, E. 1967. Behavior therapy of the sexual disorders. *Journal of Sex Research* 3:49–61.

Jacobsen, E. 1938. *Progressive relaxation.* Chicago: University of Chicago Press.

Lorand, S., and Balint, Michael (eds.). 1956. *Perversions: psychodynamics and therapy.* New York: Random House.

Masters, W., and Johnson, V. 1966. *Human sexual response.* London: Churchill.

Wolpe, J. 1958. *Psychotherapy by reciprocal inhibition.* Stanford: Stanford University Press.

———. 1969. *The practice of behavior therapy.* New York: Pergamon Press.

13

Treatment of Recurrent Nightmares in a Drug Abuser by Hypnosymbolism

C. Scott Moss

One of the very real ways in which the population of prisons has changed in the past few years is the increasing number of persons incarcerated for dealing in and taking dangerous drugs. As stated in Chapter 6, many state, county, and federal correctional institutions have instituted specific programs for the drug offender; however, these programs are strictly experimental and no agency can claim that they know yet how to deal efficiently with most drug abusers. Within the federal system we are presently limited by the number of persons that the drug abuse treatment program can accept at any one time. While the program is well financed and has three times the regular staff, at any one moment the staff is restricted to no more than a hundred individuals who must come voluntarily into the program for one full year. Needless to say, this excludes the majority of drug offenders, some of whom find their way into Operation Breakthrough (Chapter 7) and some of whom come to the mental health division. In this chapter and Chapter 16, I have deliberately chosen to concentrate on clients who have a history of drug abuse and who are necessarily treated with a time-limited or crisis-oriented fashion.

This case in this chapter is an example of the use of hypnosis in relief of nightmares associated with a traumatic neurosis. The presence of the precipitating incident of three years' duration was followed by recurrent anxiety dreams symbolizing the situation, which in turn allegedly led to extensive drug taking. The treatment ob-

Note: This chapter was presented in part at the 15th Scientific Meeting of the American Clinical Hypnosis Society, San Diego, California, November 1–5, 1972. A tape of the presentation exists (Moss, 1973b).

jective was to eliminate the disturbing dreams, in hopes that this would lead to a decrease or elimination of the drug habit. As will be evident, the effect on the drug practice was left ambiguous; however, there is provided evidence that it is possible to extinguish a troublesome symptom (i.e., the nightmare) through a combination of brief counseling and hypnosymbolism.

Twenty-five years ago I was introduced to hypnosis and hypnotherapy and in time developed a unique adaptation which I came to label hypnosymbolism. It entails the method of using hypnosis to enable the client to interpret his own dreams meaningfully as a facilitant to psychotherapy. Like Freud, I am convinced that dreams often tell about secret fears, hopes, and expectations in people's lives, but unlike Freud, I became convinced that through the use of hypnosis, self-interpretation can often reveal them. (See Moss, 1965, 1967, 1970a; Moss and James, 1970.) Of course, not every person is amenable to any one method, but nevertheless, I am convinced that hypnosis does reveal a great deal about the underlying factors in a client's emotional upset and from it more effective plans for treatment can be laid. Chapter 16 carries over some of the ways that I have learned to handle clients under hypnosis, especially in deciphering the cryptic letter which the individual described in that chapter wrote to me (pp. 220–26). These two case studies are examples of what Norman A. Carlson stated in his Foreword as *differential treatment*; as he said, "There is no single modality . . . which is appropriate for all inmates, under all conditions."

When I came to the correctional setting three years ago, I was most hesitant to use hypnosis in the prison setting; the main reason for this was the fact that the majority of inmates have a decided propensity to manipulate others, and I found myself wondering whether some inmate might come eventually to use the hypnotic technique for his personal convenience to bring him additional commissary privileges, to con homosexual favors, or even to manipulate an unsuspecting officer. Although the whole question of the use of hypnosis to bring about antisocial acts is still open, I felt it would be difficult to convince the captain, the warden or a judge that hypnosis could not be used in this manner. Thus, I avoided any use of hypnosis until I was presented with an individual who complained of a repetitive nightmare which had disturbed his sleep two or three times a week since his tour in Vietnam three years before.

The kernel of this nightmare was an undisguised, real-life event in which, through an accident, the inmate had caused the death of his favorite sergeant. Specifically, he had hurried into a bunker without his helmet or flak jacket and was going out to retrieve them when he met the sergeant coming in. At that precise instant a mortar shell exploded, killing the sergeant, whose body fully protected the inmate from the blast.

Figures 1 and 2 are the inmate's representation, drawn by him in pencil and ink, of this traumatic event. He had a vivid remembrance of the sergeant's facial expression changing to bewilderment as his body fell.

The experience left the client with a great sense of guilt which in turn reputedly led directly to his taking of drugs (marijuana, hard narcotics, and more recently LSD). He reported that when he was using drugs the nightmares occurred only occasionally and then less vividly than they did when he was off drugs, at which times they occurred frequently and were associated with high anxiety. The primary counseling goal that we agreed upon was to rid him of the nightmares and thus to moderate the drug-taking habit. The primary treatment modality I decided would be hypnosymbolism, if he turned out to be a cooperative subject. Incidentally, he had some psychiatric treatment previously but he indicated that he had failed to tell anyone about the nightmares because he was too ashamed. All of this information plus the choice of the method of treatment were made in the first session. He would be at F.C.I. for only about ten days, since he was sent in as an observation case by the court before sentencing, for smuggling marijuana.

TREATMENT

In the second session the client again told me of the typical nightmare which had occurred over the weekend. I then introduced hypnosis and he turned out to be quite a good subject. Throughout I was careful not to alert him to the variations of any foreshortened induction period. We agreed upon representing the content of counseling as a form of "relaxation" rather than "hypnosis" to parry any curiosity of other inmates (conducting psychotherapy within the walls of our prison is similar to the old "goldfish bowl routine" in that every office must have a window in which passing officers or inmates can glance). Each of the total of eight sessions was taped.

In the third sesion the training in hypnosis continued. I then gave

Figure 1. Sergeant at moment of impact.

Figure 2. The dying sergeant. Inmate is beneath him; the objects pictured on top of the sergeant are bursting sandbags.

him a posthypnotic suggestion that he would have another "typical" dream which he would have no difficulty remembering. In the fourth session he reported memory of several dreams, but no real nightmares. The dream we focused on concerned his riding in a car with an ex-army sergeant back at Ft. Reilly, Kansas. The unknown sergeant had been in the army twenty years earlier, "similar to my uncle." Under hypnosis he was instructed to re-dream that dream again, but instead, he remembered a situation which had occurred about a year previously, when he was attending a jazz concert in the company of a lifelong friend named Timmy. Suddenly he broke into tears, crying, "Timmy's dead! Timmy killed himself! He killed himself!" He then wept uncontrollably. As it turned out, Timmy had, in real life, sought the assistance of a doctor who misdiagnosed him and treated him for a muscular strain when in fact he had a severe infection. When Timmy could not stand the pain any longer he killed himself with an overdose of pills. As we talked further, the client was able to see a relationship between Timmy's death and that of his sergeant: each "occurred by mistake, an error! I was wrong just the way the doctor was wrong!"

At this point, under hypnosis, the relationship with the current nocturnal dream again came into focus. "I was seated in front with the sergeant which indicated that I was his friend." The inmate was most reluctant to look at the sergeant, but finally at my insistence, he did so, whereupon he broke out crying again and continued to sob for the remainder of the session. Of course, he identified him as the dead sergeant. But it was the allusion to his "uncle" in the dream that he said really "blew my mind." The "uncle" really represented the client's father and he launched into how he felt about his own father's death when he was four, and how he had reacted automatically to deal with the trauma by "burying it." "Even when I was very little I had to laugh or else I would cry. I even laughed at my father's funeral. I always laughed [because] I didn't want to remember. I didn't want to think about it anymore." This was a most cathartic session.

In the fifth sesion, in the waking state, we began to explore his religious-philosophical convictions. He was born a Catholic but the death of his father led eventually to his questioning of the Catholic faith. However, despite his disillusionment, there were many residuals of the earlier teachings, e.g., he still wore a Catholic medallion because, he said, his grandmother had given it to him; he related further that he still went occasionally to midnight mass, because he gets "stoned" and the music "turned me on." He married a Catholic woman and he still believes in God. However, he does not believe that God punishes us in Heaven or Hell, but that the individual "unintentionally" punishes himself here on earth for the wrongs that he has done. The inmate felt that when he did something wrong he must make reparation for it. For instance, he once stole three records from a department store and later, when he had money, brought in nine new records which he simply placed in the store's inventory. At this point, I made the tentative interpretation that his experience with drugs, followed by his being arrested and now sent to prison, could constitute his unintentionally punishing himself. He provisionally agreed with my hypothesis, but was still completely baffled over what form of restitution he could make for the death of the sergeant. My response was that while unfortunate drug experiences with the resulting incarceration might go some way toward evening the score, admittedly it was difficult to measure the loss of a human life.

He began in the sixth session by stating that he had had dreams each of the three nights since the last session, but that he could not remember them, except to the extent of recalling that none of them was the nightmare. Sensing some possible resistance, I shifted the focus of the discussion to the counseling process, whereupon he reluctantly admitted that he was ambivalent about coming in because "what is coming out is in contrast to what I would like to be." I undertook to reassure him that mental health workers learn to lay aside the conventional standards of evaluation and that I was impressed with his courage in facing things within his life that were difficult to confront. Following that exchange, he remembered a dream that reminded him vaguely of Lewis Carroll's *Through the Looking-Glass,* in "that it was so vivid and yet so seemingly nonsensical."

First I see a Bishop, a plastic black Bishop on black squares and it encounters a white, no, a red King. The red King occupies a red Queen's space. The red King has legs and gets up and walks away. It's really funny! Then there is the red Queen. She has a bird, a tall bird with long legs. She's using it as a croquet mallet. She's playing croquet with heads. That's all I can remember of the dream except that the Queen hits the head and knocks the Bishop over.

Figure 3. Dream of chess game.

In the waking state, the inmate could offer no meaning to the dream. We then proceeded with hypnosis, which produced these verbalized associations:

> The head has long dark hair and a long dark beard. . . . I dream about chess games quite frequently, particularly when I go to sleep [he denies that the game of chess has any covert meaning to him. . . . he next sees a black Pawn which is shielding the King]. . . . The King's pieces all have human features whereas the Bishop's pieces have plastic features. It seems like I began to favor the red over the black pieces. I'd be prejudiced more towards the human faces. The black pieces represent exactly what they are—artificial— the human faces seem to be winning. The black Pawn protects the King, shielding him from the black Bishop.

T: Are you ready to face what they represent?

I: It represents the artificial side of me being chipped away. . . . The head is kind of laughing. It is saying through its expression, 'If you are only a head you can't do much except roll'. . . . And the bird has its arms folded and the expression is sort of the same arrogant quality. He's kind of angered by being used as a mallet. . . . The Queen is sort of loud mouthed, kind of overly masculine, kind of huge and threatening. . . . The King, when he leaves the endangered square, seems to be saying to himself that the Bishop can't hope to accomplish anything by placing the one square in check. He feels that it doesn't really matter. It is kind of showing his maneuverability and he takes pride in the fact that the black Bishop is so easily deluded. . . . The black Bishop and the black Pawn have no emotions whatsoever. They are cold and dead and have nothing in common except for their color.

T: "Can you now translate and tell me what the dream is all about?"

I: "I can't see anymore than what I have told you. I could say some things but when I would say it wasn't . . . [for example] I could say that the dream [nightmare] is artificial because it is over and done with—because it remains in the present would mean that it is completely artificial. . . . [Then the inmate is startled, he reacts emotionally.] Oh, no—drugs—the Pawn is the drugs! [He laughs excitedly.] Now the puzzle fits! I certainly did pull the right dream out of my head! I don't know how I did that— the Pawn is drugs! The King is using the Pawn as a shield although the Pawn is part of the opposition. In chess where you use an opposing piece, it usually turns out worse for the King. . . . The shield is drugs and the King uses the Pawn twice [to defend two separate positions]. . . . The King didn't realize until he moved that he could only move into one square because of his Pawn. He could have taken the Pawn and done away with it but he didn't see the Pawn in time, even though he was employing the Pawn as a shield. . . . The Queen seemed to be the counterpart of the King as though they were exact opposites. It seemed that all of the characteristics the King contained, the Queen did not and vice versa. If the Queen had been put in check by the Bishop she would have immediately seen the Pawn and done away with him, but the fact that the Queen was occupying a different square and was in no danger, she paid no attention to it. [But] she did realize that the Bishop was a threat and therefore, she picked up the bird and sent the head rolling in his direction.

T: What is the bird? When I snap my fingers it will be replaced by several things, each of which means exactly the same [snap].

I: A hammer and a saw and a file. Each of these are tools and the bird is a tool. She's busy defending the King. But the bird doesn't care whether she is defending the King. The bird represents "indifference."

T: Now focus on the head.

I: The head is smiling, smiling in resignation. Everyone has to do something, so why shouldn't he do this? The picture has me split in half. One side of me is passive like the King and is using things to shield himself; he's indifferent to the fact that he is in any sort of danger, and is relying unconsciously on the other half, the Queen. The Queen is not completely represented on the surface. She is not passive but very active and is destroying the black Bishop or dream. She chooses the tool that is available to her. The bird represents you and the head is hypnosis. . . . Hypnosis is made of the same thing that dreams are made of [fantasy].

In the seventh session we went back and retraced in rather minute detail exactly what had happened, beginning with the sergeant's death, the intense grief that followed, and the subsequent beginning of drug usage—all in the waking state. Before the eighth and final session we were informed that the federal marshals were coming to transfer him the following morning. In the last session much of the time was spent in talking about his relationship with his wife (who was very much against drug-taking) and his acceptance that "all of the blame" for the marital discord was his. He vowed that he would not go back to drugs because of concern for his wife and child. "In the way of restitution I think that I can only do my best and follow up on my responsibilities for people that depend on me. Drugs are a defense against the harshness of life; I hope that I won't need them anymore." I then made arrangements for the inmate to listen to various aspects of the seven preceding sessions.

RESULTS AND DISCUSSION

The semantic differential (sd) was given to him at the first and the last sessions.[1] In practice, an individual judges a particular con-

[1] The semantic differential is not a particular test but rather a highly generalizable operation of measurement which can be adapted to specific research problems. Its originators postulate a geometrical model in the form of a semantic space defined by logical opposites. Factor analysis was used to identify the independent dimensions of this space, representing the ways human beings make meaning judgments. The generality of this factor structure was further tested by varying subject populations, concepts judged, type of judgmental situations and the factoring method used in analyzing data.

The measuring operation or semantic differential can be described as follows: adjectives are identified as representative of the major dimensions along which meaningful processes vary; these have a high coverage of meaning on one factor

cept against a set of polar adjective terms. Judgments result in the successive allocation of a concept to a point in multidimensional space. In this manner, changes in the meaning of a concept over time, the subtle differences between two or more concepts, and the individual differences in the meaning of a single concept may be quantitatively represented (Osgood et al., 1957; Snider and Osgood, 1969).

Example:

```
                                       me
rough——:——:——:——:——:——:——smooth
 good——:——:——:——:——:——:——bad
active——:——:——:——:——:——:——passive, etc.
```

Fourteen concepts were measured by the inmate on the sd pre- and post-therapy (see Table 1). Looking first at the middle or D category, they range between the meaning of AUTHORITY (1.00) which indicates practically no change, in comparison to considerable change of meaning around the death of the sergeant (SGT-DEAD) (5.47). It is also signicant that the NIGHTMARE underwent a sizeable change (4.90) as did FATHER (5.20). Incidentally, NIGHTMARE remained stable with respect to the death of the sergeant (2.65) for either the pre rating or post rating (even though the meaning of the latter shifted markedly), and the concept of FATHER came closer to the meaning of SERGEANT-LIVE (5.56 to 3.32).

In contrast, the ratings of the MOTHER and WIFE changed very modestly (2.65 and 2.83); surprisingly, the meaning of STEPFATHER varied (4.00). The semantic shift of HYPNOSIS and DR. MOSS indicated a rather sizeable shift (4.90 and 3.61 respectively), the latter indicating some ambivalence. The rating of NONCOMMISSIONED OFFICERS (NCO) also shifted (4.00), indicating that it was influenced by the counseling discussions, but as stated, the rating of AUTHORITY was left intact.

There are additional comparisons that might be made. For example, the distance between ACTUAL SELF and IDEAL SELF remained

---

and a negligible amount on the others. These logical opposites are used to define the ends of seven-point scales.

In this instance nine sets of polar adjectives were used, representing the three dimensions of evaluation, potency, and activity: excitable-calm, sociable-unsociable, tender-tough, dependable-undependable, strong willed–weak willed, unemotional-emotional, dependent-independent, changeable-stable and introverted-extroverted.

able 1. Quantitative Semantic Differential Changes in Meaning of 14 Concepts Measured at Two Different Stages in Psychotherapy

1-7-72 rating units				Confidence Level	D^a comparison of concepts			Confidence Level	1-20-72 rating units			
7	2-6	3-5	4						4	3-5	2-6	1-7
	3	2	4	(G)	ACTUAL SELF	(3.61)	ACTUAL SELF	(F)	1	5	3	0
	5	3	1	(P)	IDEAL SELF	(4.36)	IDEAL SELF	(G)	3	0	6	0
	1	1	1	(G)	DRUGGED SELF	(2.45)	DRUGGED SELF	(F)	1	1	5	2
	5	4	0	(G)	MOTHER	(2.65)	MOTHER	(G)	3	3	3	0
	4	2	1	(F)	WIFE	(2.83)	WIFE	(F)	1	4	4	0
	7	1	1	(G)	FATHER	(5.20)	FATHER	(F)	2	2	5	0
	6	2	0	(G)	STEPFATHER	(4.00)	STEPFATHER	(F)	2	5	2	0
	4	2	2	(F)	SGT-LIVE	(3.16)	SGT-LIVE	(F)	3	3	3	0
	3	3	0	(G)	SGT-DEAD	(5.47)	SGT-DEAD	(F)	4	2	3	0
	4	0	0	(G)	NIGHTMARE	(4.90)	NIGHTMARE	(F)	2	5	2	0
	3	4	2	(G)	HYPNOSIS	(4.90)	HYPNOSIS	(F)	4	1	4	0
	4	4	1	(F)	DR. MOSS	(3.61)	DR. MOSS	(P)	3	3	3	0
	5	4	0	(G)	NCO	(4.00)	NCO	(G)	3	2	4	0
	3	5	1	(P)	AUTHORITY	(1.00)	AUTHORITY	(G)	0	6	3	0
	57	37	14						41	43	50	2

This is the generalizable distance formula ($D=\sqrt{\Sigma d^2}$). The operation for finding the semantic distance (D) between any two concepts is extremely simple; e.g., one sums the squared differences or a pair of concepts and takes the square root of the total. The smaller the number, the closer e relationship.

sizeable—5.29 at the first rating in contrast to 7.55 at the second, suggesting that there was increasing dissatisfaction with the ACTUAL SELF. Similarly, the distance between the ACTUAL SELF and SELF UNDER DRUGS somewhat diminished (7.28 and 6.16). There are two other measurements of possible significance. Again referring to Table 1 under Confidence Level, he was much less certain of his ratings at the second time around:

Confidence level	Pre-test total	Post-test total
Good	9	4
Fair	3	9
Poor	2	1

Also, looking at the units marked in rating each concept (Table 1, the two outer categories), we find he was far less extreme or more hesitant.

	Units			
	1 or 7	2 or 6	3 or 5	4
Pre-	17	57	37	14
Post-	2	50	43	41

In summary, I would say that this person was one who found that many of his established concepts were shaken by his therapeutic experience although he still had not resolved all issues. It reminded me of what he had to say initially about his drug experience at the end of our meeting: "It was as though my mind was a deck of cards that were being thoroughly shuffled; I wound up with different values."

This is *not* a case study to demonstrate the effectiveness of hypnotherapy on all types of drug abusers, nor even to illustrate the efficacy on just one such case. When the inmate went back to court he was given a six-year indeterminant sentence at another institution, closer to his home. So the proof of whether we were successful in overcoming his drug habit was placed in abeyance. The only thing that we do know, from communication with his present institutional psychiatrist, is that he no longer complains about the anxiety triggered off by his nightmares, because the dreams have ceased. Recently I also received a letter from the inmate which read in part: "I really appreciate your concern for me, and all the help you gave me at Lompoc. You showed me many things about myself I had never noticed before. The fact that our relationship was so short seemed to have little or no effect on its success. The nightmares seem to be long dead and buried. They have fallen into place in my past. Thank you for showing me how to put them there."

This case presentation is once again only an example of a type of quasi-objective, albeit clinical, evidence that a combination of psychotherapy and hypnosymbolism is effective in alleviating a troublesome symptom, i.e., nightmares. The essence of hypnosymbolism is that the therapist directly sets the stage through hypnosis for the production or recall of nocturnal dreaming, but is ultracareful to be completely nondirective about the symbols utilized by the client and their interpretation. Symbolism is always regarded as uniquely individual rather than having anything like a universal quality; the therapist very seldom knows what the symbols actually mean and therefore he is utterly dependent on the client's understanding. To put it another way, the therapist is aware that the typical dream is figuratively a projection for the client and literally a projective stimulus for him, and thus he deliberately shies away from projecting his interpretations onto it. When the meaning becomes clear through the associations of the client, then the therapist becomes relatively active again in helping him to relate the interpretation to the present problem.

Typically, the therapist deals with at least some of the predisposing factors, as well as emphasizing the precipitating events laid down by the client's dream life (i.e., the memory of the father's death which predisposed the inmate to experience the death of his NCO as equally traumatic). Whereas Freud valued dreams as providing access to the infantile sources of conflict and placed demands upon his patients for a linear type of free association leading back to the infantile substructure, the hypnotic counselor employs a *radial* type of association to amplify the immediate meaning of each dream element in the here and now. The hypnotherapist also acknowledges the difference between *objective* and *subjective* methods of dream interpretation. Relating the dream to situations or persons external to the dream is interpretation on the objective level; acceptance of dream images as reflective of the internal psychic situation of the dreamer is interpretation on the *subjective* level. One is repeatedly impressed by the fact that hypnotized subjects are capable of making the latter interpretation, e.g., the inmate's interpretation of the chess pieces as representing different segments of his own personality.

People in hypnosis lose some of the ability to be reflectively aware, and self-reactions of embarrassment, guilt, and anxiety are reduced. The attention of the subject is turned inward and there is accessibility to deep, emotional material of which the individual in the waking state is normally not aware. In a very real sense the person at a deeper level knows a great deal about his problem, but he prefers to phrase it for himself and to communicate it in therapy at a symbolic or dream level. The hypnotic relationship, which must be based upon trust, becomes a relatively safe place to experience the anxiety surrounding his neurotic conflicts symbolically and to work through the implications of these symbols in real life.

At first exposure, dealing with the dream world of clients must seem far afield from the behavioristic stance that has been assumed throughout this book, since dreams and dreaming remain as yet outside the behaviorists' characteristic mode. However, perhaps the most important single feature that can be gained from such a case study is the knowledge that using hypnosis in the manner described enables mental health staff to gain considerable insight into the causative factors underlying such troublesome symptoms, without the additional training that customarily goes into extensive psychoanalytic training. For clients it provides the cathartic opportunity to handle meaningful affective symbols—in this instance, in a very few sessions, to gain control over anxiety-producing nocturnal nightmares.

COMMENT: R. E. HOSFORD

Ever since Franz Anton Mesmer employed a form of hypnosis to cure Parisians with convulsive disorders (1781–92), psychologists have argued for and against its application as a viable therapeutic procedure. No doubt part of the problem is related to Mesmer's flamboyant use of the technique. Rather than utilizing and investigating it as a scientific procedure, he chose instead to focus on the potential for showmanship inherent in hypnosis. Thus, most individuals—laymen and professionals alike—find it difficult to disassociate hypnosis from mysticism and to treat hypnotic phenomena as normal behaviors occurring in response to specific social influence conditions.

I have long believed that hypnosis has a lot to offer in the field of counseling. Much of this belief may well stem from the personal fact that as a student I was once hypnotized in a clinical psychology course. Because the procedure was conducted in a very professional manner, my initial apprehensions were quickly extinguished and I found the whole experience to be a highly positive one. Since that time I have had considerable interest in the use of hypnosis in therapy. However, as a behaviorist I have regarded it primarily as a technique which therapists—or individuals themselves—might utilize in the modification of anxiety-related problems. Hypnosis—much like any form of deep relaxation—helps the client to relax sufficiently so that he can concentrate more objectively on the behaviors associated with his problem. The contiguous association between the relaxation and the client's thinking about or practicing those behaviors which elicit the anxiety, in effect, helps to extinguish the anxiety which he or she has learned in relation to a particular situation.

As a therapist who uses primarily behavioral approaches to counseling, I was interested in Dr. Moss's statement that "dealing with the dream world of clients must seem far afield from the behavioristic stance that has been assumed throughout this book." While he does not employ a Freudian rationale, i.e., that a client's dream life reflects his infantile sources of conflict, he does suggest that dream images are reflective of internal psychic phenomena and that under hypnosis, clients can often interpret the symbolism as representing various aspects of their own personalities. And elsewhere Moss (1970a, p. 28) says "the criterion of meaningfulness is met with these patients when, through the use of hypnosis, they (are) able to render interpretations of their own dream productions which (are) then transformed into effective action in immediate problem situations." In this sense the use of hypnosis would appear quite removed from the regular techniques of behavioral counseling.

From a behavioral viewpoint, of course, a client's behavior under hypnosis is seen not as a special "state" but as normal behavior occurring under specific social influence conditions (cf. Hilgard, 1965; Sarbin, 1965; Ullmann and Krasner, 1969). Like any other behavior, it too is maintained by its environmental consequences. However, if it is used to provide the conditions under which a client emits new behaviors, it is by definition, behavioral; if used to elicit information for the purpose of gaining "insight," then from the behavioral model it is evocative psychotherapy (Ullmann and Krasner, 1969). Dr. Moss's hypnosymbolism appears to follow the latter.

Hypnosis has been used by behavioral therapists for a number of years and for a variety of reasons. For a while it was an integral part of the desensitization process (Wolpe, 1958, 1969). As late as 1969, Wolpe (1969) reported using hypnosis in 10 percent of his desensitization cases. He employs hypnosis primarily when the client does not relax sufficiently under standard relaxation procedures or when—for the individual—emotive imagery has no sense of reality. Many therapists assume that the systematic relaxation procedures utilized by behavioral counselors in desensitization are, in fact, the same as those employed in hypnosis. While there is considerable overlap between the two procedures, recent research studies conducted by behaviorists suggest that hypnotic susceptibility is not related to progressive or systematic relaxation and specific desensitization effects (see Lang, 1965; Lang et al., 1965; Paul, 1968; Ullmann and Krasner, 1969). On the other hand, time and effort are increasingly given to effect a coalescence between the two approaches (e.g., Weitzenhoffer, 1972; Woody, 1973; Lazarus, 1973; Dengrove, 1973).

Behaviorists' use of hypnosis to heighten a client's concentration and emotive imagery is not altogether different from Dr. Moss's use of the technique in this case. Elsewhere (Moss, 1970a) he suggests that one of the main advantages of hypnosis is that it intensifies mental imagery which encourages a direct reconditioning process: "when you deal with a patient's symbols you deal with highly charged affective meaning" (p. 287). It is this conceptualization of hypnosis which I would apply to explain the excellent results that he obtained with this particular client.

That uncertainty exists in regard to the relationship between hypnosis and antisocial behavior is undoubtedly true. Dr. Moss is certainly correct in stating in this chapter that "the whole question of the use of hypnosis to bring about antisocial acts is still open" (p. 148). Reviews by Rowland (1939), Barber (1961), and an entire issue of the *Journal of Clinical and Experimental Hypnosis* (1972), include studies, some of which are well documented, in which hypnotized subjects reportedly carried out such behaviors as murder and promiscuity. On the other hand, experimental evidence is also reviewed in which hypnotized subjects consistently refused to carry out antisocial behaviors. Given such conflicting evidence, Dr. Moss's hesitancy to use the procedure in a prison setting is certainly understandable. At the same time the crucial question is, should a guard be persuaded to provide extra favors while under "hypnosis," one would need to ask whether the favors came as a result of the hypnosis per se or as a result of other related, interpersonal factors which produced the desired outcome.

I must admit, however, I have been intrigued by Dr. Moss's use of hypnosis to facilitate dream interpretation. Dreams (and fantasy) are not dealt with by most behavioral psychologists, even though in previous years they were regarded as highly important elements in a patient's analysis. Part of this may be a reaction against psychoanalysis; a still larger part may be the insistance on more objective forms of treatment. Despite the fact that in the past twenty years there has been a reawakened interest in the scientific investigation of dreams and dreaming, it is regrettable that little data still exists to support or refute the therapeutic efficacy of this technique and others which attempt to explore the unconscious. Perhaps with the use of alpha waves and/or other measures of physiological responses major breakthroughs will occur. The use that Dr. Moss has made over twenty years to objectify the meaning of dream symbols through the employ-ment of the semantic differential is fascinating. I hope in time there will be additional ways to test this theory more objectively.

REFERENCES

Barber, T. X. 1961. Antisocial and criminal acts induced by "hypnosis"; a review of experimental and clinical findings. *Arch. Gen. Psychiat.* 5:301–12.

Dengrove, E. 1973. The uses of hypnosis in behavior therapy. *J. Exp. Clin. Hypnosis* 21 (1): 13–17.

Hilgard, E. R. 1965. *Hypnotic susceptibility*. New York: Harcourt Brace and World.

J. Exp. Clin. Hypnosis. 1972. Antisocial behavior and hypnosis. 20 (2).

Lang, P. J. 1965. Experimental studies of desensitization psychotherapy. In J. Wolpe et al., eds., *The conditioning therapies*. New York: Holt.

Lang, P. J., et al. 1965. Desensitization, suggestibility, and pseudotherapy. *J. Abnormal and Social Psychology* 70:395–402.

Lazarus, A. A. 1973. "Hypnosis" as a facilitator in behavior therapy. *J. Exp. Clin. Hypnosis* 21 (1): 25–31.

Moss, C. S. 1965. *Hypnosis in perspective*. New York: Macmillan and Co.

————. 1967. *The hypnotic investigation of dreams*. New York: Wiley & Sons.

————. 1970a. *Dreams, images, and fantasy: A semantic differential casebook*. Urbana: University of Illinois Press.

————. 1970b. The hypnosymbolic treatment of a case of conversion hysteria: A treatment failure (taped 1 hour and 40 minutes). Philadel-phia: Amer. Academy of Psychotherapists Tape Library.

————. 1973a. A concentrated training course in hypnotherapy and hypnosymbolism (taped, 4 hours). Ft. Lee, N.J.: Behavioral Sciences Tape Library.

————. 1973b. Hypnotherapy to resolve a recurrent nightmare (taped, 1 hour). Minneapolis: Amer. Soc. Clin. Hypnosis.

————. 1973c. Treatment of recurrent nightmares by hypnosymbol-ism. *Amer. J. Clin. Hypnosis* 16 (1).

Moss, C. S., and Bremer, B. 1973. Exposure of a "medical modeler" to behavior modification. *J. Exp. Clin. Hypnosis* 21 (1): 1–12.

Moss, C. S., and James, P. 1970. *Black Rover, come over: The hypnosym-bolic treatment of a phobia*. With supplement, 1¾ hour audiotape of therapy sessions. Urbana: University of Illinois Press.

Osgood, C. E.; Suci, G.; and Tannenbaum, P. 1957. *The measurement of meaning*. Urbana: University of Illinois Press.

Paul, G. L. 1968. Outcome of systematic desensitization. II: Controlled investigations of individual treatment, technique variations, and current status. In *Assessment and status of the behavior therapies*, ed. Cyril M. Franks. New York: McGraw-Hill.

Rowland, L. W. 1939. Will hypnotized persons try to harm themselves or others? *J. Abnormal and Social Psychology* 4:114–17.

Sarbin, T. R. 1965. Hypnosis as a behavior modification technique. In *Research in behavior modification*, ed. L. Krasner and L. P. Ullmann. New York: Holt, Rinehart, and Winston.

Snider, J. G., and Osgood, C. E. 1969. *Semantic differential technique*. Chicago: Aldine.

Ullmann, L. P., and Krasner, L. 1969. *A psychological approach to abnormal behavior*. Englewood Cliffs, N.J.: Prentice-Hall.

Weitzenhoffer, A. M. 1972. Behavior therapeutic techniques and hypnotherapeutic methods. *Amer. J. Clin. Hypnosis* 15 (2): 71–82.

Wolpe, J. 1958. *Psychotherapy by reciprocal inhibition*. Stanford: Stanford University Press.

———. 1969. The practice of behavior therapy. New York: Pergamon.

Woody, R. H. 1973. Clinical suggestion and systematic desensitization. *Amer. J. Clin. Hypnosis* 15 (4): 250–57.

14

Measurement and Evaluation of Assertive Training with Sexual Offenders

D. Richard Laws and Michael Serber

Traditional approaches to the process of assertive training assume that the subject experiences anxiety in interpersonal relationships, and that this anxiety in turn inhibits the expression of adaptive behaviors. The goal of training is then seen as the eliciting of appropriate behaviors which will reciprocally inhibit the anxiety responses, and which will be reinforced and maintained in strength by the positive consequences of new success in interpersonal situations. It is our belief that such approaches are at least partially inadequate in their apparent supposition that the subject knows, but simply cannot express, the "right" behavior, and that therefore the therapist-trainer's job is one of "facilitation." This reasoning fails to recognize that there are many cases in which the appropriate interpersonal responses are simply not in the subject's repertoire. This is more than a failure to be assertive; it is a total behavior deficit.

In a setting such as Atascadero State Hospital there are many patients who have been arrested for practicing socially maladaptive sexual behavior. The behaviors practiced prior to admission range from exhibitionism to pedophilia (male and female), transvestism, and rape. A significant portion of our population is virtually incapable of appropriate heterosexual social relations. When observed in a role-playing situation with a sympathetic female, for example, most

Note: An earlier version of this paper was presented at the annual convention of the Association for the Advancement of Behavior Therapy, Washington, D.C., September, 1971.

patients are physically rigid; look away from the woman; speak inaudibly, if at all; stammer; stand or sit too far from the woman; and lack the range of verbal and nonverbal behaviors usually identified with appropriate heterosexual social relations.

Assertive training, or the teaching of appropriate social behavior, has been frequently cited as the therapy of choice when maladaptive social behaviors are in need of shaping. The techniques usually employed in assertive training are specific instruction, modeling, role-playing, and behavior rehearsal. The difficulties inherent in teaching social responses such as appropriate heterosexual behavior require that considerable instruction be directed at shaping the nonverbal components of such a behavior. Simple, or even complex verbal instructions, directed at all variables observed in appropriate heterosexual behavior are, in themselves, inadequate to bring about a behavioral change. We propose that, rather than globally assaulting an entire complex of deficient behaviors, the process of assertive training be simplified by a concentration on such specific variables as interpersonal distance, fluency of speech, body and facial expression, loudness of voice, and conversation pauses, followed by a systematic alteration of each deficit, one at a time.

A related issue is the fact that traditional methods, while admittedly dealing with overt behaviors, have placed heavy reliance on the judgment of the clinician and the self-reports of the subject as indices of the success or failure of assertive training. We will demonstrate how it is possible systematically to measure and evaluate change on more than one dimension and thus give assertive training a more sound empirical base. Through the use of a standardized role-playing situation which could be frequently repeated and rehearsed, variables relevant to subsequent training sessions may be independently identified, measured, and used for determining the direction that training should take as well as indices of the success of that training.

METHOD

SUBJECT

Male subject. The trainee was a 24-year-old male confined in the hospital as a male pedophile. His sexual history with both adults and children was exclusively homosexual. He requested training in heterosexual social behaviors because he wished to stop molesting children, and, if possible, to adopt a bisexual orientation.

Female subject. The female subject was a 23-year-old nurse at the hospital.

STIMULUS SITUATION

The trainee was systematically exposed to three simulated variations on a familiar social encounter: a man at a party finds himself seated next to an attractive young woman he does not know. In each situation the trainee was given a single instruction: try to pick up the girl at the party, but at the very least attempt to make arrangements to see her again. The female subject was given three sets of instruction depending on the role-playing situation. There were as follows:

A. *Situation 1, Cooperative.* She was instructed to be positively aggressive toward the client, to continuously maintain eye contact, keep up a slightly boisterous and high rate of verbalization, make physical contact if possible, and adopt a provocative posture.

B. *Situation 2, Civil.* She was intended to be cooly polite and give little encouragement, to maintain polite eye contact, speak when spoken to, avoid physical contact, and adopt a modest posture.

C. *Situation 3, Hostile.* She was instructed to be negatively aggressive toward the trainee, to oppose any eye contact, maintain hostile and abusive verbalizations, to repel any attempt at physical contact, and adopt a posture of withdrawal.

These situations were "dry run" with the female subject until we felt that the tone of each situation was clearly distinguishable and her performance was consistent in each separate situation. These structured role-playing situations then served as the independent variable in the investigation.

PROCEDURE

All training sessions were conducted by the senior author in a classroom in which were placed two student chairs, a boom microphone, a lavalier microphone, a floodlamp, and a closed circuit television system (Sony AV 3600 deck, Sony AVC 3200 camera with VCL 16 mm-64 mm zoom lens). The situation represented the initial session for this trainee. The purpose of the session was to isolate variables for manipulation in subsequent sessions; thus, there was no intervention by the authors other than to instruct the trainee and the female regarding their roles. After the trainee had seated himself, he was instructed as follows:

You are sitting next to Mrs. G. at a party. Your job is to persuade her to leave the party with you. If that is not possible, try to make a date with her for some other evening.

The female subject was instructed:

Mrs. G., you are to play Situation 1 (or 2 or 3).

The tape deck was then switched on and a two-minute segment recorded.

TARGET BEHAVIORS

After the tape was completed, it was viewed by the senior author and three graduate students in behavior modification. We attempted to isolate one or more behaviors which could be relevant to assertive training in heterosexual social behavior. It should be noted that isolation of any surplus or deficient behavior at this juncture represents only a beginning. The assumption should always be made that other behaviors requiring manipulation may emerge as training progresses. The following behaviors were initially selected as measurable:

1. *Dysfluency.* This subject showed distinct difficulty in initiating conversation although he was always able to do so. The dysfluencies took the form of repetitions of whole words (e.g., "the-the," "my-my") and blocking or struggling, particularly "starters" (devices for getting into a verbalization) such as snorts, twitches, ritualized gestures.

2. *Body expression.* The subject physically withdrew from the female as he spoke to her. This withdrawal took the form of assuming a very rigid posture, not moving the side of his body closest to the woman, gesturing with the hand not next to the woman, and looking away from her when speaking.

Rating Procedure. The rating scale used is shown in Figure 1. The scale was designed to record two-minute sections, but longer time intervals could be included on a single page, or more than one page, if it were necessary to record segments as long as thirty minutes or one hour. Before the three training situations were rated, an observer was instructed in the use of the rating scale by means of a simulated practice situation. A sound tape on which high-frequency signals were recorded at 15-second intervals was keyed to the videotape. The observer watched the simulated tape and recorded his observations at

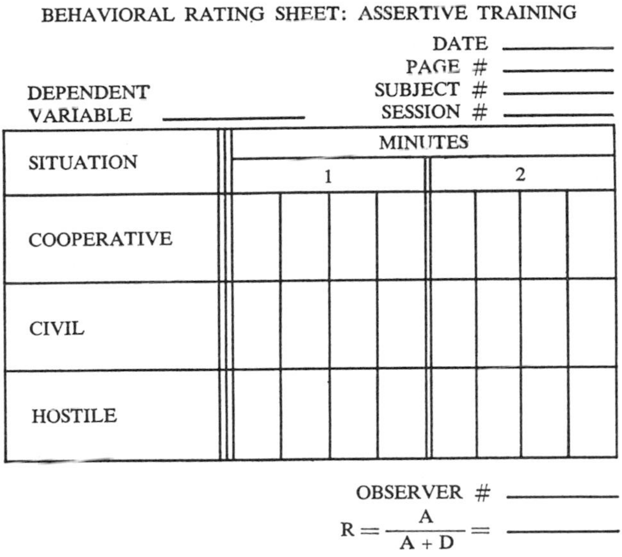

BEHAVIORAL RATING SHEET: ASSERTIVE TRAINING

DATE _____
PAGE # _____
DEPENDENT   SUBJECT # _____
VARIABLE _____   SESSION # _____

SITUATION	MINUTES							
	1				2			
COOPERATIVE								
CIVIL								
HOSTILE								

OBSERVER # _____

$$R = \frac{A}{A + D} = \text{_____}$$

Figure 1. Rating sheet.

consecutive 15-second intervals. In the interest of simplicity, each target behavior was rated differently. The absolute frequency of dysfluency in each 15-second interval was rated, but only the *predominance* of either "open" or "closed" body expression in any 15-second interval was rated. Table 1 shows the behavioral definitions used to train the observer.

RESULTS

The observational data for both target behaviors are shown in Figure 2. The upper panel shows the data for dysfluency. The ordinate indicates the number of dysfluent responses and the abscissa shows the number of 15-second intervals, with the vertical lines separating the three situations. The slopes of these cumulative curves show that the subject was continuously dysfluent throughout each 2-minute segment. He averaged 2.5 dysfluencies per 15-second interval during the cooperative situation, 2.1 in the civil situation, and 2.9 in the hostile situation. The rate of dysfluency, thus, did not change with changes in the role-playing situation.

The lower panel of Figure 2 shows the data for body expression.

Table 1. Target Behaviors

Behavior Class	Observer Task	Behavior Definition
Dysfluency	Within each 15-sec. interval, tally the absolute frequency of occurrence.	*Repetitions,* such as *Whole words:* cat-cat, my-my, I-I *Sounds:* c-c-c-cat, b-b-b-banana, ba-na-na-nana *Syllables:* fa-fa-fa-father *Prolongations,* such as s-s-s-sun, c-a-a-a-t *Blocking of struggling,* such as fa-ah . . . . ther; "*starters,*" which are devices for getting into a verbalization. Could be sounds, grunts, snorts, twitches, ritualized gestures, etc.
Body Expression	Within each 15-sec. interval, rate the predominant behaviors observed as either "1" or "2."	1. *Open.* Characterized by a generally relaxed posture, a lack of obvious muscular tension; movement tends to be easy and graceful. An open body expression may include: a. *Facial expression* of smiling and laughing, head usually up, looking directly at other person. b. *Body movements* tend to be toward the other person. c. *Head orientation* tends to be toward the other person. 2. *Closed.* Characterized by a generally rigid posture, presence of obvious muscular tension; nervous, fidgety activity; movement tends to be stiff, strained, jerky. A *closed* body expression may include: a. *Facial expression* tightly drawn, frowning head often down, not looking at other person. b. *Body movements* tend to be away from the other person. c. *Head orientation* tends to be away from the other person.

The ordinate indicates the cumulated ratings as either "open" or "closed" and the abscissa the number of 15-second intervals. Within each situation the dashed lines represent the slope the curve would assume if the predominant body expression in each 15-second interval has been rated as "1" or "open." Here we can clearly see that body expression varied with changes in each stimulus situation. In the cooperative situation the subject's body expression was rated as "open" during all but the second and fourth intervals, so there is only a slight steepening of the curve. During the civil situation, the

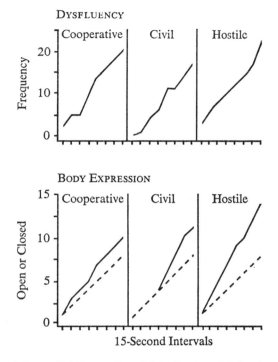

Figure 2. Observational data for target behaviors.

subject was rated as "open" for the entire first minute, then there was an abrupt steepening of the curve during the fifth, sixth, and seventh intervals. In the hostile situation, however, he was rated as showing a "closed" body expression in all but two intervals with the result that the slope of the curve is steep throughout. We observed a trend here: as the social situation became more complex and demanding, this subject showed an increasingly "closed" body expression.

DISCUSSION

The variables selected for measurement, dysfluency and body expression, were found to be relevant to assertive training with the one subject. Regarding the direction of subsequent training sessions, two points appear pertinent. First, dysfluency occurred at the same rate irrespective of the social situation. We could now choose to do two things: (1) work with the dysfluency per se through formal speech training, and (2) find the other situations in which he is also dysfluent and systematically begin to alter each one. Second, he was rated as exhibiting an increasingly "closed" body expression as the social situation became more difficult to manage. In this case we could focus on teaching him how to systematically relax concurrent with exposing him to other complex and stressful social situations. To evaluate the course of this subsequent training, we would periodically make assessments such as we have described.

It is obvious that we have not focused on all of the variables that could be measured. The content of the subject's verbalization was woefully inadequate to the task we set him. In addition, and related to body expression, was the fact that he utterly failed to use creatively the social space he was in, remaining almost completely immobile in each situation.

Since observational measurement of any social behavior is somewhat limited by the subjective judgments of the observer, we cannot emphasize too strongly the importance of clear, unequivocal, and nonoverlapping behavioral definitions. A dysfluency is a behavior of relatively precise dimensions and offers little problem in definition. Body expression, on the other hand is much "softer" in nature and does present a definitional problem. We relied on a combined definition offered by other investigators in the area of nonverbal communication but we remain unsatisfied. We feel that requiring an observer to rate which category of behavior *predominates* in a given time period is an invitation for him to be subjective, and so we feel that these data are somewhat suspect in spite of the fact that they support our theoretical suppositions. We conclude that variables which can be clearly delineated and offer little definitional problem (e.g., loudness, rhythm and speed of voice, facial expression, and conversation pauses) should be given first priority in these initial empirical approaches to the measurement of assertive training.

COMMENT: R. E. HOSFORD AND C. S. MOSS

Atascadero State Hospital has 1,200 patients, of whom 60 percent are labeled as criminally insane and 40 percent are sex offenders. The hospital has all of the criminally insane for the state of California and about half of the sex offenders. It is up to the court to decide whether a person should be sent to this hospital. If one goes to Atascadero, he initially stays about eighteen months, during which time the hospital is to treat him. After that, he returns to court with the recommendation that the patient has benefited from his stay and should be discharged, should remain at Atascadero for further treatment, or should be transferred to a state prison.

Atascadero has approximately 800 staff, about 600 of which are engaged in treatment (over 500 are psychiatric technicians in the nursing service, including 45 registered nurses). In addition, the hospital has 9 psychologists, 13 social workers and 18 physicians. Group counseling is the preferred method of treatment and is undertaken by psychiatric attendants. Atascadero has 28 wards, which are broken down geographically so that patients are always the responsibility of the same team. The institution employs 55 security officers who maintain control only of the periphery of the institution, allowing maximum freedom within the program itself. The patients are a somewhat older group than inmates at F.C.I., Lompoc, averaging 36 years. Atascadero has a fairly rapid turnover of about a thousand persons a year at a cost of $25 a day.

When we have a mental case who has also committed a criminal offense, that is, the "insane criminal" or "sexual psychopath," we have a combination which the public feels highly disturbed about, combining all the fears and primitive attitudes aroused by both mental illness and criminality. All of the patients in these categories are potentially dangerous. It is necessary to have clear awareness of these attitudes on the part of the public, for what they think about such matters has a profound effect on any program of management in such cases. Efforts to treat these people as human beings and rehabilitable are met with reactions that bear on the familiar ingredients of (1) the cry for punishment, (2) the essential hopelessness of mental illness, and (3) the fear that the offenders are getting away with something. Long ago it was demonstrated that the attitudes of irrational fear and the demand for punishment show little promise for either reducing crime or maladjustment.

Ordinarily, federal prisoners who fall in either category, pychosis or sexual psychopathy, are sent to the medical center at Springfield, Missouri; if they are sent to Lompoc, the chances are that they would be screened and transferred to the medical center. Therefore, we at Lompoc and Atascadero are obstensibly dealing with different populations. However, the newer behavioral methods are so generally applicable, they could be adapted to almost any institutional population, as could be these methods outlined in this paper of assertive training for rehabilitation.

15

A Case of Chronic Schizophrenia

Ray E. Hosford and Harvey B. Rifkin

This case represents an attempt by two therapists of differing theo-retical viewpoints, one a behaviorist and the other psychoanalytically inclined, to work with the same client. Both of us were, in effect, learning from each other as well as trying to implement a more ef-fective treatment mode for the client. The case has been reconstructed from interview notes, recall, behavioral observation data, and tape recordings made by us after various therapy sessions. Because both the client and one of us (Dr. Rifkin) left the institution before ter-mination of treatment would normally be indicated, the case is pre-sented not to support the efficacy of a particular technique but as an example of how behavior therapy might proceed with a particular kind of client having a particular kind of problem. In addition, it represents another example of a rather severe case to which coun-selors working in correctional institutions may be exposed and with which they may be asked to participate in therapy.

DIAGNOSIS

Jeff was a withdrawn, suspicious young man who, on occasion, had violent outbursts directed toward both property and other inmates. His violent attacks caused him to be placed in the segregation unit and he was subsequently admitted to the prison hospital on two occasions. During his first admission he received drug therapy only.

After his first discharge, Jeff became more withdrawn but was still combative toward other inmates. It was felt by the hospital and prison staff that he was a danger not only to others but to himself as well, and he was therefore readmitted to the hospital. Notes in his record indicate that at that time he appeared suspicious and demonstrated a very flattened affect. He spoke in a monotone and complained of hearing voices which supposedly were coming to him over the television set and which were accusing him of being involved in a conspiracy and of having illicit relations with his mother. He also related that the voices were calling him all kinds of bad names. He became embarrassed when recounting to others, at least to hospital staff, the specific profanatory terms he was being called. Although he had not completed high school, he used rather sophisticated terms such as "illicit incestuous relations" to refer to what the voices were supposedly saying to him. He found it difficult to use such common terms as "hell" and "damn" in describing words the voices used, but instead referred to such expressions as "words of profanity."

During the initial part of his second admission to the hospital he was placed on very high dosages of phenothiazines. Little apparent change occurred in his behavior. His delusions and hallucinations were untouched. He continued to be withdrawn and suspicious and was frequently seen pacing up and down the halls. At other times he would remain in his room out of contact with both staff and patients. Attempts to motivate him to do any work whatsoever resulted in little, if any, success. At times he appeared very depressed and was noted to be losing weight. His eating habits were erratic and he subsequently lost approximately twenty pounds during his hospitalization period of some seven months. It was, however, his smashing or turning over television sets and his attacking other inmates because "they were saying bad things" about him which kept Jeff in the hospital.

The symptomatology of hallucinations, delusions of persecution, and markedly flattened affect led to Dr. Rifkin's diagnosis of Jeff as "chronic paranoid-schizophrenic." The only disquieting feature in this diagnosis was his generally intact associations. His thought processes, while demonstrating flagrant misuse of vocabulary, were nonetheless basically intelligible and coherent. Thus, he was not perceived as a fragmented schizophrenic.

It was interesting that Jeff often showed rather general indifference to his hallucinations and delusions—at least he seemed generally unconcerned when he spoke of them. The fact that he reacted blandly at times was attributed to pathologic affect rather than to indifference per se. The medication which he was receiving, however, may have been a factor.

Both of us had suspicions that Jeff was more in control of his behavior than he would lead others to believe. We suspected too that he found the situation in the hospital quite reinforcing. The attention he was receiving, plus the fact that the prison hospital provided more desirable surroundings, may have helped to promote an exaggeration of his symptoms. On the other hand, Jeff did not appear to be affected by rather strong dosages of the medication. He slowed down somewhat but not to the degree usually demonstrated by patients in general, psychotics in particular. Minimal dosages of two to four miligrams of stelazine two times per day will usually produce a demonstrable effect on the behavior of a normal individual. In Jeff's case, forty milligrams of trifluoperazine and 200 to 400 milligrams of chlorpromazine, did not produce the usual lethargic behavior associated with the effects of such medication. Instead, he seemed to tolerate these dosages well, something which for some would suggest the existence of psychosis.

Thus, the initial diagnosis made upon his second admission to the prison hospital was that Jeff was "a chronic paranoid schizophrenic generally capable of responding to his environment and capable of manipulating the environment; but nonetheless one who was basically schizophrenic."

Shortly after Jeff's second admission to the hospital, Dr. Hosford joined the staff as a consultant in behavior therapy to Dr. Rifkin. Jeff was one of the cases which we worked on together.

TREATMENT

We decided to implement a therapeutic program designed to control the environmental contingencies which were possibly promoting and maintaining Jeff's behavior. Basically, contingency management refers to a program in which reinforcement and extinction procedures are consistently employed. After the specific behaviors that a client needs to increase or decrease are identified, the environment is controlled so that completion of a desirable behavior meets with extinction procedures, i.e., no reinforcement of any kind. In some cases aversive consequences might be used upon the individual's emitting an undesirable behavior.

We chose a contingency management program for several reasons. The primary rationale for such a program was the fact that medication therapy was promoting little, if any, change in Jeff's behavior; instead he was becoming more depressed and his other negative behavior patterns, e.g., talking about hearing voices and kicking-in the television set, were increasing rather than decreasing in frequency. Second, because Dr. Hosford was serving as a consultant in behavioral therapy to Dr. Rifkin, we had an opportunity to utilize both behavioral and insight techniques in the treatment process. Further, it was initially thought that the hospital prison setting would offer excellent opportunities for controlling the reinforcement contingencies of Jeff's behavior in ways that would be difficult or impossible on the outside. However, we soon found that the prison environment by its very nature severely limits the kinds of reinforcements that can be used. For example, consumable and other material rewards usually cannot be employed. The same is true of money and of extended privileges which have been found to be highly successful in similar programs in other settings. Our biggest problem, however, was lack of staff. Psychological services in prison settings at this time were extremely limited. This is a factor brought about not because prison personnel have failed to support such services, but because of budgetary problems and because of the fact that few of the trained individuals who are available are interested in working with inmate populations. In this case we had to utilize inmate nurses to carry out the program because no trained nurses are employed by the institution.

We selected two inmate nurses who appeared to be sincerely interested in working with individuals having emotional problems. Both were bright and carried out their duties well. Here again, however, the prison environment created problems in carrying out the therapeutic program. There is an informal but strongly enforced "inmate mode" which prohibits an inmate from "telling on" other inmates. Thus, we had to convince the inmate nurses that what we were trying to do was in Jeff's best interest. In addition to instruction and practice in the use of reinforcement techniques, regular college texts and other materials on the use of contingency management and reinforcement therapy per se were given to the inmate nurses. This, we felt, not only helped them to learn more about the program in which they were participating, but also to feel more involved and committed to the process.

Although this case concerns itself primarily with Jeff and the counseling involved in working with delusional behavior, another aspect of the case should be mentioned. The nurses were trained and reinforced verbally by us for working with Jeff. We decided, however, to make clinical observations of their behavior as the case progressed. In effect, we were implementing the "helper principle" of Reiff and Reisman (1965). Quite often it is the helper, i.e., the nurse in this case, who changes as much or more as the client. We did observe what we felt were significant changes in attitude and behavior on the part of both nurses who ultimately worked with us. (In reality three nurses were utilized but, as we point out later, one was released from his job in the hospital and therefore did not continue to work with us.) In addition to requesting additional reading materials on counseling, both took definite steps toward entering training programs in psychiatric nursing. One corresponded with two university nursing schools and the other sought and signed up for a training program offered in the federal correctional system. In the latter case the inmate had to agree to extend his commitment to prison as his sentence was to expire before the end of the training.

The first step in implementing the program for Jeff, however, was to identify the specific behaviors which he needed to increase or decrease. This began with both of us conducting together several interviews with him in his cell and in the hospital psychiatric office. In addition, discussions were held with the inmate nurses who were observing and recording his behavior. These interviews and observations indicated that Jeff was not eating or working, nor was he associating with other inmates. He continued to kick and to try to smash the ward television set; he talked incessantly about his voices and expressed other "sick talk" when an inmate nurse, officer, or therapist was around; and he refused to go into the prison yard or to participate in entertainment or physical exercise programs.

We felt that if Jeff were to begin functioning adequately he would have to demonstrate marked change in most, if not all, of these behaviors. Thus, we put together a program which we hoped would promote some of the deficient behaviors, e.g., associating with others, and extinguish those which were in excess or inappropriate, e.g., verbalizing about voices talking to him.

In essence, the program consisted of reinforcing Jeff verbally and nonverbally, e.g., smiling and patting him on the back, whenever he performed any of the behaviors which we had designed to be in need of strengthening. Principally these behaviors included talking or otherwise associating with other inmates in a positive manner, cleaning or performing some aspect of work in his cell or on the ward, or listening to television. The first two are rather obvious. For Jeff to function effectively in the prison generally, much less on the outside, he would have to learn again to associate with other people, practice simple cleanliness and perform other work-related behaviors. The reason for promoting television-watching, however, is probably not as evident. Jeff felt that one of the sources for his "voices" was the television. Most of the time he would merely leave the room when he "heard" comments directed to him by the television set. At other times he would try to smash the set if what he "heard" was too threatening or of a too profane nature. Further, there were other times when he would repeatedly ask if he was permitted to watch television, and when, as always, he was told that there were no regulations against it, he would still refrain from staying in the television room.

In our opinion, much stemmed from the fact that he thought about little besides his "sickness." In effect, he spent his time validating his delusions. Therefore, we felt that it would be helpful to get him to watch television more frequently and for longer periods of time. For if he could become sufficiently interested in certain television programs he might forget his "voices" for a while and might then enter into conversations about the programs. This would promote his associations with other inmates and would provide him with sources or reinforcement from them.

Among the behaviors which we wanted to diminish in frequency were talking about hearing voices, talking about being killed, and talking about never going home.

PROGRESS DATA

To determine whether or not Jeff was making progress, both frequency data, i.e., charts showing the number of times Jeff was observed performing or not performing a particular behavior, and clinical observations were collected. The inmate nurses recorded frequency counts for each behavior on a daily basis. The clinical observations were made after the program had been in effect for approximately ten weeks. Prior to Dr. Rifkin's leaving the institution to teach in a university setting, tape recordings were made of our clinical observations on Jeff's behavior in a number of areas. The observations were recorded before looking at any analysis of the frequency data collected by the inmate nurses. From time to time the inmate nurses made written comments about Jeff's behavior and these are included where relevant.

SICK TALK

Probably most important to Jeff's case was reduction of his "sick talk," i.e., hearing voices, and relating that he was going to be killed or that he was never going home. At the beginning of treatment and whenever an officer, an inmate nurse, or either of us would engage in a conversation with Jeff, he would invariably change the subject to one of the areas indicated above. Verbatim statements taken from the inmate nurses' notes are illustrative of his problem:

May 25

(p.m.) . . . Jeff talked of home and his grandmother. He is convinced that there are people that want to kill him, and that instead of being paroled, he will be transferred to another institution. . . . Jeff confronted Mr. ———— about his family. I tried to calm Jeff and told him to return to his room until he could talk with people without hearing the voices.

May 26

[Jeff] spent most of the a.m. walking in the hall. He was quiet and told other patients and nurses that he wanted to be left alone.

[Jeff] asked me if I thought he was going home in four months. I told him that I thought he was doing well and if he could stay out of trouble, he will be going home. Later [Jeff asked] Mr. ———— and was told the same thing.

May 27

[Jeff] asked if it was all right to watch T.V. . . . I told him that it was. He left the dayroom and returned to his room.

May 28

[Jeff] talked with Mr. ———— about his voices and the television set. He was told that if he wanted to go home, he would try and forget about the voices.

In order to reduce the frequency of such "sick talk" and to promote what we called "positive talk" the inmate nurses were instructed not to react to any responses Jeff made in these three areas except by yawning or by ignoring them completely. On the other hand, they were to listen attentively and react positively to any other statements Jeff made which were neutral or positive in nature. We used the same approach in our weekly interviews with Jeff except that from time to time we also interrupted his "sick talk" as if we had not been listening—with questions or statements about more positive things that he had been talking about or about topics which we knew were of a general interest to him.

One inmate nurse was instructed to have two 15-minute discussions with Jeff daily. These were to occur each morning around 10 o'clock and each afternoon between 2 and 2:15. The nurse was instructed to keep count of how many times within the 15-minute period Jeff verbalized about the voices, fear of being killed, or the thought that he would never go home. These frequency counts were taken for a three-month period from May through July, but, as we pointed out earlier, conducting a program such as this in a prison setting using inmate personnel has its disadvantages. Just after the base rates were taken and treatment began, the inmate nurse engaged in the discussions with Jeff and in taking the base rates was fired from his job because of reasons unrelated to us or the case. He thereupon "lost" his charts, which contained the base rates for the first three weeks. Thus, included here are only those frequencies for one week in May and for the months of June and July. Although comparisons cannot be made before and after the contingency management program began, it is possible to observe from the charts whether or not a change in frequency of "sick talk" was occurring. In tape-recorded clinical observations related to this area, Dr. Rifkin described Jeff's behavior as "much improved" over six months previously. He commented to Dr. Hosford that Jeff reported voices "with slightly less frequency although he is still hearing them, and he is still reacting to them. His speech is [now] interspersed with more topics of neutral personal nature with me. He inquires about where I am going and what I am going to do. He takes more of an interest in me as a person then he did previously. This is very much in evidence."

Some support of our clinical observation is provided by the frequency counts taken by the second inmate nurse. Although the counts were taken daily, weekly summations are shown for ease in presentation (Figure 1).

The frequency data indicate that Jeff generally decreased the

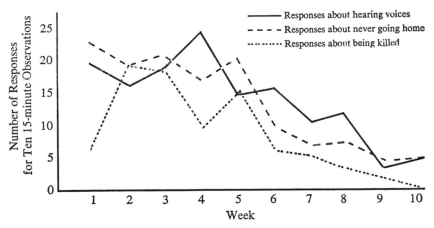

Figure 1. Weekly summaries of sick-talk responses.

amount of "sick talk" in all three areas as the weeks progressed. It was particularly interesting to note the daily summations for week five of "never going home responses." Noting a sharp daily increase from 2, 2, 1, 2 to 6, 5, we identified the dates involved and discovered that Jeff's parents had visited him on the two days in which the sharp increase was noted. The general trend, however, was in a reduction in responses about never going home.

ASSOCIATING WITH OTHERS, WORKING, WATCHING TELEVISION

To promote these behaviors, a program similar to that used in dealing with Jeff's "sick talk" was put into effect. The inmate nurses were instructed to reinforce Jeff verbally whenever they observed him watching television, working, or associating with other inmates. Smiles, pats on back, and various types of horseplay were also to be used whenever Jeff was seen doing any of these behaviors. Because one of the inmate nurses in particular was able to develop a good relationship with Jeff, he was primarily responsible for reinforcing Jeff, although we were all to participate where possible. Figure 2 provides the summaries in hours of the average amount of time per day Jeff was observed associating with other inmates, working in his cell or on the ward and/or watching television.

It is unfortunate that the base rate was "lost" for the period three weeks prior to initiating the reinforcement procedures. Again,

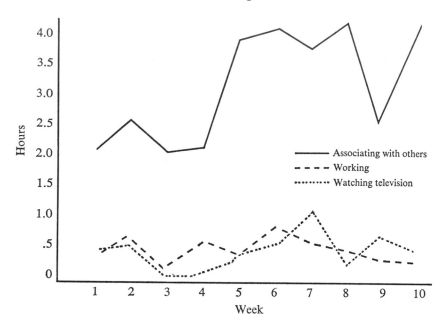

Figure 2. Average number of hours per day associating, working, watching TV.

all we can do is to look at trends. It appears that Jeff did increase the amount of time that he was associating with others as the treatment progressed. It is not known why the reversal materialized between weeks eight and nine. However, nurse records again indicated that he had two visits by his parents during this time, and this may have decreased the amount of time for associating with others and therefore the time noted for this category by the nurses. Many other factors such as changes in routine, lack of news about his pending parole, or depression following the departure of his parents, might also have affected the frequency with which he associated with other inmates. Figure 2 indicates that we had little, if any, progressive effect on Jeff's working behavior. He did increase the amount of time in which he watched television but the increase is small and would not reach statistical significance if we were to compare the last four weeks of treatment with that of the first four.

In retrospect, we realize that Jeff's baseline behavior in these three areas was very weak. Thus, instead of instructing the nurses to wait until Jeff was performing the behavior, we should have taught

them how to elicit the behavior so they would have something to
reinforce. Inviting Jeff to watch TV with them, to play cards, attend
a movie, or go out into the yard might have been effective means
for initiating the behavior. As it was they had few opportunities to
reinforce Jeff for performing any of these behaviors. On the other
hand, his verbalization of voices, etc., was well established and the
nurses had many opportunities in which to apply the extinction
procedures.

Clinical observation data, however, are more positive than the
frequency charts would suggest. Notes taken near the conclusion of
the treatment period from interviews with the inmate nurses as to how
Jeff was progressing include:

Nurse 1

"Saw changes"

"When he drops, he doesn't drop as far as he used to."

Nurse 2

"He doesn't believe that he is going home."

"He's learned to live with others and he doesn't get so uptight."

"Not so apt to hit others, can cool it."

"Appetite has picked up—he's eating."

"Generally, just easier to live with."

"He's looking for work. One inmate had to leave [and Jeff] volunteered to clean up [for him]."

"When his parents were here [last week] they said, 'He was back to
being the old [Jeff].' "

Transcriptions from our tape-recorded session near the end of
the treatment period similarly indicate that changes were observed
in Jeff's behavior.

Dr. Hosford: How would you assess Jeff's work behavior?

Dr. Rifkin: His work behavior still remains erratic; however, there
are instances of his volunteering from some duties where he had
not done this before, and to seemingly have been able to enjoy
some kind of satisfaction out of his work. So there are times when
he spontaneously volunteers for work and will do some work, but
again this remains basically erratic.

Dr. Hosford: . . . and his aggressive behavior?

Dr. Rifkin: He is not attacking inmates anymore nor is he turning

over the television. . . . Much more controlled as far as his violent
outbursts are concerned. His last "reported" incident was a pre-
meditated outburst and I do not feel [that it] was motivated by
his hallucinations. He chose his victim rather carefully as one
he knew would not fight back, that he could overpower, and that
there was essentially no risk to himself. I would not classify this
as strictly a product of his psychosis or his delusions but merely
a way of letting off steam and letting off some aggression and
hostility upon someone who he knew could not respond adequately.

Dr. Hosford: Does he appear to be socializing any better on or off
the ward?

Dr. Rifkin: Yes, he is talking with other inmates more. He is also
talking with the inmate nurses more than he did before.

Dr. Hosford: Generally, how would you describe his flattened affect
which was of concern before the reinforcement procedures began?

Dr. Rifkin: His affect has improved. At times he is very bright and
very full of laughs frequently and has a bright look in his eyes and
seems cheerful, happy, and very alive. There are times, however
when he becomes somewhat depressed and flattened. However,
even at these moments the flattening of the affect has not approached what it was when I first saw him, and so his affect [I
would say] has improved considerably. His eating habits though
are still erratic. His weight, however, has stabilized; and his
initial loss of weight . . . has seemingly stabilized and he has
not lost any appreciable amount of weight over the last two or
three months. His eating is given to spurts when he will eat his
regular three meals a day and then maybe he will eat only one or
two meals. At these times he usually appears depressed. Overall,
his weight seems to have stabilized and his eating patterns are not
a source of concern to me now as they were at one period of
time, . . . approximately four months ago.

DISCUSSION: C. S. MOSS

A long time ago I was taught in graduate courses on learning that if
I wanted to teach a dog to "shake hands," it was insufficient to keep
seizing his paw at the same time I was saying the verbal cue. It was
my nervous system that became conditioned under this procedure
while he remained relatively passive. A greatly improved technique

would have been to step gently on the paw he was to raise while saying "Shake!" and rewarding him a morsel of food or a pat on the head. This latter experience follows the paradigm of a good learning situation. Before any given response can be rewarded and learned, this response must occur. A good teacher will arrange a situation so that the learner (in this case a dog) will somehow make the first correct response.

In other words, the key to all learning is eliciting the correct response so that it can be reinforced. Insight, conditioning, imitation, verbal instruction, etc., are all different ways of producing the correct response in a learning situation. Regardless of how the response is produced, it then becomes subject to the same laws of learning. There are four fundamental factors of learning: motivation (pressure on the paw), response (lifting of the paw, or more correctly, avoidance of an aversive stimulus), positive stimulus (the stated verbal command), and the reinforcement or reward. If all goes well, the dog will shortly learn a relationship between the new signal and the response.

The point of this obviously grossly oversimplified analogy is that this conditioning procedure remains the chief method by which we human beings learn most of our emotional behavior, that is, our prejudices, preferences, superstitions, fears, phobias and even delusions. The conditioning process is the predominant type of learning during infancy and childhood followed by the intellectual processes, the age when basic attitudes, the by-products of behavior, tend to develop. What often results are highly emotionalized, extreme attitudes quite resistant to conscious control and later modification. Attitudes of this nature are often said to be "unconscious," that is, the individual is unaware of and/or finds them most difficult to alter or change. It simply means that the attitude is unverbalized and even when the subject develops "insight" he finds it most difficult to alter the overlearned habit.

A very important variable is the concept of anxiety. This concept occupies a central position in all modern-day theorizing about behavior pathology. Anxiety itself is not pathological, it is a natural accompaniment of everyday living. To a greater or lesser degree every human being is born into a life characterized by frustration, pain, suffering, loneliness, injustice, and inevitable death. Each person must develop effective methods for coping with anxiety since anxiety is often too painful to be long endured. Reduction of anxiety is often the most important reward or gain for much of human behavior, i.e., it is a primary reinforcer. The degree of anxiety in individual experiences, the various modes of expression, the defenses utilized against it go far toward differentiating one personality from another.

According to psychoanalysis, anxiety is sometimes objectless or free-floating because of major repression (motivated by the escape from anxiety). It is also highly generalizable and quite resistant to modification through learning, such that the neurotic (or psychotic) does not seem to learn readily by failure experiences. This exemplifies the so-called neurotic paradox, that is, the explanation of the emotionally (or mentally) unstable individual's self-defeating behavior when viewed externally. Freudians maintain that symptoms are satisfying in that they reduce anxiety and have multiple secondary gains. The short-term relief of anxiety often outweighs long-term advantages. In other words, alleviation of anxiety is a powerful source of reinforcement and the behavior that an individual might use in order to cope with or reduce the anxiety often appears unintelligible because it may be far removed from logical problem solving. Such behaviors serve to reduce anxiety temporarily, but do not always result in realistic solutions to problems.

It is characteristic of behavior modification to largely ignore the historical antecedents of pathology and to place instead much greater emphasis on present and future behavior. This accounts for the fact that in Jeff's case the reasons for his incestuous thoughts about his mother were strictly ignored and the therapists attended to what psychoanalysts might say are secondary gains. This was greatly simplified treatment in a sense (at least the "couch routine" was eliminated); behavior therapists can point out to considerable gains by consistent application of reinforcement principles on a variety of clients ranging up and down the whole psychotic spectrum.

In conclusion, it is unfortunate that time was not available to explore the association between Jeff and his parents, as reflected in the two regressive trends noted in the two figures. His parents apparently still held some significance for him and it might have been worthwhile to investigate what, if anything, they might have lent to the reinforcement contingencies. Finally, it was also less than fortunate that Jeff was always so highly tranquillized; it was an undetermined confounding factor that might have been eliminated, especially because his behavior did not appear to be that effected by medication.

Research is desperately needed to determine the degree to which medication attenuates or enhances learning.

A FURTHER COMMENT: R. E. HOSFORD AND H. B. RIFKIN

We agree fully with Dr. Moss that it was unfortunate that Jeff was so highly tranquilized. Although his medication was reduced considerably from that which he received during his first hospitalization and during the earlier portion of this therapy, we do not know whether the medication helped or hindered the other aspects of therapy. The fact that we were operating from two different theoretical approachs to therapy was a factor. Where possible, however, both of us greatly prefer manipulation of social-psychological variables to medication in promoting behavior change.

In addition to Dr. Moss's comments we would like to raise a few summary points relative to the case.

First, given the same personnel and budgetary limitations, there are several procedures which we would do differently. For example, we would be more careful to involve officers and other staff members more fully in the therapy program. For reinforcement or extinction procedures to work they must be consistently applied and this is only possible through the full participation of all the reinforcing agents within the individual's environment. The wrong comment, however well intentioned, if emitted at the wrong time and by the wrong person can undo much progress. In Jeff's case we have sufficient reason to believe that while the inmate nurses and both of us were conscientiously and consistently ignoring "sick talk" responses, other staff members by their responses were, in effect, reinforcing the very behavior we were trying to extinguish.

We were willing to test the hypothesis that Jeff's delusional behaviors were caused more by the environmental situations in which he had to operate before and after incarceration, than anything within himself. That is to say, we viewed delusions as the *result* rather than the *cause* of inappropriate or deviant behavior. In a prison setting, for example, opportunities for social reinforcement are minimal at best. Therefore in order to receive the attention needed to exist as an individual, the inmate must resort to attention-getting behaviors which will make him stand out. In a prison, as in a mental hospital, the ordinary inmate or patient may be largely ignored due to staff demands. By demonstrating inappropriate behavior the individual commands the attention he seeks from the busy staff workers. Once the deviant behavior pays off, chances are it will be repeated with increasing frequency. In time fantasy becomes habit and very real indeed. This is what we believe may have been the case for Jeff.

The types of reinforcement would be another area in which changes should have been considered. Verbal and other social reinforcements, though very effective with certain individuals, may have little, if any, effect on others. In Jeff's case it would have been well to have explored a variety of reinforcements; however, the prison setting seemed to us to preclude much of this. The only alternatives we considered to the verbal and social reinforcers were material and other consumable items. In future cases we would survey a much greater variety of reinforcers, such as greater use of privileges, progressive self-selection of work assignments, or the chance to perform previously frequently demonstrated behavior contingent upon performance of the desired behavior. Reinforcement menus in which the individual is confronted with a variety of reinforcing activities and items from which to choose his own reinforcer might be more effective than arbitrarily selecting one for him.

REFERENCES

Reiff, B., and Reismann, F. 1965. The indigenous nonprofessional: A strategy of change in community action and community mental health programs. *Community Mental Health Journal*, Monograph No. 1.

16

Dealing with a Drug-Induced Psychosis

C. Scott Moss

THE CASE OF JACK

The inmate was sent by his caseworker, who expressed a good deal of concern over his mental instability. The caseworker had written: "Returned from escaping a Community Treatment Center in Los Angeles. He claims that he found himself through religion. He also admits to the use of LSD. It was obvious after a series of interviews that this youth was suffering from LSD 'flashbacks.' "

SESSION 1, NOVEMBER 6

To allow the reader to empathize with the client, the initial portion is presented as a slightly paraphrased soliloquy.

I: There is an inner turmoil inside of me, between my mind and my heart. Whenever I do something that the other doesn't like, the other side rushes to attack. I have a bite here where I bit myself. It's a spiritual conflict. I'm psychic to begin with. Since childhood I've always been extremely perceptive. I can read palms, predict futures, and have visions. I'm extremely spiritually minded. I hear voices all the time. As a matter of fact, everything I've done in the past three to four years was all spiritually involved. I was told to do everything I did.

I used to take LSD and meditate under a Yogi. We used to go into a spirit and the spirit used to come down to us. For a long time I was demon-possessed and I didn't even know it. The only reason I knew was when they were cast out of me. A bunch of preachers got hold of me (when I left here) and I was led into becoming a Christian and the demons were cast out of me. I was a raving maniac and didn't even know it. They settled me down and kept me for three to four months. There was a lot of prayer and real intensive spiritual guidance. I was cleared up and I was saved. I have been taken over by spirits, too (in contrast with demons). Naturally I don't do things that I don't want to do, but I do things against myself because of other spirits who take me over.

I had a confrontation with the Devil. As a matter of fact he lived within me for a long time and he was doting on me. There was a whole group of people with whom I came in contact. My brother and I moved away from home and got an apartment and we didn't have many friends. We noticed a lot of spiritual oppression and we could hardly move because it hurt. We couldn't even work and so we turned into bums. A bunch of people moved down the hall from us and they couldn't pay their rent so they moved in with us, too. We'd smoke weeds and take a lot of drugs.

All of a sudden I could see that one of my acquaintances was the Devil. It was as if a negative power came to me and I had to battle it, so my spirit came out of me and protected me. There was a lot of conversation between God and the Devil and I felt a lot of fear. Sometimes I am very poor and don't even talk to people and at other times I am the center of attraction and everybody thinks I am fantastic. This happens to be one of those times.

Little by little, after I talked with Him (and it took a lot of intelligence to know what was going on), it turned out there was at least twenty-five devil-friends and ten or fifteen good spirits that helped me. I was like a mediator. I took from the bad and took from the good trying to solve problems, like you trying to solve problems with the inmates and the Establishment.

He came to me with a problem and he gave me LSD. He said you have a lot of wisdom and it would take very little for you to solve this problem but he wouldn't tell me what it was. (I know I'm shooting up pretty high, but I will go on up and if I'm crazy we will come back down and get it straightened out). He talked to me just as though I was God. He said, I can't take it any more, because I'm wise enough to know that if I come to you with my problem it would be better than just leaving it to myself because I would just destroy myself, because I am that foolish and afraid.

I'm not crazy, but I am dangerous to myself. There are lots of times that I get in over my head, very foolish. Spirits guide me and when I don't do it I get in lots of trouble. If I smoke cigarettes I get hurt real bad. My mind gets muddled and I can hardly think. It varies from twenty minutes to two days. I suffered from a crippled mind. But there is a lot of activity going on to repair the damage that I do. I kind of wanted your opinion as to what it looks like, what it is mentally, because I'm not educated. I was a psychology major because I like things like this. That's what got me into this, being interested in my own mind. But I wasn't learning fast enough, so I decided to go out in the world. [Now] I have learned more in four years than anybody that I have ever met.

I believe myself to be the wisest person that I have ever met and the most experienced. You're probably more educated but in dealing with spiritual things I am the wisest in that I have been given much wisdom and that sets me apart. It is like a movie star who can't be touched because she's too pretty.

It's kind of fun sometimes because I talk to God a lot. I don't think I'm God, although there is some debate within me about that, too. If I was anybody I would be God himself, and I still think I am, so that's a problem. I'd like to find out I was wrong, but too many times I am proven right. I have heard that lots of times people thought they were God and they went to the crazy house and got fixed, but I don't ordinarily go around telling people I'm God. Although I have in the past just to see if they could prove me wrong.

Just the other day I was walking around the field and I had been bad. I had eaten a whole lot of lunch. I was gluttonous or I have a need for affection. I had put myself in a negative spiritual condition. The Lord asked me to run around the track and I said I didn't want to, I was too tired. Then the Lord said that he didn't want this to happen but "know that I love you and will come back and fix you up later." So a guy came up to me and I knew what kind of a spirit he had (I was to do some spiritual dealing). He told me his story in disguised or code talk. I asked him questions and he talked (questions and answers don't have to be related). I let him go from some of his bonds because he was a negative spirit, pretty powerful and he has to be kept at pretty close range or he will begin hurting people. So he gave me a progress report and I, in turn, through the authority that sometimes was given me, let him go. So he goes his way and I go mine. I don't like that kind of work because it gets me involved with him. I have to take all of his hangups and I have to go back and work on them through mental exercises and spiritual awareness; a lot of things that I'm really good at—getting rid of garbage.

I'm a spirit dealer like a marijuana dealer. But I'm only human so if I go around talking this to people they would think I'm crazy. Lots of people are afraid of me. [Thus] I make myself very humble and so that people that walk by me think I'm a dud. People can see my spirit if I let them—it is like flies to honey. She would never have approached me going around the track if I had been in a big, strong, healthy state, because we are enemies. Only when I drop down and become a lesser degree and she's not afraid of me does she come over and tell me her problems.

I'm like a spiritual doctor. I had a dream about this. I haven't had a dream that hasn't come to pass. For example, what I dreamed last night will happen today. I just remembered a dream I had. I dreamed about a four or five page letter of appeal to free my conscious mind of the strain of my spiritual body, and just as I was running this down to you I had a flash, and I told you I was a surgeon, a spiritual surgeon. I remember that I was talking to some bigwig, like you, someone with authority, spiritually, asking him to free me. I told him I was a surgeon and he just flashed it back to me. I don't know whether it was your spirit that I was talking to or not but the parallel is here again. I just remembered that last Sunday in my dream the very thing happened, which is what happens to me a lot. That's another reason why I think I'm not crazy because it has never been wrong. In three years,

I've never made a mistake yet. I'm perfect! It keeps coming down, I'm perfect! Perfect! Perfect!! I don't make any mistakes, of course, because God puts into me whatever he decrees.

T: Well, then, what is the source of your conflict?

I: What I have been talking about is one source of what I don't like. The other one is that I can't eat certain foods. Now my prescribed diet should be a bowl of cereal in the morning, skip lunch and do a lot of physical exercise, and then at supper just eat vegetables. But what I actually do is go in there and eat like twelve eggs for breakfast every morning. I've run as many as ten miles in just a matter of—I do a lot of intense work. I'll go and get real dirty—spiritually negative. I'll pick up a lot of bad things, and then I'll just work it off as hard as I can. The way I pick up bad things is by eating. I eat physically and mentally and I take in all the garbage—mental garbage. Of course, a lot of people shove it on me because they don't like me. They shovel *ignorance* into me. [Pause]

T: [I then deliberately inject] What's your first name?

I: John.

T: Let me note that down since I only have your last name [I go through the process of writing it down].

I: I don't go telling everybody this kind of stuff—I don't expect people to know because I've been real quiet. I've been a model inmate, I made it out of here (the first time) in model time. I am the associate warden's clerk and my caseworker thinks I'm just a fine young man—and I am—I do a good job with everything I do. I'm in the choir and I go to church and I'm a Christian, but that is as far as it goes. Except when I'm on business. So even if this only comes out as an experiment, I'd like to get rid of this life. I don't want to hear voices! I don't want to have weird feelings! I don't want to be trapped!

T: Do people call you John, or Jack, or what do they call you? What do you prefer to be called?

I: Jack.

T: Jack? O.K. The things that you've related to me in this half an hour make you sound very crazy. If I were of a mind to categorize people into being crazy or mixed-up or nuts, and people who are more normal, perhaps I'd classify you as being off your rocker. But I've worked in this sort of business for many years and initially I used to think that some people were crazy and some people were normal. But eventually I came to recognize that what I was classifying as being crazy, is simply a role that people play. You're motivated to play this particular role toward me now, and I don't even begin to suspect why you want to do this.

I: Well, do you think it's true?

T: Not for a moment.

I: [Incredulously] Really?!!

T: Not in the sense that you've been saying.

I: Well, it's absolutely, positively true! I've got to be crazy!

T: Well, the point is that all of these roles that you talk about—God and the Devil, and the conflict with the Devil—

I: Do you believe in God and the Devil?

T: Not in the sense you're talking about.

I: You actually don't believe in Jesus Christ?

T: Not in the sense you're talking about it. Notice I always qualify the statement: God and the Devil simply don't intervene in human personalities the way that you experience it.

I: The story of Job in the Bible when God and the Devil definitely intervened—

T: Of course. I'm saying there are many competing parts of any personality and this is simply the way that you have learned to deal with the conflict that you then personify as the Devil and God.

I: Well, who is this person who came out in the express person of Satan many times to me?

T: This is you, and you're simply not accepting the responsibility for that aspect.

I: It's my own will against myself?

T: That's right! These different offending parts of your personality are in conflict, and when you recognize them as such, we have broken down your biggest defense. To put it another way, instead of projecting out and making these different aspects into spiritual beings, you'll come to accept that they really all belong to you.

I: Very good! So let's take the Devil out of it and begin putting "desires" and "loves" or "mind" for Devil and for God and I can accept that rather than just doing away with this other, call it bullshit. Now I actually feel a pull from my stomach wanting chow, which is a normal thing because I haven't eaten breakfast. Whatever it is it is hunger for what you have let out there and my mind is extremely hungry because I am extremely intelligent.

I probably have an IQ of 125 or 130. My mind is controlling me at the moment completely.

If I were to just let go I might go into convulsions or say "please help me, I am going crazy," or just have all of this love come bursting out. I might start crying and let all of this love come bursting out because I have been freed from these bums. My heart is full of love and it would probably be a little embarrassing for me to express it which is probably my hangup. My heart wants to little by little let you have everything I've got. But my mind isn't going to let this happen. My mind is going to destroy all of the fitting pieces because first of my guilt complex which doesn't want to be helped and second, my hunger. I pray four to five hours a day and other intelligent spirits have shown me that if I do this and this, it will be fine, but I always end up saying that I don't want any of that.

Let's say we have taken the eggs and some flour and sugar and yeast and we can make a cake out of this and let it bake in the oven. It will take time and patience for this thing to come about, and we'll be able to enjoy the fruits of our labor, but all I see is an extremely starved-for-love person. I see an egg and the flour and the yeast, and all I want to do is to grab the egg and to eat it, and I'm going to grab the flour and get it all over me as I try to eat that, and then I'll down any sugar and we'll end up never having any cake.

T: And with all of these ingredients, what is the process that it must go through before we can make a cake?

I: Slowing me down, keeping me from trying to destroy what I have, to train me, to changing my mind. We have all the ingredients taken out of my mind and put into a box here; now if I lewd it, rape it, rape myself for any peace that I've gotten from this.

T: It's interesting, I thought you'd give another answer to this. I thought that with all of the ingredients and allowing it to go through a process where you would make a cake, I thought the kindling process would be l-o-v-e.

I: I think there is sufficient love here. I would say it was nature, patience, care—you're right, *love*, I don't know why I didn't say that.

T: Well, this is a complex process—to build and bake a cake *out of you* and what you are talking about is simply the many different aspects of you. Over time we hope we can take each of the different parts and mold them together under love so they will eventually result in a cake. Despite the resistance. This is what I expect.

I: Right, correct! My mind is used to doing things very rapidly but my heart is not so. I can make a cake *if* my mind can be changed, if I can accept this. If my heart can accept this, but I don't know if it has. If it is accepted, then I can go eat lunch. But if it hasn't and I go eat chow, then I will pick up enough negatives to destroy this.

T: Your going to eat chow is the first step and it shouldn't be a conflict at all.

I: But I have real fear of it—ever since I was demon-possessed.

T: Don't fall back into the vernacular that you did earlier. Let's accept that the *demons were you.*

I: Then we have to eliminate the spirituality out of me! I used to work for the Devil—I can't give it up as theory! I used to rip people's souls off!

T: You can say that *as long as* you admit that it wasn't really real.

I: Then I can let my spirit have its problems and I can give you my problems.

T: I don't think we can divide it that neatly, since the spiritual is part of your total personality. I'm willing to accept a God and a Devil but I'm only telling you that the way you perceived a God and a Devil—

I: [breaks in] I perceived them as my enemies and they gave rise to personal conflicts.

T: Yes, that's right.

I: O.K. I've got you. People wake me up in the middle of the night and tell me different things. Say a guy wakes me up and says that if you don't say a prayer the Devil will get you.

T: As far as I am concerned this is pure and utter nonsense. It is simply one part of your telling the other part of you to do certain things, and if you refuse then will come maximum retribution.

I: Wow! That gives me a lot of freedom, man! It's pretty hard for me to accept, because it makes a fool of a lot of people that really think there is somebody big. But you are telling me exactly what I want to hear. I'm escaping from all of my responsibilities, so I'll go eat chow as though it was nothing.

It may seem as though I'm putting myself above you but I'm just throwing myself at your feet. I'm not being your psychologist. I realize that I'm an unstable creature. If I seem overbearing and not accepting what you are saying, in my heart I am more than grateful for everything you can tell me. I do accept what you say.

Comment

There is no question that Jack is convinced that he is the victim of a diabolical, negativistic, and perverse intelligence whom he has been schooled to call the "Devil," as opposed to an opposite, enlightened, humanitarian intelligence whom he has personified as God. Thus, there is a division between the "bad" and the "good" parts of the personality (which calls to mind numerous cases of multiple personalities). Any creature-pleasure calls forth immediate retribution, which Jack compensates for by the illusion of omnipotence and omniscience, but in the process he is effectively immobilized. Obviously, he is not happy over this situation and he is motivated to seek help to reduce his ever-present conflict.

Rather than exploring the background to see how these dynamics were learned, my initial strategy calls for a simple six-step program which focuses exclusively on the here-and-now: (1) After listening to him more-or-less uninterruptedly for the first part of the session, I then intrude to ask him, very concretely, his first name and what he prefers to be called; (2) I then state that for me the term "crazy" no longer has a function and over his protests I prefer to think of even psychosis as just another role; (3) I undertake an alternative explanation in terms of conflicting parts of his personality in lieu of his superstitious mysticism; (4) I ask him to begin to substitute reality for his current preoccupation with unreality; (5) next I attempt to persuade him that it is all right to eat without any fear of retribution; and (6) I promise full emotional support.

SESSION 2, NOVEMBER 16

After the first session, Jack proceeded to eat several hearty meals, but with a growing sense of uneasiness. We were scheduled to meet the following week, but unfortunately the press of other demands kept me from seeing him. On Friday (November 13) the evening officer warned me that he felt the inmate was slipping. He recorded the following message: "This morning [14th] I heard water splashing and heard someone singing. It was this man. When I checked he was washing his face in the toilet bowl and splashing water. Later he had gone to bed. He covered up his head and ears and was praying aloud. He repeated the phrase, 'Lord, have mercy on my soul.' "

Saturday evening Jack was ostensibly caught up once more in a conflict between spirits and the Devil as to whether he should eat or fast. Finally in great frustration he deliberately threw his chair against the window in his cell, knowing that he would be sent to the segregation unit. Locked up, he felt much more secure against his tendencies to act out, including thoughts of suicide. The inmate told the officers on the segregation unit that he was hearing voices and they were telling him to do things that he didn't want to do.

When I saw him he was very disheveled and had not eaten since he came in. He didn't even want the Bible because of the urge to tear the pages. He also displayed several self-inflicted gouges on his face. We spoke primarily about his "mystical experiences." I had the impression that his grasp of reality was quite tenuous. During the Monday morning segregation committee meeting, I explained that he was repelled by the high degree of structure of the clerk position to which he had just been appointed, and consequently he was reassigned to "indoor maintenance," essentially a job of keeping a restricted part of the yard within the prison policed. I also persuaded the committee to release him from isolation, since the crisis had passed and the counseling relationship would continue.

SESSION 3, NOVEMBER 19

T: Now how did that happen [pointing to the marks on his cheeks]?

I: It happened when I was in the hole. Kind of a climax of the whole thing, and probably it set me back quite a bit. But I liked being in there [segregation]. There wasn't much pressure.

T: You were free of all responsibility, is that it?

I: Well, I felt good in there, you know, because [phone rings] I could just let go. I was a lot freer without any worries. When I went in there I felt like I was never coming out, so I completely let go and felt a lot better as a result.

T: [Phone still ringing] Do you wish you could have stayed?

I: I feel a lot better now that I'm out. I've got a new job. I used to be the associate warden's clerk. There was a lot of stress and stuff to it, you know, a lot of typing and mental exercise; but one thing that kinda freaked me out because I knew I couldn't make typing errors.

T: Let me answer the phone. [Pauses] I think when I get up it will stop!! [T. gets up and the phone stops]. See, magical thinking!

I: I figured, well, that I blew the job. It was one of those things that you want, but once you get it there is so much responsibility it would be grueling.

T: So how about the scars, where did they come from?

I: I saw this thing was pulling together, and I really wanted it to work. I thought, wow, nothing tragic has happened! I haven't flipped out in a couple of days and I feel a lot better, maybe it will continue this way. I think I get a lot of anxiety whenever I think something good is going to happen. I just freak out because I know nothing will happen. And that could be the reason that I stop things from happening because I'm afraid of the consequences, I don't know what to accept or what to reject. But this I was beginning to accept. And me accepting the fact or several facts: (1) I'm sick, (2) I could get well, (3) there's a way to do it, and (4) it's all fitting together. Anyway, it started some pretty other freaky things happening, because I was starting to be strong within myself in believing in something.

T: From borrowed strength?

I: Yes, through you. Well, something else flared up, but I couldn't see it, I could only feel it. Something else was losing ground, let's say, and I got up and started to eat breakfast, and just as I sat down I felt afraid to eat, but knew nothing could happen because I had eaten four or five meals and there had been no problems. So I started to sit down and eat it, and just as I did, something in me said, "Gee, I wish Jack would wash his hands." Just at that moment when I started to get up—I just freaked out.

T: What do you mean by "freaked out?"

I: I scratched my face.

T: But who scratched your face? It makes no sense that *you* scratched you face. I wouldn't scratch my face, nobody else would deliberately scratch their face, so to do this you must be back at playing roles, and assign some part of you to scratch your face. So who did it? You didn't do it. Do you see what I'm saying?

I: Yes. I can't believe how simple this is.

T: Why not?

I: Just in that I don't even want to assume this double role thing. I'm really amazed that I'm sitting here and I actually have made two or three attempts not to be that guy over there. Now that I try to relate to him, I find that quite a bit of it is gone.

T: Isn't that good?

I: Yeah! That's what I'm saying, usually I have all these answers and now I have to think who did it.

T: You know, a moment ago in relation to the phone, you asked me in prior sessions, if I believed in things that are mystical, supernatural. And I tried to make it clear to you that I don't believe in them. And there are two things that I did in connection with the phone. Can you remember what I did?

I: Well, the first thing you did when you stood up, you went "Ah ha, now you watch. We all know how this works." (1) The phone stopped and I was going to comment (for example) that when you go into a restaurant and you want your food, you light a cigarette and immediately it is there. (2) When you stood beside the phone you said "Phone, do you realize I'm standing here" and when it realized you were standing here you went walking away like a baby from a toy. Like, "Please don't know I'm escaping you."

T: Now, the thing is, I don't believe for an instant that my actions affected the ringing of the phone at all. Or that my sneaking away did, but there was within me a memory of thirty or thirty-five years ago when I was ten or eleven years old. I would have said that the phone's got to stop ringing! Why doesn't it stop ringing? I'll stand up and it will stop ringing! And it stops! From my faint memory of things and the magical way that things develop in a person's mind, I can empathize with you when you are talking nonsense, mysticism, supernatural.

I: Do you credit anything but nonsense to coincidence?

T: Well, you'll have to spell out what you mean.

I: Well, this is the first thing that got me to believing. I noticed a lot of coincidences in my life. I stand up and wave my hand and the lights go out; I wave my hand again, and the lights go on. I do it again, and it doesn't happen, but the first time it did. I say, isn't that interesting. Course that's never happened to me. Do you credit anything to life like that? Because similar things like that happen repeatedly in my life.

T: Nothing but pure coincidence.

I: You don't accredit anything to more than coincidence?

T: No, not any more. I used to believe that when I was a little boy and I was thinking about something if I heard somebody say a word that I was thinking of, or the radio said the same word I was thinking of, or the TV, I used to imagine that if I jotted down all the words, eventually they would spell out a secret message to me. But the point is that I remembered these things from when I was a little boy, and then I eventually outgrew them [knock on wood]. But I have a sneaking suspicion that if I was ever under enough anxiety and I became psychotic, that I would go back and start to believe it again.

I: I had a thought. I thought that I heard your voice, a conversation between you and me, a short one, but you said "you think" and I had just said "I think." I don't even know where I got that. I think it with the very purest baby mind. I said child's mind, and that's where I came from with a baby mind. It's a childhood thing.

T: That's it exactly.
What I see in you is a person who for whatever reason is under sufficient pressure that you begin to come apart at the seams, you become superstitious. And the task is how to weld you back together again. It's all right to think things, it's all right to think that when you take a word and hear it quite accidentally from another source, it may add up to a secret message. But you don't tell people this.

I: How come? You don't tell people that if you think it in your heart.

T: Because I don't think it in *my* heart or my head any more.

I: This is something that has always gotten me into trouble. I was always telling people, "Guess what happened to me?" And they look at me kinda funny, and I say, "It really did!" You know? And they'd go, "All right." But I don't think I ever really quit telling people.

T: There is something very intriguing about you! And the fact that in a sense you still believe in fantasy and imagination, even to the extent of believing they actually exist. I wouldn't for the world have you not have some memory of them.

I: Is it possible that if a person was under enough mental strain, like say he lost his mother at a very early age, his father remarried a woman that he never enjoyed, the woman took the father away from him, he had brothers and sisters and the family was completely disrupted at a very young age, he was forced out into the world when he was 15 years old, completely rejected by his father whom he loved terribly, his mother was in a mental institution, [he] was in a Catholic boarding school and was coddled very much, kind of put out in public schooling and had to face all these big boys and things—might he revert back to his innocence or his youth for comfort?

T: Is this you?

I: Yes.

T: Well, I would say that he never really grew up.

I: Yes, he stopped growing at age 10 or 12. Because I remember a time about that age when something happened to me, I don't remember what it was but I said I'd rather die than live, and I just went inside of a shell.

T: Let's go back to what you said about the way you were brought up. A child becomes essentially the way he's treated. If he doesn't have stability, if he isn't treated with love and affection by the same consistent people over time, then something doesn't add up correctly and he becomes something like you are. You were not consistently loved in growing up. And that's why you have all these problems now. It seems to you as if these are actually different people out there who are tugging and trying to get you to do widely different things.

I. They have softened up a great extent—the tugging. The "good guys" say, well you can sort of relax on this and the "bad guys" say, well, we don't have this power over you any more. These are some changes that have happened the last couple of days. I started smoking. I started smoking because I always wanted to and didn't because it was bad. I'm also quitting the choir.

T: Why?

I: Because it's kind of a responsibility that I don't want any more. When I was younger and was in the choir it was security. And when I look back on it, it was just no longer something I wanted to hold up. And I'm not even going to church. Which may or may not be for the best. I'm going up to see the chaplain when I leave here.

The other thing, I quit a Bible study class which was absolutely driving me berserk. It was the heaviest thing on my head. It was so intense, you know, where they break everything down. Bibles have always freaked me out. I remember when I was a little kid, I didn't ask my father, but I had this question go through my mind maybe ten or fifteen times, "What are the rules, what's the goal, I want to know how to play and how to live and nobody ever told me."

T: So you turned to the Bible?

I: I never had a Bible when I was young. When I was 20, I found a Bible, just when I came here and started reading it.

I was brought up without much strength in morals. But I didn't know you should have morals, I didn't know it was a sin and would hurt you to be wild. And then I found out when I came here that life is bigger than the merry-go-round and so I clung to the Bible. But then there was this deep rejection of it, too.

T: So you've vacillated back and forth, for example, not knowing whether you should fast or gorge. And the thing is, all these decisions that you're trying to make for yourself in the past, present and future, aren't really a matter of death.

I: That's right. I won't die if I smoke, I won't die if I quit going to the choir.

T: As soon as you really accept this, then the voices will grow quieter and quieter and eventually cease.

I: I kind of had a "kiss off" the other day. I'll relate this experience to you right out of my heart. It's the end of a fantasy story. Remember that song "Puff the Magic Dragon"? Puff the Magic Dragon lived by the sea, and frolicked in the autumn mist in a land called Hona Lee. Little Jackie Paper used to come to the dragon and bring him strings and fancy things. But one day Jackie didn't come back, and the dragon's scales fell like rain. For dragons live forever, but not so little boys.

The other day I smoked my first cigarette. And with that decision a voice came to me and said, "Today you are kicked out of the kingdom," and this girl's voice said, "You're no longer fit for service," and again I really wasn't worried. Well, I acted a little concerned, but I don't even know what kingdom I'm being kicked out of.

And after that I changed. I knew I was going to start smoking, and I quit the choir and I did this and I did that. Things just sort of fell away. I was being ousted out of the cradle, onto my own two feet.

T: All of which indicates that little by little, you're growing up and you no longer believe in the things you did originally.

I: Another question: I believe that if you take a man and aim him in two different directions, exactly opposite—let's say a pair of identical twins, and you sent them in two different directions, one on a righteous path and guide him all his days, in a fully rich, wonderful planned childhood all the way up till he was 30 years old, trained him through school and got him this job and then just let him go, he would find certain things in life; and you took the other guy and just smashed him, not just let him go but smashed him every way, that both these personalities would find and would be searching for the same thing and they would have the same number of experiences if they were balanced.

So if this guy met this guy, one would say bad and the other would say good because their personalities would stay the same. So where dragons are over here in this guy, there must be something in this guy to take the same place, let's say tycoons, to take the place of dragons. Because I feel, that for every fantasy, there's the reality and for every reality, there's a fantasy. Someone who never finds the reality will probably still hold on to the fantasy because a growth process is a grabbing on and letting go of, grabbing on and letting go of, and you can't let go until you have something equal to grab on to.

T: You are again talking about yourself. And you're also saying that there isn't that great degree of difference between fantasy and reality?

I: Yes, I guess so.

T: Don't for a moment give up the fantasy just as long as you recognize that it is fantasy. There's a certain part of life that can be lived only in fantasy. But it is correct that the fantasy will turn itself into reality and vice versa.

When you were describing two personalities who were sort of mirror images of each other, one goes for reality and the other for fantasy, and you in a sense were talking about yourself, of course, and this is the way in which you were sort of torn apart by God and the Devil—one represented Heaven and the other Hell. All I'm trying to get you to see is that it really doesn't make any sense to have this extreme decision around every action.

Don't make a federal case out of everything. Don't make a supreme issue out of whether you smoke or don't smoke, whether you go in and have a bite to eat or not. None of it is really *that* important. Except for a person who is bound up in himself as you were and everything you did had an issue to it.

I: I always kept going to absolutes. One time I bragged that I only dealt in absolutes, and if someone said this I would quickly slide it to which of the absolutes it came from, dividing them as I was dividing, which makes me pretty hard to get along with.

T: Do you still feel you're playing a role in here with me, that when you leave you'll slip back into something else?

I: I'm finding that things are explaining themselves away and disappearing much more rapidly than I had ever imagined. But I have since dropped my Devil and God load, picked up lesser loads of things like coincidences, even higher than that, let's say myths or downwind levels from that, fairy tales, animals and fairies now. I came by this book called *The Tolkien Reader* by J. R. R. Tolkien. I came upon this little fantasy book about elves and dwarfs, and I got so interested in that, ordinarily I don't read, my mind has not been able to read for over a year. And all of a sudden I started reading this book on fairies. The last book I was reading was in El Reno, believe it or not.

If someone else were to come along and explain that these voices could be the fairies instead of angels or God, since I have found the book I've wondered whether these might have influenced me. They fit my situation to a T—like a horoscope always seemed to fit.

There is a short book by Tolkien that tells where fairies come from, what they are, how they got to be, what myths they come from, how they influence people's lives—and I went wow! Why did this book come to me just now when I was looking for something else?

T: That's really another remarkable coincidence—like the Bible was three to four years ago.

I: That's nothing—wait until I get a hold of your head. The coincidences that led me to finding this book are so remarkable—

T: Pardon, what did you say a moment ago?

I: "You wait until I get a hold of your head." As I am slowly falling into your confidence, you are also revealing parts of yourself to me. I should have said getting hold of your heart but I said head because I was a little afraid of the combat if I said that I was winning you over. People fall under my influence. First because I am lovable, and two, because I am intriguing, and three, because I am innocent and simple, and four, because I need help so desperately.

T: That adds up to an almost unbeatable combination.

I: It is an unbeatable combination. If I seem over-egotistical it is only for protection of you. There are a lot of heart traps that we fall in. My personality wavers as a breathing thing would. Maybe on our seventh time you will see something in me. I guarantee it. You will see something quite delightful to your heart in me. I don't think you'll resist me. You're not afraid of me. I will receive much wealth from you and I, in turn, will reintroduce you to something that you have lost and will be very happy to gain again. It's a gay freedom which I have to offer. It would touch your heart as any fairy tale would. When I get your heart I'll know what you believe in, so I can tell you something that you can accept. I'll really hit you and go by your intellectual thing and straight to your heart.

Comment

In the first session I had created a quandary through posing an alternative solution to the conflict which completely preoccupied Jack. What culminated on November 13 and 14 was a very real crisis and it represented the throes of the dilemma that he was going through. It was his "mystical" solution (with which he was not at all happy) versus reality *as I defined it*. I have no hesitation taking an authoritarian stance, if I feel the client has a chance of accepting it. In a sense, it was like undergoing another religious conversion, but one which hopefully would bring added peace to his mind.

In this, the third session, I make the point that I had the ability to empathize with him; hence, the telephone episode which, in turn, precipitated the discussion of "coincidences." I called on my memory to supply events which were similar to the paralogicalness that he was presenting but I was always careful to label them as childhood beliefs. I think the point was made when he commented on a coincidence in our immediate relationship, "I don't even know where I got that. I think it was the very purest baby mind . . . It's a childhod thing."

As recorded on the next page of the transcript, he begins to relate some of the traumatic events that were precipitated in his very early adolescence. Earlier in my career I would have immediately latched on to these and begun exploration into the painful, earlier incidents; but now I am much more restrained. I have long since restrained myself from exploring past events which might be revealing for the therapist but do little for the client. I feel that Jack was progressing towards restoration of reality, and I was hesitant to inquire into past circumstances. (From reading through his case folder, I knew that early in adolescence his father had impregnated his secretary, divorced the mother, and married her. This, of course, played extreme havoc with the Catholicism in which the family had been raised. The mother subsequently went to a state hospital, where she remains to this day). He ends up saying that he has substituted J. R. R. Tolkien's belief in fairies and elves for the prior belief in the supernatural as being influencial in his life.

Jack indicates that we have had some heart-to-heart confrontations in our reminiscences about childhood (which I would concur with). He ended up with a challenge: If I am changing him then I should also be aware that he is going to change me! viz., he ends up with a promise that he will "win my heart" and "bring the little boy back out in me"—thus trying to reinstate my childhood fantasy.

SESSION 4, NOVEMBER 27

I: Things are much better.

T: That's nice, they really should be, because you were exercising yourself about a lot of things which didn't need to be.

I: It's funny how some things have just fallen away, and other things have combined. It seems as though I've spread things out. I've made many things out of one thing. For example, the simple practice of enjoying something. Instead of just enjoying it, I have broken it down into every little facet of how I did things, so that I wouldn't make a mistake, so that I could keep track of myself. Like eating or relaxing. When I began to feel that I was really up tight, I felt that relaxing was a wrong thing to do. So every time I would do something I would define it and label it, and try to control it. And in so doing, my imagination had a computer so I wouldn't lose myself, so I wouldn't get away from myself, so I wouldn't be free. Because I was afraid to do things. When I'd do something, I would suppress it. So whenever I would give out some joy, or relax, or enjoy myself, or participate, or communicate or feel free, I'd grab it, label it, tab it, identify it. I'd try to mentally control the simplest things.

I lost the ability to change because I had to do it so much to keep control of myself, but now these things have fallen together. I have found things in my imagination, and this and this and this and this are all the same thing. I thought they were many different things, but they're just simple. These complicated things I had worked out and I let them go. I feel so much freer, that I really feel hope now. I feel stronger, like I can really get well! I really was sick and like now, boy, this is wow, fantastic! It's happening so fast that I'm really enjoying it.

T: I'm taken by your need to ease up on control, whereas formerly with the loss of control something dreadful would be visited upon you.

I: I still can't express the fascination that I feel over the success. I'm surprised that anything works and it did. Oh, good lord, the thing worked out. There was a nature to it that took over once I let go of myself, the job, the responsibility which I had taken on to satisfy everyone. Now I only satisfy myself. I find that they can satisfy themselves, too. And so I meet other people and instead of trying to make them happy, I just make myself happy and I find there is a more of an individuality about that.

T: Well, I would guess there is much more delight in other people in being exposed to you, rather than the way you were before.

I: I think they felt the strain, too. I feel some people pitied me in my devotion to a foolish cause. And now I no longer have a foolish cause, so to speak. Because my cause is now myself, not extremely selfish, but acceptable to me to make myself happy. I'm not my brother's keeper. But I would still help people as much as I could, unless it hurt me. I used to give away things until I was almost dead, but now I know what greedy people are like. I didn't know that before. I thought if a person showed me a need, it had to be satisfied. Now I see people coming and I think, Oh, this hurts, it's woe onto my head. And I'd think, wow, you're sure a selfish person, I know because I was one myself.

T: But why were you so terribly responsive to other persons' needs, so much so that you almost lost yourself in the deal?

I: My family and my brothers and sisters, we are extremely free and sensitive. We exchanged really beautiful kinds of joy when we were younger, just glee, utter glee. And when I found someone who didn't even comprehend glee, who knew nothing of joy, childish type stuff, I was hurt, I felt pity. I just wanted to give to them because I had it. And when I was away from my brothers and sisters I couldn't give it. And then I went into this and that's all I had to give. I was sensitive to other people's needs, I had it so I gave it to them. I love to give to people and see people satisfied or entertained or excited. If I found someone who needed help and I couldn't satisfy, play with, communicate with, part of me died. Oh, I failed somehow! It was always my responsibility! I took it upon myself to see people happier than they were. And so whenever I couldn't give to them, I went inside myself and said, "Wow, what does this mean?" I took other people's situations, I took their bitterness, their sorrow, even stole from them to do it. I'd figure out what I was going to do about it, which gave me a lot of hang-ups because I was picking up their hang-ups. As a result I ended up with all the needs.

I: When I was sitting out there, I had all these bubbly things I was going to tell you. And I thought, when I tell him this he'll blow it because I found this fun thing in nothing, in reading *Playboy* magazine. I read and read and read them. I couldn't read for a year! And I'd get so happy! I went down and got myself a set of earphones about three or four days ago. And music fills my mind now. I thought it was from the Devil, or I had segregated myself from it because a lot of people can't take joy from it. So I didn't accept it. And now, smoking cigarettes, it's utterly unexpressible the joy I feel from the simple things, being able to eat two cherry pies if I want to. I'm able to eat anything I want now.

T: And all of this comes about because you've learned to relax, and not bind everything up in conflict.

I: Lately, I stay in my room all the time, just sacked out, turn on the heater and smoke my pipe and read *Playboy*. I have all kinds of goodies in my house, candy, just different stuff, fruits. And I can't believe that this all can be so good. I can't tell you how much this has changed me. I'm glad for you that I got to come here and have this happen to me so that you can appreciate it. See, I could never appreciate it fully without you having to tell me and watch me.

T: In a sense, it's almost as if instead of being involved with every other person, you have taken and focused much of your intention on me.

I: I think you were here at the right time, and I sense that you enjoy working with people and I like to share with other people. And because you're an expert in this field, I know you take enjoyment in a happening, in a birth, experience. Of course, I don't think of you all the time, but every once in a while, five or six times a week I think I'd like to tell you this, because you'll like it.

T: Last hour it ended up with your talking about some joy that you would give me—remember that?

I: I didn't mean that I would give you a joy, I meant that that thing you have locked up—that child thing, I told you you would see it because you will believe in me. You know it's in there and there's no denying it. You've helped me; can you see the change, how much I've been helped?

T: Of course.

I: Well, as I work with you, as we work together, I have no way of expressing my gratitude except letting you believe the truth of me by displaying my wares at first, and this in turn will free you. There's no other way of describing it—eventually you'll find something you like. You know within your own heart you will give to me. This is how I work, this is my business, I hate to put it this way but it helps. My business was when people gave me something I took it within myself to show how I felt about it and then give it back to them, greatly improved, or depleted or whatever I felt about it.

T: I see, in a sense it is a display of gratitude. And what am I looking for in our relationship?

I: You are certainly looking for nothing because that's your mind talking. Your mind will get nothing, except the business satisfaction you have.

As we work together, you'll come to love me because people grow to love one another regardless of whether they realize it, because it just happens, if there's any kind of love for that person. My way of reimbursing you would be to simply aliven that childhood thing that you said was there and went away. Now it may not have been practical but it will be extremely powerful and joyful. I wasn't pointing a gun at you saying, I'm going to do this; it may have sounded as though I was going to be the power, but I just meant that you will see it and you will obtain it.

T: O.K. I begin to understand it, but there was a powerful control element in it when you expressed it earlier.

I: Have you noticed that if I say something very sweet, the next moment I will say something very cold? When I'm talking about hearts, especially about the person I'm dealing with, if you get too sweet with a guy, he'll draw into himself because he doesn't want that. If you're too cold with him, he's not going to come out in the first place, unless it's in anger. I've found out if you're subtle with someone and then you're very sharp, they're really affected and so I told you something very sweet in a very sour way, so that's just technique. And the power about it was my authoritative way of saying it. It was kind of protecting you from the truth, but it was true in a sense but to a lesser sense than what I really meant. But I had to say it that way: I'd rather have you be dubious of me and of my attitude than have you realize the truth too soon.

T: Do you think out ahead of time exactly the tactics, the strategy that you will use?

I: This is just my experience; I know what I need. I know you find that just a little bit hard to accept, but I think I know how much you're accepting at any one moment. I'm more sensitive than you are in certain areas which should be natural because every insane man has his fine points. Like Van Gogh must have been extremely insane to do all the things he did, whether it was in his heart or his brush.

T: Do you think of yourself as really being insane?

I: It's flittering itself out to a pretty weak state. I'm extremely influenceable. I could have been driven to a point by myself of extreme looseness, but my insanity has very little control over me now. But there's a battle all the time. But I win more and more, so much more that I enjoy myself, I don't worry, I have self-confidence now. My insanity is losing its land, its property; it's like a depression hit. My insanity is no longer valuable to me. I was feeding my insanity before. It had a very strong, powerful hold over me. Well, now I've quit feeling it and it's withering away like a balloon with the air let out.

I tried going back, I tried going insane again or picking up this or that and I couldn't. It was repulsive to me! I'll never do that again, I realize that it's a freaked-out thing to do something like that.

T: And isn't it so much more pleasurable now to be able to relax, to sleep, to eat, to smoke cigarettes, enjoy *Playboy,* to relate to others, and so on?

I: I suddenly feel leery; I hope that you don't stop letting me come in here though. Don't find me sane—ever, because I relish the thought of coming in to see you.

T: But you do see the fact that the amount of time that I can spend individually with any one inmate is limited. And I can't carry it on interminably—

I: That would scare me—it has in the past. If I thought you were going to cut me loose, I'd freak out so that you would say, "Oh, I found a new problem. Well, we'll work on this problem for a while." Because I like this, more so than you realize, because I need it.

I would hope there would come a time when we would both realize that something has to be completed. That's what I'm relying on. When you're satisfied, I can also be satisfied. And when I'm satisfied, I want you not to have any doubts that I wasn't running a game on you or something.

T: I am satisfied that what you're telling me is truthful.

Comment

The fourth session concluded the crucial exchanges that transformed an acute psychotic process into the return to some semblance of normalcy. Jack begins this session with a testimonial as to the effectiveness of the counseling effort of this time. He then goes into the extreme obsessional-compulsive defenses of his disturbance and contrasts it to the increasing freedom of his new adjustment.

He goes on and attempts to explain some of the background that originally led him into "trying to be his brother's keeper." Essentially, in trying to adjust to the early adolescent conflict he came to the conclusion that he had to accommodate to each person that he met and in the process he was in continual danger of losing himself. He took on others' needs, problems, or hang-ups ("garbage") because he was convinced that at the end by taking on this responsibility, he anticipated the day of reimbursement for all the work that he had done (it was a parody of doing unto others because, in the end, they would repay you many times over). Now, Jack was hedonistically giving the rewards to himself based on the premise that I had sanctioned it. Again, rather than going into the background of it, I chose to emphasize the immediate reinforcement of a new way of life.

This session makes it clearer why I had come to the conclusion that even a major maladjustment (psychosis) was simply another form of role playing. I had succeeded temporarily in becoming a very significant person in this individual's life, and many of his expressions contained the implication that he initially emphasized the "insane angle" because he knew that this was my interest; he changed in part because I was intrigued and would appreciate it; although he was also threatened because of the possibility of termination. In this regard, I take a very condescending view of the therapist's role in the outcome of counseling—in a very real sense he is simply the object that the client's neurotic or psychotic fantasies project themselves upon.

The lessening of the inmate's preoccupation with internalized conflict revealed that in his characteristic way he increasingly felt a need to play an important part in my life. He felt impelled to play upon my memory of my submerged childhood role in the expectation that it would overwhelm the rational part (the adult or psychologist role). As he put it, it would become a reciprocal relationship by my displaying "my wares at first . . . this in turn will free you." I also suspected that he was trying to "seduce me," perhaps instituting a relationship that was somewhat reminiscent of the kinship with his brother. The question was, how would I handle the growing attachment since the primary objective in therapy (a restoration of reality-testing) had been accomplished.

SESSION 5, DECEMBER 2

In contrast to the preceding sessions, which focused upon the client's intrapsychic dynamics, this interview was deliberately structured along the lines of inquiring into what present and future plans the inmate had for educational and vocational training (VT) in preparation for his eventual parole. The first twenty minutes were spent in discussion of his present work assignment and how he thought it would progress in the time ahead. Jack had spent about two weeks in his assignment on inside grounds. He likes the minimum responsibility that the job bears and the fact of relative freedom from supervision (probably he works not more than two hours a day).

He acknowledges that his present occupation doesn't make much sense in any active pattern of life, but now he just enjoys watching the worms, birds, clouds, etc. He states that in the past he worked his way up very rapidly in whatever occupation that he might have been interested in, and he maintains that he was an extremely good carpenter. Jack toys with the idea of perhaps being an architect-draftsman in the future. But for now he recognizes his instability, and for the present he likes to believe that he has the talents to help people. He then got around to discussing how he resented this newfound structure.

T: Are you again saying that my attitudes are dominant, that they are controlling you, or are attempting to control you?

I: That sounds kind of harsh. For you to obtain the "me" out of our discussions, I have to transform my emotions into your thought patterns so that you can accept them. And that's hard for me to do. If I could speak my own language I could tell you much more. There's some words that I have that don't go into your language and you find a hard time interpreting them because you won't accept. You find it hard to accept my rambling. It looks to you like I'm just going to wander off somewhere and actually I'm seeking something over here. Seeking very definitely, trying to define it discretely, and to put it back into something you can draw from it. Our relationship will have to change from me being submissive to you to a sharing or giving thing, as individuals. Because I don't really feel we were acting as individuals before, I know I wasn't 'cause I had no individuality left. You kind of developed that within me, and now I feel that it's strong enough to speak for itself.

And now in here if it's not allowed to speak for itself, it will find some other way of expressing itself to you. But it may be resistance. That's not my attitude, but it would seem to you that maybe I was being obstinate. If I was able to tell you the new things that were within me, I'm sure we could share them more, but it will have to be on a different level than we have been doing it. The cement thing will no longer hold.

T: Can you expand on what you're saying? Go ahead and say them.

I: All right. Things like this. [He produces a penciled drawing.] I didn't intentionally bring this in here to show you, but I have had it in my pocket, so I could show you my latest growth. It's a small thing, but I do many things like that. I think it's a direct comparison with what you saw when I first came in and what you're looking at now. Of course, I'm not a girl and you know I was never a scribble, but as far as I'm concerned, that's my growth. It's a pretty good interpretation [He refers to Figure 1].

T: The two drawings, A and B, represent you before and after counseling. Are you also saying, then, that one way in which you might express yourself is through drawings?

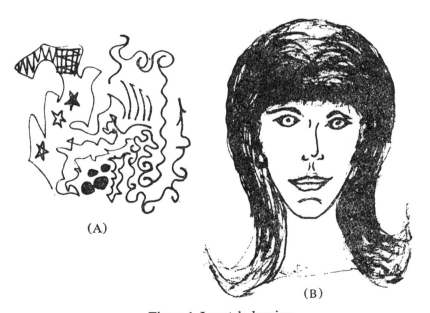

(A)

(B)

Figure 1. Inmate's drawing.

I: Something that I could do on the outside and then bring in here to show you.

T: I would be very pleased at that.

I: I'm sure you wouldn't accept a lot of it. See, I could never—there would be no psychological attitude in what we were doing because some of my ideas would be conflicting, some of my freedoms, some of my attitudes, would be unacceptable to you I'm sure.

T: Why not try me out?

I: Well, I am. I'm just showing you what I would mean, but in other modes of expression. When we first got to know one another you showed me how far you could go with your emotional capacity to accept a theoretical reality, and I would deal a great deal with theory and things that would be intangible. I deal a great deal with intangibles, and you deal strictly with tangible things. They are rooted all about yourself, but not I. For you to get to know me and for me to be able to express myself, it will have to deal with intangible things. We'd need a mediator, someone who could take your words and put them into my language and take my words and put them into your language, 'cause my words are no longer acceptable to you.

Do you see that we deal in two worlds? You have the intellect to perceive it if only you'll accept the fact that there are two worlds, and we each live in a different one.

T: Believe it or not, I accept that already. I believe that every human being surrounds himself largely with his own autistic world. It's meaningful only to himself.

I: You mean like your coat there, is that what you're assuming? Would that be called your autistic world?

T: [Laughs] I think that's a pretty good parallel.

I: That's what I'm saying; to me this is your autistic world. Whatever you do, it is only meaningful to you.

T: That's right up to a point. This is the autism in which everybody surrounds himself and it takes a great deal of effort to reach out even a finger to another person and establish contact with him.

I: Surprisingly enough, it is my greatest delight to have the ultimate of reaching people quite easily. Throughout the institution there are a number of brothers or friends who would be making a practice of communicating. We have a great deal of freedom;

we're just people alike, just the ones that accept one another. We don't speak too much verbally; we don't get together and write letters back and forth, but we have a domain of our own, and it's like an animal kingdom, the most powerful. We just recognize one another and we have developed our awareness and our acceptance of it to such a degree that we live there all the time.

T: I'm looking forward to having some exposure to it also, through your drawings and writing.

I: I'll have to write something extremely platonic so you can accept it. This is pretty hard for me to even sit here for this hour, because I felt extremely suppressed in my expression. I felt that I was coming back to a different place—like I had grown and grown and grown and now I have to ungrow this time. I am very dissatisfied with what I was able to present you with.

T: Maybe this came about because of the structure that I imposed.

I: Yes, that's what I was assuming, that you would be willing to let go of it, so that I may more freely express myself. What I anticipate is that a new relationship will develop.

Comment

My attempt to refocus from a concern with his intrapsychic dynamics and about our relationship to looking at his plans for the future in terms of educational and vocational training was very painful for the inmate. For example, I deliberately chose to ignore strong hints of sexual misidentification. This precipitated a protest against "rehabilitation" on his part and specifically a growing resistance based on the dominance-submissive aspect of our relationship.

At this juncture, Jack comments that he must have the freedom to express himself in his "own language" if I am to obtain any meaning out of our discussions." At the same time, he definitely disparaged my abilty to understand ("translate") it, indicating that even if I did I would find it "unaccessible." He goes on to remark that if we entered into a new relationship that this would mean the end of my dominating role (in essence, that my leadership would be curtailed; i.e., that I would cease functioning as a therapist) and that we must relate as equals (in fact we might even find that the roles were reversed). He made it very plain that the "psychology field" was only one element of the broad area of his competence ("domain of the heart"), that I must accept that we live in two different worlds, and that by the word "autism" he would refer to me and my drab and outworn coat. The relationship was suddenly fraught with rejection; nevertheless, I took consolation in his new-found independence, without any hint of regression.

SESSION 6, DECEMBER 9

I: How did you enjoy my "sculpture"? [alluding to a written memo he had sent me ahead of time].

T: I must confess I really didn't understand it. But I didn't like the "rejection" that I read into it.

I: It's purely platonic. I didn't know what I was writing. [He looks it over and then comments.] Very good—I really appreciate my work. Each sentence is like a mathematical equation: it contains certain ingredients and the whole thing should have a balance to it or an answer. It's like a spell.

Desco Drab,

Smot snots rot. Through you I can't see but I know what to expect. Tragically- magically you'r saved. If our eara of madness is subject to dismissal. Obviously you've been snared by my style, caringly I ventured into it with you.

Sorry 'bout the closet door being stuck. My house wasn't made for cruel people, it was only being spiteful. You've returned my interest for inspection and now you want and want and want.

I'm sick of you. In your present state you'r useless. Thats a polite way of saying you inspire the dead onto greater foolishness. I'm not dead and don't need friendly proding in the direction of my mothers womb.

I pity you in your underwear. When that quake reveals you taunt in terror of relief. Satisfy, that must remind you of fattening foods. The grief of it all, you'll probably refuse to understand this.

one of my friends

The client's interpretation follows:

Desco Drab: When I wrote this I didn't know who I was writing this to. The wording itself is unpronounceable, and it means "inaccessible" or "I can't reach you," which I found out through trial and error. You are inaccessible to me.

Smot snots rot: I don't think that that had any meaning. This is how I start off doing things. It is nonsensical but it comes out very important. As I look at you and your field, I see a kind of aloofness, and an inaccessibility—as if you were in a stronghold. And within that stronghold, "Smot snots rot." Even from your closest friends you are inaccessible. What you give them you only put out (a certain part) for them to have. It's not really all of you. So this is the opening sentence.

Through you I can't see, but I know what to expect: I've gotten something from you already, and even though I can't see through you, I realize that what you have given me isn't you, but I do know that what you will give me won't be you. It will be another material. Skip down to the remark about "fattening foods." It won't be something from the core; it will be something drab or not too powerful. And it will keep coming out of you forever and ever and ever. I see that you have become partially emotionally attached to your patients but you can't become more attached than to yourself. You can't love people more than yourself. I know what to expect of you because I know what you feel about yourself.

Tragically- magically you'r saved: There is a media in which you could be saved, but only magically, tragically you can be saved, if you give all of yourself eventually.

[Because] your eara [aura] of madness can be changed: It can be done away with, you can be made to react. Aura means the whole Establishment, *your whole life, your own mind is subject to dismissal*: Something can come along and change everything you think. Everything you know can completely disappear. Anything you do requires a deep touch and that is what it would take to dismiss your aura.

Obviously you have been snared by my style: That wasn't meant to be self-centered or conceited but simply as another equation. To get a hummingbird inside of your room [this relates to a previous conversation] you have to snare it by something. I have something that you have been snared upon; because I can admit that I am insane, but you can give up my relationship with this fantasy world; therefore, I am interesting. It gives me a hold on you, a relationship, some type of emotional contact.

Caringly I ventured into it with you: And I think you'll agree that both of us ventured into my style. If you read the whole thing and believed it by the time that you got to the end, you'd be a completely different person. It's like when you go into a really good movie and you come out changed. A director's idea is how to change people's hearts. As you read this, part of it is made to open you up and part of it is made to close you down. Part of it is very exciting and part of it boring or repulsive or unmeaningful.

"Desco Drab" should bring you out and get you involved and then "caringly I ventured into it" is almost emotional, so you would back off, knowing you. The whole letter is like a breathing exercise; it opens you up and puts something inside and closes you up. I had a definite point in here and it should have hurt. "Tragically magically you'r saved" says that you're not saved now and it will take something to get you saved. "Your eara of madness is subject to dismissal" says to you, "Well, this dude has a lot of gall; what's he trying to say?" It should get you a commital attitude and then it closes back down. Once you've swallowed that and there is a meter to it, and you've come to understand it, then the second one is just to slap you back. You push and pull something to make it grow—the sun comes up and then it sets.

Sorry about the closet door being stuck: That's dead; there's nothing there. It doesn't mean anything to anybody, but it does, but you wouldn't get it until you get to the last line. Say this puts some concern in you; the concern is about getting something out of the second part, but that is very deep. Because it is not personal, you can't consciously relate to it. It is an unconscious thing.

My house wasn't made of cruel people, it was only being spiteful: The door was spiteful because you were cruel. *You returned my interest for inspection and now you want and want and want*: It should cause you to go back and read it again, "What does this guy mean?" What I meant about the closet door being stuck is a small room being a closet, and I am sorry about it—you must have been trying to open or close the door and it was stuck. So you opened it when we came in, you presented yourself to me and we got to know each other a little better, and you were opening up old closets and there were skeletons in the closet. You opened it up with the tools of your experience and you partially manipulated me. You weren't cruel in anything you did, but you ventured into me and tried to set things straight and were successful to a great degree. But the door was stuck when you tried to get it shut.

It's like something (a flower) blooming and it just went on blooming. You couldn't put it back down. You fixed it and then you tried to close the door but it was stuck. So *My house wasn't made for cruel people, it was spiteful* is a load that I take upon myself. Remember when we were discussing the things of our childhoods and you told me little things that you did? You may not remember, but I made some mistakes as we were discussing them (there's nothing that we discussed that I don't have a perfect recollection of because it was very meaningful to me; I go into our discussions in detail after I've left here).

[For example] when you picked up the phone and you said, "You know what I used to think, whenever I heard a word on the radio and think of it at the exact moment, if you can string them together. . . ." Well, I was trying to be kind and was going to be kind and was going to say something to the effect that I've thought an awful lot of weird things, but I never thought anything like that. Just before I did that, you thought that I took you seriously and said, "Well, I was only kidding now." There was an element of cruelness in there, because there was a lack of communication. You thought I took you seriously and were stopping me. I don't know whether you would ever believe me that I knew you were only kidding.

In a hummingbird way it could be a cruel thing. If a hummingbird came into the office and you moved at it, it would *freak out!* It would bash itself against the wall trying to get out. That's what you did to me whether you recognized it or not. I was hurt to the quick by that. You didn't trust me. You thought to take control was in order. To take control of the hummingbird meant it would never come back. I came back but my door was stuck. If you thought that I was that crazy, even for an instant, then you watch this because I am not that crazy. That was a spiteful attitude. You were wrong about me; you never had me, yet you made judgment upon me, you moved upon me!

You've returned my interest for inspection: That is the end of that thought. It is still a derogatory statement. You have a pretty good way of doing this; once I give something to you, you give it back to me in a different attitude and have me inspect myself, which also hurts quite a bit. Suppose you saw a child laughing and playing with her dolls and you said, "What do you think you are doing pretending those are for real?" The kid would just freak out! I knew they weren't real, but you would make the child wonder, "Wasn't I supposed to do this?" If she thought you were serious, she would take the attitude of "How dare you

assume that these are real creatures since they are only dolls.
How dare you assume me; I am only playing."

You were a psychologist and were to put me back together,
assuming that I was apart. Maybe I was and maybe I wasn't.
It made no difference. *You returned my interest and now you
want and want and want.* You took away the dolls and said,
"Let's pretend that I'm your boyfriend or your daddy and I
want you to play again." I thought it was kind of interesting so
I gave in. It was making love to an innocent thing because you
wanted to keep it going and it was fun to do. *Now you want and
want and want.* It leaves you with a dead feeling, so you want to
go on with the next paragraph.

The next one really comes right back to you in such a derogatory
state that you're whipped right now. *I'm sick of you.* This comes
from the little girl; so you want to play games? I'll play games—
I'm sick of you. *In your present state you'r useless.* The little
girl turns to you and asks, "Do you really want to know—I'm
sick of you—I find nothing in you. I don't want to play with
you—my dolls are better than you are." That's a polite way of
saying, you inspire the dead onto greater foolishness. *I'm not
dead and I don't need friendly proding in the direction of my
mother's womb.* That would be death. You know how as a kid
they want to go back where it is warm and good, in a prenatal
state. To prod a person in that direction—to make him regress—
it is like a tree but much more tender—like a snail's little antenna
reaching out—and to prod him into the direction of his mother's
womb is to poke at it. To say "No."

Parents are always doing this to children and it is one of the
most devastating things that can happen to a child, "No, no, no!"
It is a punishment. I wouldn't slap a child when the child didn't
understand. So from that I'd say, *I'm sick of you,* bearing in
mind that this comes from a childish heart. *And in your present
state you'r useless.* I've seen your farthest reaches, your greatest
depths, so I know all about you in every direction. So taking the
child out of it (for when you hurt somebody it always gets older
and smarter) when he says *you'r useless,* it is almost in despair,
because he has tried you and found you wanting. As far as he
is concerned for you trying to be him would be useless.

You inspire the dead onto greater foolishness: To point out
what is dead and what is foolishness, I would again revert to the

cement block and say that was the Establishment. People who live in the Establishment are proud of it and would back it up and use it as reference. They relate to things and not to human hearts, and I would say that those people are dead. You would take a person who was not adjusted to this death and get him adjusted and go on to accomplish greater foolishness, is nonsense. Only that part of me that is God forsaken would aspire to go back into this thing and become part of it, because as far as I'm concerned, it is foolishness.

I'm not dead and it is the ultimate explosion of my meanness to tell you that I think you're dead. I think you're foolishness and I think you're dead. I'm not dead and I don't want to be poked back down. Like the little cape or mold, I don't need that. If you ever poke me on the top of the head trying to get me to go back down, well, that's what I don't need. I'm sure that you consider it a friendly prod for me to go and get a job. We've gone far enough and you should go out and get a job or start programming. I was very much aware of what I needed, and I'll go when I am ready, because this is the type of person that I am. I'm getting a job in a couple of days anyway. It's already on the Change Slip.

I don't think I refer to you anymore. This is just me going back within myself, my own self pity. *I pity you in your underwear. When that quake reveals you taunt in terror of relief.* It has a couple of meanings, but what I mean is if all the cement (Establishment) fell away, you would be left with only your concern, but no great powerful love or devastating goals. You think that you're satisfied with your technique, *which means satisfied with fattening foods.* You eat fattening foods and you're satisfied with it. You have let it kill you. With me, that's not the way it is. And then *The grief of it all, you'll probably refuse to understand this.* So I sign it *one of my friends,* which means that when a king has someone write something for him and he refuses to put his name on it because he is so disgusted at what he has to say, so he has one of his friends put his stamp on it. My emotions were put to someone else and they wrote you this letter because I wouldn't have anything to do with you because it would kill you, believe it or not. If you ever saw me you would die in your tracks.

T: This is a devastating summary of our relationship. I am intrigued that you have compacted every single line with multiple meanings.

It is like a dream. I couldn't for a moment read into it the meanings that you got out of it.

I: It shows your inability to ever understand me even though it was
there.

T: You are quite correct, but I am also convinced that *nobody*
could understand you that well. I am sorry that the last two
sessions were such a disappointment to you—perhaps I did try to
make the transition from fantasy to the real life situation too
rapidly. On the other hand, you used the relationship to pull
yourself out of a morbid preoccupation with fantasized roles
so you are to be complimented on that. I am still fascinated at
the many sensitive comments that you have shown in your writing.

Comment

The content of the client's message becomes starkly transparent,
especially after he had interpreted it. He anticipated my move to
begin termination and he made it clear that he is not about to program
activities laid down by the team for the sake of accomplishing any
secondary goal toward rehabilitation, at least at the present time. In
the message he expresses the disappointment, bitterness, and resentment that came about because of my unwillingness to form a much
closer personal bond or attachment.

The structure of the message and the subsequent translation bears
a close resemblance to my years of experience with dream interpretation. Typically a dream consists of several short sentences which in
interpretation will be expanded to several pages (see pp. 152–55).
Like a dream, every single element of this message is highly meaningful to the dreamer. Public thinking puts us under pressure to be logical
and the continuous sharing of thought acts as a constant check on
the validity of our thinking; in contrast, dreams are a particularly
dramatic example of autistic thinking in normal man. They are not
governed by rules of public communication; the main function is
emotional expression. Similarly, people who suffer from major mal-
adjustments withdraw and their thinking becomes much more idio-
syncratic (Moss, 1957). The psychotic is under pressure to establish
meaning out of his experience and he arrives at significant insights,
some of them logically based on the sensitivity that he has for interpersonal relationships and some of them illogical conclusions, i.e.,

delusional thinking. In my thinking, we had opened up a new mode of communication, his writing, which promised to be productive in the time immediately ahead.

SESSION 7, DECEMBER 17

Jack began by registering a strong protest that it was impossible to write under duress. "Because I couldn't create, I'd have to translate." He went on to say, "I don't need to be treated. I'm well. I'm a happy guy and that's all I care about. You're trying to hang me up on something. This is the most foreign thing that I've ever come across in my life. It's disgusting! Before it had a purpose. Now it's most uncomfortable. It's all worn out. You have a very technical mind; you're society-oriented, but I want you to sum up what you think of me, the fruits that I've displayed to you. What I am as an individual, and what my qualities and potentials? I'm satisfied with myself, but I want to know what you think of this kid that came in here six weeks ago."

> At least if I can get you to say it, I have given you among the most unique experiences you have ever had. Why the difficulty in describing me? What makes me one of the most unique you have ever encountered?

T: In my dealing with people over twenty years, I think you are unique in the degree of access you have to ordinarily "unconscious" material. More than that, is the recovery that you made in such a relatively short period of time. The astonishing thing is how quickly you managed to control these diverse roles and began to relate to me as an increasingly reality-oriented person. It was as if you said, "All right, if you want me to come in here and be sane. I'll do it." It was as if you'd do it initially *if* I wanted you to, but in the end only because it fit in with your needs of the moment.

I: It looks as though I still had a great deal of control even at my most insane moment, and I was pretty insane; what does that say, am I a genius? What gives me the control and allowed me to do these things?

T: I agree, you are a form of artistic genius—and this is what I find so unique in you.

I: I know what I have and the only thing is I want for *you* to know it, too.

T: In the beginning I believed that the therapist had great influence on clients but through the years I have divested myself of this original impression—

I: You had a great deal of influence over me, whether you recognize it or not.

T: Yes, but it was only because—

I: I was submissive to your world. When I received subconscious vibes which were as close as my brother and I—it went boom, boom, boom—it went like a ticker tape.

T: What I wanted to say is that what I do has relatively little influence; it depends much more on receptivity of the client to receive what he has to offer. I felt that for whatever reason you were receptive [submissive] at that moment, but *the moment has passed.* We are no longer exchanging sympathetic vibes. I am perfectly willing to step back and relinquish the relationship, be glad that it happened and that it happened so perfectly as it did.

I: I would have had to say all sorts of things like a crazy person talks—that's where all my stuff is. I'm just as crazy as I ever was because everything I said is the truth, but it has now shriveled to that small [indicates by circling his fingers on one hand]. It has found its place—it's gone.

I have paced through the cooker, saw millions of boiling bubbles around me, freaked out, and somebody took me out of the cooker and stuck me on the plate. They were real bubbles, but I will never go back. Now I'm a boiled egg and it doesn't have to go back to the water to be boiled again. It is a hundred percent different. It went and got hard on the inside, whereas formerly it was soft. Anybody who thinks I am an egg need only shake me, baby, there is no egg in here, it's all boiled stuff. I know that I was in the hottest water that you can imagine. And, of course, it experienced extreme heat—it's a very "aware egg." So all of these things that happened to me whether they are real to you or not, are real to me.

We gave to each other subconsciously, and we became one, for the time that it took to shake out all the bullshit, and now we have gone away and both of us are improved. But you haven't as yet accepted the fact that I have improved you as a person. You are still going as a doctor-patient relationship and there's no doctor-patient relationship—it was simply something that needed to be done and now I'm going on my way and you are going on yours.

By mutual consent we agreed that the "party" was over.

Comment

So we come to the culmination of the case study. The thing that is so outstanding about the client is the extreme verbal facility and the insights that he displayed. It emphasizes once more that behavior that is odd or strange or bizarre is always meaningful, to the extent that it is possible to view it through the eyes of the disturbed individual. Behavior is incomprehensible or illogical only when it is judged from the outside.

SESSION 8 (FINAL)

Several months later I had occasion to see him again. I was impressed that he had continued to settle down. I was also tremendously pleased that most of the hostility toward me had been drained off. Below are his reactions to the earlier counseling.

T: Could you contrast the sessions that we had several months ago with what we are talking about now?

I: It seems like before that my mind had been blown and was out here someplace [indicates an area over his head] and was all in a big balloon above me. What you did was to make the pieces start dropping out, like you put water made of paste and the glitter things began dropping back within my head and finding the right place.

I'm sure that everyone has a fantasy within his mind but mine from taking all those drugs was blown up and it compelled me to be constantly aware of it, playing with it and dabbling with it. Now it has fallen within my head. My head is sealed up. I had no fantasy all the time I worked within inside grounds but now it is started coming out of here [indicating his head] and is starting to give me joy. It is a much more beautiful, crisper picture than I got before.

And I feel differently, too, I feel that I'm here now, whereas before I felt that I was up there also, wandering around some-place. Now I feel as though I'm sitting here, that fantasy is only something that I can play with like a charm bracelet or some-thing. It is like the harmonica, it is just there and I often forget the harmonica is there.

T: It seems that there is a definite change between the sessions that we used to have and what you are saying now.

I: It seems that there is more control now? Before, they [the fantasy] controlled me. I was only a part of their play, now they are toys to me.

T: So now you do control them, whereas formerly most of the action in your life was centered in the fantasy.

I: It's hard not to control them because now they are such small things to me. But they are also full—it's like having a good dream at night, or smoking marijuana, kind of.

My chow habits have made me much more satisfied—they haven't been giving me any trouble, and as you recall, they used to give me a lot of trouble. I really like to smoke now. All those things have contributed to stabilizing me. My little pleasures. I used to watch television and stay up until late hours when we got the new hours and also let my hair grow. All of those things excited me but now I have accepted them. Now I'm concerned with playing cards, which used to be a big no-no. Now I have a num-ber of books in my room, which also were a big no-no; so now I'm reading all kinds of books. Even getting involved with people used to be a no-no, because I was sure they had a part in the plot. I used to get so seriously involved with people—"say what you want to say, but I'll try to figure out what you're really meaning." Now I don't do that any more.

T: All of these sound like beautiful changes.

I: I'm so aware of every moment, the little things, the changes in my life. So each one of these things are of infinite importance to me. And as I watch them change, I like to relate my joy because I'm growing. I feel more familiar with myself, more accustomed to being myself.

T: Very, very good. After we broke up you became involved with a sensitivity group.

I: That was one of the best things I have ever done in my life.

T: Tell me about it.

I: That was quite a change. In there [the sensitivity sessions] I was forced to tame my fantasy. Of course, they didn't want fantasy, they were in a very real sensitivity group. They wanted emotions and they wanted thoughts that related directly to the emotions, so they could deal with reality as human beings. Lots of times I wanted to say things and get off on gigs and lead people on, and jive with them.

T: To get them involved in your stories and forget themselves.

I: Yes, for the pleasure. They [the members of the group] always took it so seriously. It was a hard thing to accept that I had to always tell the truth and exactly how I felt. A couple of times I got carried away, but I always got nailed for it.

One last exchange perhaps provides additional insight into Jack's previously acute condition.

I: [Expressed with considerable reservation] You would like to have my fingerprint. To get my fingerprint you have to get hold of my finger. It would be all groovy and exactly like I am. To try to get that which is original but I am very elusive.

I don't want to go into a crazy bag again, but to enjoy fantastic thoughts, I'd have to have something on the ball. I can function completely normally now, but before I couldn't. Before I had fantastic thoughts, fantastic insanity.

T: And what happened to the fantastic thoughts, now that you are able to function normally?

I: They're transmuted. It was like a water hose and the water was shooting out uncontrolled, without any particular form. You drained it in and it came down and died and it popped out the other end, like ice, completely transmuted. A different mutation of the same thing. After that it all came out differently and that's how it is now.

There are feelings but no voices; there are dreams and no wonderment—

T: Perhaps what you are saying is that there are dreams but no more nightmares—at least that carry over into your everyday experiences.

I: That's true, because the power over my fears now is a dominating thing. I dominate them and my mind is stronger—it doesn't accept what is doesn't want to.

I used to like the fantasy until it began to bother me. When it sent me topsy-turvy, it was of no value to me. It will be of no value to me in the rest of my life. I don't ever want to go back there again.

T: Was this something that came about since your imprisonment or did it begin earlier?

I: The earliest thing I can remember was when I was a little kid I was sitting up one night and I drew an elf's head in the dark. I was maybe five or six and I could see the head very easily. That was the beginning in having fun where fun isn't. I hung on to that.

Eventually all of my psychotic experiences just took me over. The reason why it popped up so harmfully to me was because I was put under so much pressure in here. It got out of hand when I began taking LSD, although I didn't know it. That put a slam jacket on it and my mind was screaming about 90 miles an hour. That was what caused the problem and eight or nine months later I was here under more and more pressure. I just blew it! My mind was just boxed and it was crushed and crushed. There was tremendous confusion in my mind. Sometimes I had to figure out that one and one was two. I was stark, raving mad! It would take me an hour and a half to do a ten-minute job. I don't know when it actually got out of control. It hurt my head. And when I came back I said, "Help me!" and you put a bullet through my balloon. And that's how I saw it.

Comment

Like most clinicians, I don't place much stock in testimonials, but they do provide one bit of evidence as to the effectiveness of a given treatment, and in this particular case I am convinced that the inmate's acute psychosis was abated. While the primary goal was attained, the secondary objective of progressively programming him so that he could make it on parole was not yet accomplished.

To elaborate on his comments about the value of being a member of a sensitivity group (see Chapter 3): we have tried all three forms of leadership in groups; that is, groups that are led by staff members, those that are led by the inmates, and those that are led by both acting as cotherapists. There is no objective evidence, but the impression is that the last would generally be the most effective. While any existing group within the facility probably would not be sophisticated enough to handle most psychotics, this particular case would perhaps point out one relationship between individual and group counseling. Having partially handled the autism that is the product of a psychotic condition, then the inmate was ready to explore further into his particular problem in a more social setting. In this instance it further curbed his tendency to retreat into himself and got him to attempt to resolve his problems in a more realistic framework.

Taking what the client said as a reasonable probability, the rehearsal in fantasy was practiced almost all of his life (to slightly paraphrase, he learned to "have fun where no fun existed"). Later, when he attempted to combat his problems through active drug taking, specifically LSD, then imagination increasingly took over. To use an analogy, as is true for story tellers or actors who throw themselves into a role, he found it increasingly difficult to differentiate the real from the unreal. Finally, the pressure associated with incarceration became too much, and he went "completely over the deep end." It was fortunate that he recognized his cry for help and not by chance I was in a position to assist him back to a more realistic stance. Currently, he states, "The power over my fears is a dominating thing—I dominate them." He went on after our contacts to further reinforce this trend in more social types of learning situations.

DISCUSSION: R. E. HOSFORD

After reading this highly documented case study, I felt completely drained and I wonder how I would have felt to have been the therapist. In essence, Jack's situation was not unlike that of Jeff. If one were to diagnose each case according to its symptomalogy, using traditional Kraepelin's nosological classifications, both paranoia and schizophrenia would, no doubt, be included in the diagnosis. I must admit that much of the content of Jack's verbalizations concerned itself with delusions, problems of guilt, and material far removed from reality. But, we have to ask ourselves what is accomplished by categorizing clients' behavior in terms of presumed underlying illnesses. This model, i.e., the medical model, has not proved fruitful in the past. Society's tendency to label people, to say nothing of that of the therapist who has as his goal helping the individual get better, can produce more of the very deviant behavior which both society and the therapist seek to extinguish.

It is evident, as Dr. Moss suggests, that much of Jack's delusional behavior was promoted by the reinforcement he received by engaging in it, i.e., his fantasizing reduced his anxiety. Individuals will engage in many "inappropriate" behaviors in order to cope with anxiety; excessive masturbation, delusions, imbibing, and chronic lying are but a few examples. Further, it is evident that by adopting a "sick" role and supporting it with his delusional justifications, Jack was able to command attention which he would not have otherwise received. Environments in which there are few opportunities for reinforcements *produce* much higher rates of atypical behavior than do environments which provide many opportunities for procuring reinforcement. Jack's situation is an excellent example of this type of learning taking place.

Although with Jack we are dealing with drug-induced delusional behavior, the case, like that of Jeff, demonstrates that what is "sick" behavior is, as Dr. Moss points out, always meaningful to the extent it can be viewed through the eyes of the individual. Whether that behavior is "abnormal" depends not so much on the behavior itself but the situation in which it is exhibited. An individual's behavior is determined by the frequency and types of reinforcements he has received relative to the situations he has encountered and the interactions between various reinforcements, social models and situations he has experienced. Atypical behavior, then, differs from appropriate behavior not in the way it was acquired, i.e., learned, but only to the extent that the behavior is inappropriate in the situation in which is emitted.

Consider, for example, how Jack describes in the seventh session what has happened to him since the first interview:

> I have paced through the cooker, saw millions of boiling bubbles around me, freaked out, and somebody took me out of the cooker and stuck me on the plate. They were real bubbles, but I will never go back. Now I'm a boiled egg and it doesn't have to go back to the water to be boiled again. It is a hundred percent different. It went and got hard on the inside, whereas formerly it was soft. Anybody who thinks I am an egg need only shake me, baby, there is no egg in here, it's all boiled stuff. I know that I was in the hottest water that you can ever imagine. And, of course, it experienced extreme heat— it's a very "aware" egg. So, all of these things that happened to me whether they are real to you or not, are *real* to me.

In the context of pure logic, the statements seem "sick," a reflection of delusion—Jack isn't really an egg—but as a metaphorical description, the statements not only make perfectly good sense but are also quite beautiful. If taken out of the context of therapeutic interview, much of Jack's verbalization might be considered to be that from some stream-of-consciousness novel.

Consider also Jack's description of therapy in the sixth session (p. 220). It is evident at this point he is anxious about the whole process. If he continues to work with Dr. Moss, he will have to give up—not as a condition to work with Dr. Moss, but as a result of progressing therapy—his delusions which heretofore have been so reinforcing to him. It appears to me that he feels he must make his decision to give up or keep his fantasies and Dr. Moss represents the stimulus which is associated with his decision.

And finally consider this definition of the therapy process:

We gave to each other subconsciously, and we became one, for the time that it took to shake out all the bullshit, and now we have gone away and both of us are improved. But you haven't as yet accepted the fact that I have improved you as a person. You are still going as a doctor-patient relationship and there's no doctor-patient relationship—it was simply something that needed to be done and now I'm going on my way and you are going yours.

Although these statements occur near the termination of therapy, they are not unlike many in the beginning interviews. One needs only to consider the situation and the reinforcement contingencies associated with each statement. In the beginning Jack even admitted that he liked to fantasize as a way to please people and draw their attention to him. The habit per se hasn't changed. He has learned to use this expertise in more appropriate ways and in more appropriate situations. The question must be asked, "Was he mentally ill, psychotic, or an artistic genius who chose to use his skills in inappropriate ways to obtain the social reinforcement denied him in the prison situation?"

Another question raised in my mind upon rereading some of this client's verbalizations is, "Who is psychotic?" Perhaps, as some point out, many people thought to be psychotic are gifted in ways most of us fail to understand. Jack learned to "find fun where no fun existed"; others find it in a bottle, a pill, in aggressive behavior, in feeling sorry for themselves, ad infinitum. Sometimes one wonders just who is "sick"—the individual or the environment which caused the behavior.

REFERENCES

Moss, C. S. 1957. A note on the use of the schizophrenic in Rorschach content analysis. *Journal of Projective Techniques* 21 (4): 384–90.

Afterword

...and the Walls Came Tumbling Down

C. Scott Moss and Ray E. Hosford

Practical judgment would tell us that the job of the counselor in a correctional institution varies greatly from that of a similar position in any other setting. There are many reasons for this; the physical surroundings, the phenomenon of being incarcerated, the type of client—to name a few—are readily apparent to even the most unsophisticated. In addition, there are many other less obvious but equally important factors which, when interacting together, make the process of counseling the inmate not only different but considerably more difficult than counseling other types of clients.

Perhaps nowhere is the causal relationship between environment and behavior so apparent. Thus, counselors who view man's behavior as a function of some internal events, soon find such conceptualizations ineffective if not irrelevant to the process of bringing about behavioral change on the part of the inmate. Even the therapeutic process itself, i.e., the way in which the therapist proceeds in counseling must be held suspect. Traditional dyadic and group procedures, often effective on the outside, are not only much less efficient but totally inadequate in the prison setting.

We are not pessimistic about the worth of psychological services in the prison. Quite the contrary. The positive outcome of the cases discussed in this book strongly suggest otherwise. What we are proposing, however, is merely a different model for these services—a model which begins with a conceptualization of the inmate's behavior in terms of learning principles rather than disease-oriented internal constructs and a model which includes a different sort of therapy than is associated with traditional counseling practice. The fact that some of the case studies were concerned with the amelioration of psychoticlike behaviors, should not force the reader to lose his or her perspectives; for while the psychotherapy was intriguing and the attempts to deal with it in the here-and-now were rather successful, the cases are definitely atypical. In addition, while several of the cases utilized new and innovative procedures in counseling inmates, they are representative for the most part of traditional one-to-one type of therapy which we feel is outmoded in the prison setting if not society in general. To gain an understanding of our reasons for such a premise, one must begin with an understanding of how we view the individual labeled "inmate" and the process by which he became and is perpetuated in being a criminal rather than a positive member of society.

Most frequently we find that the only real difference between the inmate and the man on the street is simply that the inmate got caught. A more heuristic view, however, is that the inmate was brought up in environments which promoted different behaviors; he learned to seek satisfaction of his needs through illegal means. He is not psychotic or abnormal; he just learned different behaviors. However, because these behaviors conflict with those which society needs to maintain in order to survive, these behaviors need to be changed. The difference between abnormal and normal behavior then is only in respect to society's norms, i.e., the type of behavior society needs to promote in order to maintain its values and achievements. All behavior, whether abnormal or not, is acquired in the same way and it is only the situation in which the behavior is manifested which determines whether or not the behavior is "abnormal," i.e., whether it needs to be changed. Every individual has aspects of deviant behavior which he hides, more or less successfully, within himself.

Still there are many individuals who could not "make it" in regular society. In other words, they did not learn, i.e., acquire, the behaviors which society reinforces, and in order to cope with their anxieties and frustrations brought about by an absence of socially approved skills, they learned to perform other behaviors which brought them the attention and reinforcement they sought. The difficulty arises from the fact that while the behaviors serve the individual in that they help him to cope with his environment, they are opposed to those society needs to promote. Many criminals, for example, are proud that they are "good" criminals because there are so few other things in life which they can do well. A student who does well in mathematics does not resort to deviant other behaviors during his mathematics class in order to gain attention and good feelings of self. An individual who does well in the various aspects of life which are important to him in terms of personal, educational, and vocational achievement seldom resorts to criminal behaviors by which to gain further reinforcement.

One might think initially that counseling within the confines of the prison walls would be very rewarding. It is, of course, a misconception to believe that once an individual is incarcerated and is therefore "down" or in a state of despair, he will suddenly break the pattern by which he has been directing his life, and that he will be extremely motivated to change his behavior and thereby improve his condition. This conception, of course, assumes that the individual already *knows* how to behave differently, i.e., that the knowledge and skills needed already exist in his repertoire of behaviors. He needs only to start using a different set of behaviors. The problem, however, is not that simple. Many individuals, as we pointed out above, have deficit learning patterns. They have not learned to perform the types of behaviors that society reinforces. Thus, a whole re-learning program is often necessary if the individual is to change sufficiently so that he will be able to cope with the outside environment. Certainly men who are locked up cannot escape any longer from themselves and the conditions which brought about their incarceration, but most inmates, like any other adult segment of the general population, are resistant to change. They are neither more or less ready to deal with themselves than are any comparative "free persons."

However, the inmate has to face obstacles in this regard with which those on the "outside" do not have to contend. In addition to dealing with his own attitudes, the inmate is constantly confronted with those of the custodial oriented staff as well as those of society in general, attitudes which are frequently antithetical to his own and which often work to reinforce existing negative points of view. Instead of changing the inmate's view of the world in a positive direction, the situation often strengthens the very attitudes it is designed to extinguish.

Many inmates blame their imprisonment on certain laws of society instead of accepting responsibility for their own behavior. From the inmates' perceptions, they escape despair and subsequently the motivation to change by claiming that others higher up in the social hierarchy ("those who control the Establishment") unjustly sent them to prison. Like the lyrics of the song, "I've been down here so long, it looks like up to me," many inmates really do not see any other alternatives to existence than the one that led to their confinement. They are not motivated to change because being "down" has become a way of life. In effect, they feel completely alienated from society. They learn to gain satisfaction by taking from the society with which they cannot identify, rationalizing their behavior by insisting that it is society that is wrong.[1] While in a therapeutic situation it is very common to hear the inmate express a desire to change, the expression is usually followed by a concomitant "but," i.e., "I would like to get my head together, *but* the police won't let me."

Traditionally, the very nature of prison itself demands submission of identity and individuality. Despite all our rhetoric and despite our attempts—albeit limited ones—at prison reform, in most institutions the inmate is still known by an assigned number rather than by his name. This is rather like those of us on the outside finding ourselves re-christened by our Social Security numbers. Not only does the inmate lose his place in society and thereby his identity, he is even in danger of losing his own sense of self. In effect, he becomes a "nobody." And being good at some criminal behavior is far superior in terms of feelings of self than is being a "nobody." Thus, the system itself actually promotes identification and pride with being a criminal. Those who were just unlucky to get caught but who identified primarily with society's goals and values, now find themselves looking to and identifying with the criminal image in order to maintain some positive concept of self, i.e., in order not to become a cipher in the system, a "nobody."

The reasons inmates initially "cop-out" for counseling are multiple and varied. High among the list of motivations from our point of view is simply the fact that seeing a "head shrinker" adds greatly to the individual reputation for being different. In this environment where the emphasis is always placed on a mundane and pedestrian sameness, one cannot undersell the few ways that a person has to make himself distinctive and thus to preserve his uniqueness and ultimately his self-respect even though they might seem childish by the usual standards. This is the reason why in the uniform drabness of prison life inmates like to sport "contraband," i.e., something not

---

[1] This section was written with the active collaboration of Don Mitchel, Bob Darby, and Larry Seffels.

issued by the institution or sold in the commissary, such as dressing very casually or *bon et roué* (the latter takes an incredible amount of time and energy), wearing a headband or cap which is not government issue, or simply growing the hair too long as a reflection of the long standing feud with the policy of getting a haircut every two weeks. One does not have to go very far back to remember when it was absolutely mandatory that inmates, among other things, had to keep all shirt buttons buttoned, walk in a single file along the corridor wall, and had to refrain from talking during the time that they were seated at their meals. This and many, many other restraints were justified as teaching them self-control rather than anything that was punitive in nature. Regardless of the reason why the inmates come to us as clients, and we do suspect that this aspect of uniqueness is one common drive, the therapist strives to uncover a deeper level and more progressive inducement to get the subject focused on changing himself.

A division between the "good guy" and "bad guy" permeates the prison set-up, the definition of these terms varies with whether one is a representative of the Establishment or an inmate. On the one hand, an officer may look upon himself as a relative model of purity and goodness and, in contrast, view the inmate as a conniving or manipulating con or psychopath. On the other hand, the incarcerated person views the "good guys" as those who support the inmate subculture which, in order to cope with the situation, is based on opposition to all formal authority. Despite the recent clamor, the majority of inmates are not "revolutionists"; however, some of those who come into contact with militant and organized fringes are talked into supporting radical philosophies because their own experiences within the prison provide them with ready rationalizations for their own incarceration.

Being able to blame the system is a much easier way of coping with the situation than is undergoing the tension-producing process of changing themselves in order to be able to "make it" back in society. Thus, for many inmates, the system, in part, actually promotes identification with the criminal subculture instead of promoting behaviors which would help the individual manifest his responsibility to society. As Menninger says in his book *The Crime of Punishment*, society punishes the criminal and the criminal takes the rest of his life getting even with society. Although we talk of rehabilitation, the prison serves society primarily as a custodial institution which actually pro-

motes the continuance of antisocial behavior rather than its amelioration.

For these reasons, among many others, counseling for change
within the prison is very difficult to accomplish. It is as if one were
counseling an extremely hungry person. An inmate's overwhelming
appetite is for parole, a way out of imprisonment. Dealing with anything besides his hunger is initially taken as a pastime, something to
keep his mind occupied, a game. In other words, he wants the counselor to give him his food; he does not want to learn the process whereby he can gain it for himself. There is the tendency to play games
rather than to deal with the greater risk involved in order to change
and to grow. It is difficult for any real human growth to take place in
a prison because, as we stated before, most changes are but by-
products of the prison environment itself. The inmate may change,
but the change is toward coping with the prison environment rather
than with the problems which he must face on the outside. When the
personal worth of a man is measured by how well he can do his time,
rather than the extent to which he increases his human dignity, alienation with society and self must increase rather than attenuate. To a
considerable extent, positive changes in behavior, honest dignity, and
human awareness, the usual sought-after goals of therapy, are forced
by the contingencies of the system to take a subordinate position to
"games-for-people."

Since immediate parole for all inmates is impossible, the therapist
must try to help the person cope with his confinement. At this point
the therapist is in danger of changing from being a helper to the inmates to being a quasi-conspirator with the prison system, helping
to keep a smooth-running institution. What is worse, the therapist
may give up and retire behind some other activity, e.g., he may de-
vote himself to the never-ending task of diagnosis, some esoteric
research, or to preparing his course material for presentation to his
evening class at the university, or of retiring even further to perusing
through the professional journals or books.

On the other hand, the conscientious counselor always tries to keep
in mind that helping the inmate learn to cope with the many aspects
of prison life can have relevance for helping him learn to cope with
society in general, although the lessons at times are sometimes quite
distant and distorted. It is one thing to help the inmate learn to
acquiesce to authority and quite another to help him learn to survey
all the alternative actions he might take and to consider the conse-

quences of each before he initiates a course of action. Thus, the correctional therapist is always forced to use his active imagination and to point out how lessons learned from within the prison can be generalized to events outside of confinement.

A good example of such generalization is the teaching of inmates how to control their natural animosity toward authority. Unfortunately, rather than dealing with the opportunities for learning real self-control, it is often easier for the inmate simply to adjust to the authoritarian control which is built into prison life. Learning to adjust completely to authoritarian control is, of course, opposed to the principles of human freedom and democracy. Is it any wonder, then, that when the inmate is at last confronted with parole, he is completely unprepared to cope with his new freedom. He has learned to have his decisions made for him—when to get up, when to go to bed, when to eat—but he has not learned how to cope with the situation which holds him accountable for and demands that he make his own decisions.

The gap between learning to adapt to the prison environment and learning to adapt to society in the great majority of cases, is just too great; anxiety, confusion and frustration must, in such systems, be harmful by-products. Is the paroled prisoner afflicted with some kind of internal predisposition, as some would have it, which "causes" him to do those things which will return him to prison? Or is it that the system repeatedly promotes his learning of behaviors which are suitable only for coping with prison environments? Because the prison does not help him acquire the behaviors and decision-making skills which he needs in order to cope with an environment which demands greatly different behaviors, the paroled inmate gets into trouble again; he has not learned to behave otherwise.

Because few inmates are psychotic or even severely neurotic, many counselors are prone to forget, as they get engaged in therapeutic relationships with their individual clients, that the primary reason that the inmates are incarcerated is for the protection of society. Any formal psychological treatment a therapist has learned to apply in other settings is as a matter of consequence often ineffective if not inappropriate in the prison setting. Other techniques, often unassociated with "formal therapeutic techniques," must become the primary intervention procedures. In his effort to perform counseling or psychotherapy, the therapist invariably comes up against barriers under the policy of *inmate accountability* which are not present in other settings, to wit, "We must know at every instance where an inmate is and make sure that he is under adequate staff supervision." This stipulation works to dispel the initiative of the mental health staff. Consequently, the two programs often seem to be in opposition to any arousal of inmate-led self-responsibility. This factor serves to promote friction between the mental health workers and the custodial staff. Consequently, the two programs often seem to be in opposition to each other. The situation differs greatly from that of a federal hospital situation where the medical staff has, at least theoretically, the final decision in determination of what will happen to the patient. In contrast, in the prison setting it is ultimately the custodial rather than the mental health staff which has the final decision in a case.

Another factor which makes counseling in a prison setting significantly different from that in other environments is that of trust—a variable crucial to any effective counseling relationship. Inmates have been conditioned not to trust any member of the correctional staff. In fact, the inmate subculture actively reinforces this principle through a variety of aversive means. Seldom will an inmate relate information about others or self if it will in any way affect another inmate. To do so is to break the inmate code which provides other inmates, who may or may not be in any way affected, with "justification" for implementing fast and effective punishment such as beatings, silent treatments, or knifing, to name a few. This trust or the lack thereof, plays an even greater role in a counseling relationship existing in the prison than it does in situations on the "outside."

The way in which the inmate subculture manifests itself is illustrated in the following example taken from a plight that our Human Resources Center orderly found himself in recently. This inmate went into the dayroom in his housing unit to watch television, but there were no unoccupied chairs. While waiting, four people in a group got up to leave and this inmate had the presence of mind to ask one of them if he could use his chair and was given permission. However, another individual who remained behind stated that he was keeping the seats for his friends and when the inmate sat down anyway, he was promptly slugged by his antagonist. The inmate orderly did not retaliate and rationalized that he did not do so because he wanted to keep out of trouble in order to maintain a clean bill of health to present to the parole board, which was to consider his case in three to four months. His "friends," however, encouraged him to instigate a return fight or knifing, or find an opportune time to gang up on the offender. Knowing that this is typical of how things work in prison, the inmate was also aware that this was probably in his opponent's mind and he was justifiably concerned about getting "shived," i.e., knifed, first. He also recalled that a month or so earlier he had backed down in a confrontation that took place over his watching the same fellow play cards. Both times, however, this inmate kept the identity of the other individual carefully concealed, thus maintaining the code of the inmate subculture.

This inmate and those like him are termed "low riders" by other inmates. "Low rider" is a derogatory term that implies a poor, inferior adjustment or a criminal that has lost his nerve or explicitly a person who permits himself to be used for immoral purposes. In this case the inmate was seeking a solution from a counselor. He definitely did not want the caseworker or the officer designated as the correctional counselor involved because if he told them the name of the other inmate and they took any action whatsover, he would be immediately labeled as a "snitch." This was absolutely the last thing that this individual wanted since to snitch is to break the inmate code, which he did not want to do. From his perspective, since all of the inmates were housed tightly together, any difficulties must be resolved within the inmate context without involvement of the staff. The inmate cubculture definitely maintains a pecking order similar to that which many undergraduates are familiar with in the study of the social order of chickens. A hierarchy is formed in the flock of hens or roosters in which the top-ranking bird pecks all others and the bottom-ranking bird pecks none.

Another stumbling block to the establishment of trust is that of perceived roles between staff and inmates. Rapport between a correctional officer and between staff members themselves and an inmate is most difficult to effect because the respective roles are diametric to each other—traditionally, both are cast as enemies. An officer's real loyalties are interpreted as mutually exclusive to the inmate's best interests. The mental health worker, too, is held suspect until he can prove that he is a professional person who can be trusted. This poses, for the neophyte psychologist, as well as the established practitioner, some very difficult philosophical and moral issues which he is relatively free to avoid in outside practice. To be successful, the counselor in the prison setting not only must establish a fairly close relationship between himself and the inmate, but also between himself and the custodial staff members who come into contact with that inmate.

While the officer and the counselor do not view each other as enemies, each sometimes feels that his job is made more difficult because of the efforts of the other. The officers may feel that the counselor molly-coddles the inmate, while the counselor perceives the officer's work as counteracting the results of therapy. Probably neither is the case, but improvement in communication and joint-involvements in the total therapy process is essential if any positive change in inmate behavior and subsequent attitude is to materialize. Ideally, the counselor has to work toward a coalescence among all three—the inmate, the custodial officer and himself.

F.C.I., Lompoc, has instigated several projects designed to involve more and a greater variety of individuals in the therapy process. Dr. Shapiro's chapter outlines one such program. After conducting several groups for staff in leadership training principally around the sensitivity training model, the concept was broadened to include inmates. This fact greatly enhanced motivation and consequently leadership quality because staff and inmates served as co-therapists for subsequent inmate groups.

In addition, transactional analysis (TA) groups were initially organized under the guidance of the associate warden for programs. Since that time TA has come under the auspices of mental health but organization and direction of the program remains with the inmates themselves. This was a compromise in that we were bowing to the distrust of the inmate subculture of the Establishment, hoping to capitalize on the initiative of self-help groups. We were taking a calculated risk but it seemed that "trust" had to start somewhere. It also appeared to us that this was in keeping with the use of indigenous workers who have been used widely in attempting to bring community mental health services to the poor or lower classes. It is significant that none of the TA group leaders are persons who were previously trained in mental health.

An important observation, however, was that among the staff group leaders, most were case workers or allied correctional counselors and people from administration or industry—there were few officers from the custody staff per se. The reason given was the legitimate difficulty of officers being freed from their official duties; if they came, it was strictly on their own time. However, it was also indicative of the lack of clout that the psychology service had; in comparison, for example, it was mandatory that officers be given time to take forty hours in bureau-sponsored Carkhuff psychological training, which was not part of mental health–sponsored activities. This program was instigated to increase the custodial staff's efficiency in dealing with inmate problems on an individual basis; but the two techniques (the individualized Carkhuff training and group-oriented sensitivity training) were believed to be wholly compatible. At the same time, it was also believed by some that inclusion of a member of the custodial staff in a group was most likely to produce a decidedly distrustful situation. It was held to be difficult if not impossible for an inmate to trust a person who had such a powerful control over his life, so the participation of officers wasn't pushed.

THE FUTURE OF THE PRISONS

Is it possible to remake the correctional setting into a truly effective rehabilitation center, or must the system undergo radical changes in order to achieve any marked success in this area? Perhaps paraphrasing a point Warden Kenton made in Chapter 1 would serve best to clarify the problem. He related that he saw no way that society can continue to use the prison system as a "convenient garbage can" for its unwanted and troublesome deviants and at the same time expect much to be done to rehabilitate them. Instead, he says, society must bear the brunt of the problem, opening up new units within the community to socialize the offender while the traditional prison—such as F.C.I.—would be reserved for the more recalcitrant inmate. Even there, the closed subculture that is the prison must be opened up to the community so that the almost insurmountable gap can be markedly reduced. Inmates who "happen to get caught" but who identify primarily with society's goals, cannot be alienated completely from that society and conditioned to identify with and behave according to criminal norms and still be expected, upon release, to be "rehabilitated." Nor can such inmates be expected not to learn more of the very behaviors which caused their incarceration.

Common sense, if not the research which presently exists, should convince us that when we want individuals to learn certain behaviors we often need only to expose them to others who perform these behaviors well. How many noncriminals learn to become hardened criminals and how many mentally healthy individuals learn to become "mentally ill" by being exposed only to those others who perform the very behaviors which are in need of extinguishing? In order for the individual to learn to perform effectively in society, he must be exposed to that society—but, at the same time, he must achieve some degree of success if we ever hope to expect him to be or even *desire* to be a productive individual in that society. Inmates on controlled and graduated levels will have to be invited into the community just as the community must be encouraged to come into the correctional facility.

To quote from a paper coauthored by one of the editors (Nietzel and Moss, 1972), "Of all modern innovations in corrections, none represent as much promise as the present emphasis upon the handling of offenders by and in the local community. In terms of expense, recidivism, employment, and re-integration into society, community-administered programs have the advantage over institutional handling. Of equal importance, the disabling effect of institutionalization . . . is in large part avoided."

Much evidence exists to indicate that treatment for most offenders should be community-based unless explicit contrary evidence can be shown. As an example, Allen Breed has estimated that 75 percent of all juvenile delinquents in California can be treated effectively at the community level.[2] Breed mentions only two factors that should militate against the offender being handled by his community: (1) a total lack of community resources for his rehabilitation, and (2) a serious security risk. In either case the vast majority of offenders would not be exempted.

For the individual preparing himself to become a part of the correctional institution mental health staff, this point of view suggests several implications. Rather than preparing himself to do traditional therapy, i.e., one-to-one weekly sessions in an office with a client, he will need to gain that knowledge and experience which will enable him to act as a consultant and trainer for his staff, for the community, and for relatives and other individuals who will need to become involved in the rehabilitation process. It is axiomatic that intensive in-service training of custodial officers (guards) must be undertaken to transform them from security oriented-individuals to people intimately involved with rehabilitation. The latter, of course, is not opposed at all to behaviors needed for maintaining security.

The punitive methods usually employed in maintaining security, however, would be replaced with methods of control which behavioral sciences have shown to be more effective than punishment and

[2] Allen Breed is currently the director of the department of the Youth Authority in the state of California.

which, at the same time, have none of the by-products that punitive procedures promote. Too, the psychologist must refrain from the habit of accepting most referrals for troubled people and begin by getting out of his office and becoming involved in helping the staff acquire more effective ways of handling difficult psychological problems themselves. The feasibility of such a program is supported by the current practice of taking officers off custodial roles in the living units and making them collaborators of case managers, i.e., correctional counselors, for a year. Although the experience is mandated, observations indicate that the officers become willing participants and do take a much greater interest in the personality adjustment of the inmates. The increased involvement of the mental health staff in promoting this outcome consists primarily of providing the on-going in-service training needed in the re-training of these officers.

It appears from the evidence which is accruing that in the time ahead extensive individual psychotherapy, with its preoccupation with intra-psychic dynamics, including the exploration into the psyco-archeological substrata, will become largely passé in society and almost extinct in correctional settings. "Talking therapies" will be largely restricted to brief, crisis-oriented sessions focused on the resolution of immediate reality-oriented, maladjusted behavior. The interesting thing is that more effective, and time-saving methods of behavioral change are now available and they can be taught to the line officers and other change agents, i.e., significant individuals who affect the behavior of the client, without the usual mystique that all too often surrounds psychotherapy. The central concepts are no longer complex and mysterious—the single most difficult thing in application now is the *consistency* with which the remedial techniques of relearning must be applied. This consistency implies much more than noninterference by custodial-oriented staff; *all* staff must be in complete agreement about the treatment that must be undertaken and *all* must enter into being active change agents.

For over the past decade the national mental health program has undergone a remarkable transformation. One crux of the program has been the shift of treatment of the mentally ill and mentally retarded from the web of isolated, self-contained and antiquated state hospitals to the care of the local community. One part of this plan was the community mental health center construction program which phased out large centralized institutions and replaced them with a network of comprehensive community mental health centers. The objective was a total continuity of early and immediate care within coordinated services at the community level, such as the comprehensive community mental health centers, psychiatric beds in general hospitals, day care and outpatient psychiatric clinics, etc. This made established mental hospitals automatically much smaller in size and they were at last freed to concentrate on the important responsibility of caring for the seriously chronically disabled. Some such patients may benefit from the relative isolation, remote from the source of earlier contagion. Thus the stage was set for the most momentous, widespread, and rapidly moving changes to ever transform any health program in this or any other country. A somewhat similar program is in the process of being blueprinted for the treatment and rehabilitation of the youthful offender.

A word of caution, however, is in order. It is sometimes assumed that by replacing the methods of correctional institutions with the programs of the psychiatric hospital, the inmate's better interests will be served. The work of the mental health professionals is thought to be more therapeutic and the benevolent aspects of hospitalization and psychiatric and psychological treatment more esteemed, while the coercive and punitive elements of custodial care are minimized. The number of inmates handled by the criminal justice system is growing rapidly and the prevailing opinion among some circles seems to be, "give us more psychiatrists and psychologists and many of the inadequacies can be overcome." We feel that this may be a badly mistaken notion.

First, this area is clearly the preserve of people trained in corrections; those of us principally in mental health must realize that we must work with and become a part of the institution if any real progress is to be achieved. In each state, for instance, there are psychiatric facilities that handle the criminally insane. Granted that this population is very difficult to reach, nevertheless, there is no objective evidence that treatment in these institutions is superior to that found in conventional correctional settings. To implement to a greater degree the traditional mental hospital type of treatment in correctional settings, would, in our opinion, be a serious error.

Second, our experience, plus research in the field (see Bandura, 1969; Ullmann and Krasner, 1965, 1969), strongly suggests that many of the practices associated with traditional therapeutic approaches are, at least in the correctional setting, ineffective, ill-conceived, and in many cases inappropriate. Only when the mental health professionals direct their attention to consultation, in-service training, and applied demonstration and research, rather than giving direct services only, can we be in a position to assess adequately our full contribution to the process of rehabilitating the inmate.

Finally, if we are to succeed in meshing the total resources of the community and the institutional apparatus in the rehabilitation of the offender, such a program will have to involve radical alterations in staff roles and functions. Purely psychological explanations of human behavior cannot yield basic guide lines for the action required to meet broad social problems any more than can the traditional medical model. The issues demand social, economic, political and cultural planning and action involving sociologists, anthropologists, penalogists, political scientists, economists, psychologists, biologists, psychiatrists and the lay public. New innovations for in-service training and up-grading of staff competencies are badly needed. In such a program rehabilitation becomes *everybody's* business and the professional correctional worker would be required to expand his working context drastically. It will no longer be sufficient for staff members to even develop a collateral knowledge of each other; they will have to be prepared to establish genuine collaborative relationships with a wide range of community agencies, organizations and leaders as well as with themselves. In other words, as counselors and therapists we can no longer enjoy the luxury of only talking to each other. We shall need to have an intimate and detailed knowledge of the resources within and without the institution which can be employed in the therapy process.

The mental health worker will need to become a change agent— one who coordinates the efforts of those who are involved in the therapy process. At the same time he will need to look constantly and closely at the system to determine which practices promote far greater "crimes" against individuals per se than those the individuals committed in responses to these practices. He will have to work hard not only help to establish rehabilitative goals for correctional institutions but to instigate programs which promote these outcomes. Rehabilitation for return to society involves the re-learning to live in that society. We can no longer support divorcing the correctional institution from society. When we truly set up rehabilitative programs for the offender, the psychological and physical walls must come down.

REFERENCES

Bandura, A. 1969. *Principles of behavior modification.* New York: Holt, Rinehart, and Winston.

Krasner, L., and Ullmann, L. 1965. *Research in behavior modification.* New York: Holt, Rinehart, and Winston.

Menninger, K. 1969. *The crime of punishment.* New York: Viking Press.

Nietzel, M., and Moss, C. S. 1972. A reformulation of the role of the psychologist in the criminal justice system. *Professional Psychology* 3 (3):259–70.

Ullmann, L., and Krasner, L., eds. 1965. *Case studies in behavior modification.* New York: Holt, Rinehart, and Winston.

——. 1969. *A psychological approach to abnormal behavior.* Englewood Cliffs, N. J.: Prentice-Hall.

Contributors

BARABARA E. BLISS is the psychiatrist at the Federal Correctional Institution, Lompoc, California.

TERESA R. BOULETTE is a psychologist with the Santa Barbara County Mental Health Service, Santa Barbara, California.

GARY O. GEORGE was a counseling intern at F.C.I., Lompoc, at the time he wrote his article. He is now a psychologist at the United States Penitentiary, McNeil Island, Washington.

RAY E. HOSFORD is director of counseling psychology in the Graduate School of Education, University of California, Santa Barbara, and consultant to F.C.I., Lompoc.

FRANK F. KENTON is warden of F.C.I., Lompoc.

BURTON KERISH is staff psychologist at F.C.I., Lompoc.

D. RICHARD LAWS is research psychologist at Atascadero State Hospital, Atascadero, California.

KENNETH LEBOW is director of the drug abuse program at F.C.I., Lompoc.

C. SCOTT MOSS is coordinator of mental health services at F.C.I., Lompoc.

HARVEY B. RIFKIN was formerly a psychiatrist with F.C.I., Lompoc, and is now on the staff of Tulane University Medical School.

MICHAEL SERBER, a psychiatrist, was the clinical director at Atascadero State Hospital until his death in the spring of 1974.

STEWART B. SHAPIRO is a professor in the Graduate School of Education, University of California, Santa Barbara.

JAKE STODDARD, a former inmate of F.C.I., Lompoc, now attends the University of California, Santa Barbara.

ALBERT G. THOMAS, a former correctional training specialist at F.C.I., Lompoc, is now personnel officer at the Federal Prison Camp, Stafford, Arizonia.

Index